To: JACK.

Lots oF Love: M

Nov. 20/99

HELL ISLAND

Dan McCaffery

James Lorimer & Company, Publishers
Toronto, 1998

First publication in the United States 1999

James Lorimer & Company Ltd. acknowledges the support of the Department of Canadian Heritage and the Ontario Arts Council in the development of writing and publishing in Canada. We acknowledge the support of the Canada Council for the Arts for our publishing program.

Cover illustration: Paul Tuttle

Canadian Cataloguing in Publication Data

McCaffery, Dan
   Hell island

Includes index.
ISBN 1-55028-625-0

1. Malta, Battle of, 1940-1943. 2. World War, 1939-1945 — Aerial operations, Canadian. I. Title.

D756.3.M35M33 1998   940.54'4971   C98-932349-8

James Lorimer & Company Ltd.,
Publishers
35 Britain Street
Toronto, Ontario M5A 1R7

Distributed in the U.S by:
Seven Hills Book Distributors
1531 Tremont Street
Cincinnati, Ohio 45214

Printed and bound in Canada

CONTENTS

This book is dedicated to Mary-Jane Egan for her unfailing support and friendship.

ACKNOWLEDGEMENTS

It is with a great deal of pleasure that I acknowledge the invaluable assistance of the dozens of people who helped me write this book.

First and foremost, my thanks go out to the former servicemen, both Allied and Axis, who were involved in the epic Second World War siege of Malta. They were extremely generous with their time, whether it was to sit down for interviews or to write letters. Some lent me diaries, unpublished memoirs, old letters and photographs that proved invaluable to my research.

Former British Commonwealth fighter pilots who helped me included Eric Crist, Johnny Sherlock, Bob Middlemiss, Noel "Buzz" Ogilvie, Bob Taggart, Jerry Billing, D.J. Dewan, Carl Fumerton and Dennis Parker. Thanks also to Ben Miller, whose late father, Harold, flew a Spitfire from Malta, and to Mrs. Lorne Archer, whose brother, Gordon Foley, died defending the embattled island in a Hurricane.

Former bomber crewmen who provided me with riveting stories about what it was like to attack enemy shipping from Malta air bases included Peter Hoad, Alex Stittle, Kenneth Boyle, Wilfred Baynton and Reg Thackeray.

Other Allied servicemen who helped included former Royal Air Force ground crewman Arthur Inch, and ex-Royal Canadian Air Force rigger George Demare. Thanks also to navigator Doug Appleton, who flew relief missions to Malta aboard a Dakota transport plane.

Among British soldiers who served on the island I would like to thank Harry Kennedy, John McIntyre and William Keen. Thanks also to Frank Kerley, a Royal Navy sailor who helped break the siege.

Special thanks to John Dedomenico, who was an anti-aircraft gunner on Malta throughout the long struggle.

On the Axis side, my thanks go to former Luftwaffe bomber pilot Helmut Zlitz and to former Italian airmen Renaldo Scaroni and Tony Ferri. I trust that these brave gentlemen will understand I am not referring to them, or the majority of Axis fighting men, when I write in my forward that the siege of Malta proved that the "bully" doesn't always have to win. Former Maltese civilians who told me what it was like to endure years of bombings and hunger included Vincenza Desira, Milo Vassallo, George Scerri, Ed Cauchi, George Porter, Paul Stellini, Carmel Portelli and Myriam Mifsud. Thanks also to Peter Mifsud, whose father, Joe, was a Maltese anti-aircraft gunner, and to Noel Banavage, whose mother, Lena, was a Maltese civilian living under the bombs.

Others who helped in various ways included Gary Quarrington, Dorothy Weichel, Lloyd Hunt of the Canadian Fighter Pilots' Association and Alan Mann.

Thanks also to the staffs of the University of Western Ontario Weldon Library, the Toronto Public Library and the Imperial War Museum.

Thanks also to the *Toronto Star* for publishing a letter I wrote in 1997 looking for people who took part in the siege.

Thanks also to Diane Young at James Lorimer & Company Ltd. for helping me to fine-tune the manuscript.

Finally, heartfelt thanks to my wife, Val, for understanding why I had to spend so many hundreds of hours cloistered away in my study, working on this project.

INTRODUCTION

This book is about the tiny band of young British Commonwealth fliers who overcame impossible odds during the spring, summer and fall of 1942.

More specifically, it is about the defenders of the tiny island of Malta and the role they played in turning the tide during the darkest days of the Second World War.

When the war began in September 1939, the British all but abandoned Malta because military experts did not believe it could be successfully defended. In fact, engineers working on one of the island's three airfields packed up their tools and returned to England, figuring there was no point in finishing the job. When Fascist Italy entered the war on the side of Nazi Germany in June 1940, that decision seemed to have been a sound one. Malta, after all, was now hopelessly surrounded. Axis forces controlled virtually all of mainland Europe and much of North Africa. Furthermore, large concentrations of enemy air and naval units were located only 95 kilometres to the north, on the island of Sicily, while the nearest friendly faces lay more than 1,600 kilometres away. Reinforcements could only be flown in sporadically, and then only at great risk. Both ammunition and aviation fuel had to be sneaked in by submarine, leaving precious little of either for practice flights or gunnery tests.

Before long, however, it became obvious to the British High Command that, difficulties aside, Malta *had* to be held. Sitting smack in the middle of the shortest Axis supply route from Italy to Libya, the island gave the Allies the opportunity to choke off the steady flow of reinforcements needed by German Field Marshal Erwin Rommel's dreaded Afrika Korps. In other words, it held the key to the outcome of the war in both the Mediterranean and African theatres.

This book does not look at the entire siege of Malta. I have decided instead to concentrate on the most dramatic part of the epic struggle — the air battle waged over the island during the year 1942. The important contribution made by the Royal Navy, Allied merchant sailors, Maltese civilians and ordinary British foot soldiers is recognized too, but the narrative deals mostly with the fighter pilots and bomber crews who were in the thick of the action two and three times a day, day after day, week after week and month after month.

A large number of them were Canadians, including some of the most talented pilots Canada would produce throughout the entire war. Canadian aces George Beurling and Wally McLeod combined to shoot down more enemy aircraft over Malta during the spring and summer of 1942 than the rest of the RCAF would bag during the whole year on the Western Front. Perhaps not surprisingly, therefore, many of the sources I used were Canadian. It is not my intention, however, to suggest the siege was won primarily by Canadians, or that pilots from Canada were superior to those from other countries. Nor do I wish to damn airmen from other nations with faint praise. The truth is that the air battle over Malta could not have been won without the contributions of men from every corner of the Commonwealth. It is, in fact, my opinion that Englishman Adrian Warburton was the bravest and most outstanding pilot on Malta; his story is told here in considerable detail, as are those of many other British, Canadian, Australian, New Zealand and South African pilots. When all is said and done, Malta should be viewed as a victory won by a small number of very brave fighters from all over the British Commonwealth.

Regardless of where the pilots came from, theirs is quite a story. Airmen on the island seldom had more than a few dozen planes; the enemy had 800. They had 3 airfields, the enemy 17. Their anti-aircraft guns, which were mounted in crumbling medieval fortifications, included weapons that dated back to the First World War. They had only 24 searchlights and just 2 radar stations. Initially, many of their aircraft were open cockpit biplanes, made of wood and canvas and held together with piano wire. Their enemy was flying one of the best warplanes on the planet.

Many of them had little or no battle experience. Most had never fired a shot in anger. More than a few were fresh out of flight school, with only a few dozen hours of air time in their log books since graduation. Some, like Warburton and Beurling, were undisciplined misfits whom squadron commanders in the United Kingdom had gladly shipped off to the Mediterranean just to be rid of them. Their enemy had conquered mainland Europe, half of Russia and much of North Africa.

As the siege wore on they became utterly exhausted. They flew several times a day, then spent long evenings servicing their own battered machines. Nightfall saw them trying desperately to grab a few hours of fitful sleep in dank bomb shelters or rat-infested caves. Overhead, they could hear the wail of air raid sirens, the drone of aircraft motors, the relentless thumping of flak cannons and the terrifying explosions of nearby bombs.

They were half starved. The enemy blockade meant that food had to be severely rationed. Healthy young lads who had arrived from the United Kingdom without an ounce of fat on lanky frames lost 23 kilograms after only a few months of eating sparrow-sized servings of corned beef and carrots dipped in revolting cod liver oil. Enemy officers lived in posh Sicilian villas, wolfing down loaves of homemade bread and plates of sausage, cheese and fruit.

They were often so sick they had to be hospitalized for up to a week at a time. Painful cramps, brought on by a poor diet, clouds of dust and oppressive heat put pilots on their backs with a mysterious illness that became known simply as the "Malta Dog." Those who remained on operations for any length of time were so frail they sometimes had to be helped into bomb shelters by their buddies.

They suffered punishing battle losses. One squadron lost half its planes in a single week and, before the siege lifted, nearly every pilot on the island had been shot down at least once. Almost half of them were to be killed or wounded. Many of the rest survived harrowing parachute jumps or bone-jarring crash-landings. Those who escaped without physical scars often had had their nerves stretched to the breaking point.

If they received any leave it seldom lasted for more than 48 hours, and the only places they could visit were Malta's bombed-out towns and villages. These were largely devoid of cinemas, restaurants or any other form of entertainment. If they were lucky enough to find female companionship, they soon discovered the deeply religious Maltese would not let a girl out of the house without a chaperon. Their enemies, meanwhile, took extended rest periods in Rome, Venice and Florence.

Their planes were falling to pieces, and spare parts were in short supply. Sometimes, radios, guns and even parachutes failed them at crucial moments. On paper they could not possibly win. But they did. And in the process they altered the outcome of the entire war. More than that, they proved that the "little guy" can make a difference, and that the bully does not always have to win. This is their story.

Dan McCaffery
Sarnia, Canada
April 1998

CHAPTER 1

STORM CLOUDS GATHER

Total victory was within their grasp.

German dictator Adolf Hitler and his Grand Admiral, Erich Raeder, were in agreement about that much as they stood over a table in the Berlin Reich Chancellery on February 13, 1942, as an army colonel unfolded the charts that told of their growing global domination. The Axis powers were winning on every front. Hitler's legions controlled virtually all of Western Europe and, in the east, were almost to the gates of Moscow. To the south, German and Italian troops occupied Greece, Yugoslavia and much of North Africa. Legendary Field Marshal Erwin Rommel's seemingly invincible Afrika Korps was poised to run the British Eighth Army right off the continent. After that, the Desert Fox, as Rommel was called by both friend and foe, planned to seize Egypt, the Suez Canal and the entire oil-rich Middle East. If he succeeded, the Second World War would be all but over.

Raeder was in favour of Rommel's pending offensive, but he saw one flaw in the plan. If Axis soldiers were to stay on the attack for any period of time they would need vast quantities of supplies. The Panzer divisions required 50,000 tonnes of food, fuel and ammunition per month to keep rolling. And since the previous fall, the Italian navy had only been able to get 20,000 tonnes monthly from Sicily to the giant port at Tripoli, Libya. It was only a short hop — two or three days' sailing time across the Mediterranean Sea — but British bombers and submarines operating from the tiny island of Malta were making the passage extraordinarily perilous. The Allied garrison on Malta, which was located only 60 miles directly south of Sicily, had sent two Italian transport ships to the bottom on September 18, 1941, drowning 5,000 Axis troops. Two months later, they struck an even more devastating blow when four Malta-based warships caught an Italian convoy in the moonlight, sinking all seven of its vessels. Since that time, shipping losses had reached such alarming levels that Italian merchant sailors were referring to the run from southern Europe to North Africa as "suicide alley." Put simply, unless something was done about Malta, Rommel was not going to be able to stay in business.

Italy's dictator, Benito Mussolini, knew this better than most people. He referred to Malta as an "unsinkable aircraft carrier" and had been pushing Hitler to sanction an invasion for months.[1] But the Führer was reluctant to order an amphibious assault. The year before he had lost thousands of crack paratroopers during the conquest of the island of Crete, and he was not anxious to risk his best troops again in a similar venture. Aerial photographs showed just how difficult it would be for gliders to land on Malta's rocky terrain. Hitler proposed that Rommel be given the go-ahead to drive to the Suez Canal without first subduing the island. He feared if he waited until conditions for an Egyptian offensive were perfect, the British would send enough reinforcements into Africa to gain the upper hand. "On the leaders of armies the Goddess of Battle smiles but once," he lectured Mussolini. "He who fails to grasp her favours invites a mass of future troubles."[2]

Now, however, Admiral Raeder was backing the Duce, and that also impressed the Führer. The naval commander had just humiliated England's Royal Navy by successfully sailing three battleships right through the English Channel. As far as Raeder was concerned, Malta had to be destroyed. "Suez and Basra are the western pillars of the British position in the east," he said. "Should their position collapse under the weight of concentrated Axis pressure, the consequences for the British Empire would be disastrous." The key, he continued, was the capture of Malta. "The favourable situation in the Mediterranean, so pronounced at the present time, will probably never occur again. All reports confirm that the enemy is making tremendous efforts to pour all available reinforcements into Egypt. It is therefore imperative to take Malta as soon as possible."[3]

The Desert Fox, Hitler's favourite general, concurred. "With Malta in our hands, the British would have little chance of exercising any further control over convoy traffic in the Central Mediterranean Sea," he said. "It has the lives of many thousands of Germans and Italians on its conscience."[4]

Rommel believed if he was able to get enough reinforcements he could wipe out the entire 600,000-man British Eighth Army. If that happened, coming hard on the heels of crippling English setbacks at Dunkirk in 1940 and Singapore in 1941, the Nazi high command was convinced the United Kingdom's war-weary population would demand Prime Minister Winston Churchill's resignation. That, in turn, would likely lead to a negotiated settlement in the West, leaving the Germans free to concentrate all their efforts on finishing off the Soviet Union. Hitler himself believed this. "Rommel must be given all the supplies he needs," the Führer declared. "When the Germans captured Alexandria [in Egypt] the entire British public would be thrown into a far greater rage than at the surrender of Singapore."[5]

This was not just wishful thinking. Winston Churchill himself believed Rommel could win the war for Germany — provided he could get enough supplies past Malta. Indeed, the prime minister had paid a remarkable public tribute to the Desert Fox in a speech that shocked the Allied nations. "We have a very daring and skillful opponent against us," he told a hushed House of Commons. "And, may I say across the havoc of war, a great general."[6] In a top secret message to the commander of British forces in North Africa, General Claude Auchinleck, Churchill made it clear the only way to beat Rommel was by saving Malta. The loss of the island "would be a disaster of the first magnitude to the British Empire, and probably fatal in the long run to the defence of the Nile Valley ... The starving out of this fortress would involve the surrender of over 30,000 men, army and airforce, together with several hundred guns. Its possession would give the enemy a clear and sure bridge to Africa with all the consequences flowing from that. Its loss would sever the air route upon which both you and India must depend for a substantial part of your aircraft reinforcements. Besides this, it would compromise any offensive against Italy, and future plans such as Gymnast [the proposed liberation of North Africa by Allied troops]."[7]

Churchill had one more reason to be worried. If Rommel grabbed the Suez Canal, England would lose much of its Middle East oil supply. At the start of the war, one-twelfth of Britain's oil came from that part of the world. But now that the Third Reich controlled Romania's oil fields, and U-boats were making shipments from North America unreliable, close to a quarter of the nation's oil was coming through the Suez.

Nazi paratrooper general Kurt Student now joined the debate, siding with Raeder. Student, a First World War fighter ace, had masterminded the bloody — but successful — invasion of Crete. He was confident he could take Malta too. He pointed out that Mussolini had promised to supply a parachute division, a full battalion of well-trained engineers and five field companies. At sea, the Italians could throw in 30 warships, including five mighty battlewagons. In all, Student proposed to drop 30,000 airborne troops on Malta. Another 70,000 men would storm the beaches in landing craft, giving the Axis 100,000 soldiers to pit against a defending force less than a third that size. Student, a thin-lipped man with hawk-like features, said later the formations he had assembled for an attack on Malta were at least five times as large as the one he had used against Crete.

The plan had also been scrutinized by high-ranking officers from the third Axis power, Japan. Both a Japanese airforce colonel and an Imperial Navy admiral had endorsed the scheme. These were men who had helped destroy the American Pacific fleet at Pearl Harbor on December 7, 1941. Since then, their forces had trounced Allied troops at Hong Kong, Singapore, Manila, Bataan and Wake Island. They knew a thing or two about seaborne assaults, and Hitler was impressed when they backed Raeder.

The Führer turned to Hermann Goering, Commander-in-Chief of the Luftwaffe. No invasion of Malta would be possible without air superiority. Could he provide it? Goering, a chunky, flamboyant man with a can-do attitude, answered in the affirmative. He already had 200 planes on Sicily that had been harassing Malta for months. Winter had brought operations on the Russian Front to a virtual standstill. That would allow him to free up 225 more planes almost immediately. He had five Junkers-88 bomber groups, one Stuka dive-bomber outfit, a Messerschmitt-110 fighter-bomber squadron and four crack ME-109 fighter units ready for duty in Italy. And because Mussolini already had 275 planes on Sicily, including 200 fighters and 75 bombers, that would place an incredible total of 700 warplanes within a scant 15 minutes' flying time of Malta.

Hitler, anxious to do the job right, suggested a Luftwaffe night-fighter squadron could be sent from Germany to Italy to bolster the Axis air armada still further. But even with this massive force he was still nervous. His hopes of invading England in 1940 had been dashed by the Royal Air Force and he feared a repeat of the débâcle. Would the German-Italian airforces be strong enough to deal with RAF units on Malta? Luftwaffe General Albert Kesselring, commander of all Axis air units in the Mediterranean theatre and North Africa, assured Hitler there was no cause for alarm. His pilots could knock the RAF out of action soon after spring weather permitted around-the-clock flying, probably by the end of March. He proposed to bomb Malta's airfields to rubble, essentially taking out any fighter opposition on the ground. Any RAF planes that did get airborne would not be capable of offering much resistance, he said, because Malta was equipped with hopelessly outdated Hurricane fighter planes that were no match for the German Messerschmitt-109s or the Italian Macchi-202s. The British were keeping all of their fabulous Spitfires on English soil to guard London from the threat of Nazi bombers. Most of the RAF's best airmen were also in the United Kingdom, leaving Malta defended by only a few dozen largely inexperienced flyers. Many of them, Kesselring's intelligence sources told him, had no battle experience. Taking control of the skies from them, he stated emphatically, would not be a problem.

Hitler asked about reinforcements. Couldn't the Allies fly in dozens, or even hundreds of Spitfires, once they realized what was happening? Not possible, Hermann Goering assured him. The Spitfire did not have the range to fly all the way from England to Malta, and it was not designed to take off from an aircraft carrier. The Allies could send planes from North Africa, but the RAF needed every fighter it had there if it was to have any hope of containing Rommel. Reinforcements were not a factor, Goering insisted.

Kesselring, fearing Hitler was going to veto the plan, virtually demanded that Malta be taken. "I urged Goering and Hitler to stabilize our position in the Mediterranean by taking Malta," he wrote later. "I even persuaded Rommel to back me up. It was not until February, 1942 that I succeeded in getting my plan approved. The occasion was an interview at the Führer's general headquarters. Tempers ran high. Hitler ended the interview by grasping me by the

5

arm and telling me in his Austrian dialect, 'Keep your shirt on, Field Marshal Kesselring. I'm going to do it' — a typical sidelight on the tension at headquarters."[8]

Hitler was convinced. He ordered Kesselring to move air units from just outside Moscow to Sicily. For good measure, he instructed General Bruno Loezer, an expert on fighter tactics, to head for Italy as well. Operation "Hercules" — the code name for the invasion of Malta — was going ahead. The Luftwaffe and Italy's air arm, the Regia Aeronautica, would have until May to neutralize the RAF and soften up the island's ground defences. After that, Axis troops would seize the island fortress once and for all.

The die was cast. Although few realized it at the time, the fate of the North African Campaign now rested squarely on the shoulders of a few lonely young Allied fighter pilots stationed on a dusty rock in the middle of the Mediterranean Sea.

Transporting a mighty air fleet across 5,000 kilometres from the frozen wastelands of the Soviet Union to the subtropical Mediterranean, was no easy task. The planes had to be refitted to meet radically different weather conditions. Motors had to be equipped with special air filters if Sicily's clouds of sand were to be kept from clogging cylinders. But Kesselring moved with astonishing speed, sending 190 long-range bombers south in just five days. Three of those days were taken up refitting planes and packing whatever personal possessions the air crews could store inside crowded fuselages. Two more days were spent in the air.

Bomber pilot Hajo Herrmann has left behind perhaps the best description of what it was like to transfer from one theatre of war to another in a hurry. Writing in his memoirs almost five decades later, he recalled having a difficult time just getting his heavily laden plane airborne. "Our staffel [squadron] of Ju-88s was climbing laboriously," he wrote. "We were not carrying heavy, streamlined bombs under our wings, but big, angular containers in which was stowed the equipment necessary for operations in the south. In addition, we had a fifth man on board, our ground mechanic, and there was a lot of gear squashed into the cockpit. There was scarcely enough room to move."[9]

He was certain their arrival in Sicily had been noted by Allied spies as they circled Gerbini airfield, looking for landing spots. "The roar of engines filled the landscape, rolled across villages, fields and slopes and echoed against Mount Etna. Goodbye secrecy! What the people learned there, including our Geschwader [wing] identification mark, 4-D, painted large on the aircraft, would find its way to Malta."

The milder climate and less regimented Italian lifestyle took some getting used to. "I was the last of the five crewmen to climb out of the Junkers and I felt a mild wind on my face and my neck," Herrmann wrote. "The air smelled of farmyards, mixed with the scent of a spice I didn't recognize. A motley collection of men on donkeys, attracted by the noise of our engines, had wound its way towards us from the olive and almond groves and through the cactus hedges. They brought every sort of edible and vitamin-rich commodity, which they exchanged, amid a welter of words, for anything that we could spare. A donkey, for example, changed owners for a pair of high-fashioned, lace boots."

For bomber pilot Werner Baumbach, who arrived a little later in the year, the biggest adjustment would be Sicily's scorching heat. "When we came down in a wide sweep to Comiso airfield, the snow-capped Mount Etna lay before us between the burning sky and the quivering dust-coated tarmac," he wrote later. "The sound of all the aircraft of our squadron flying in was echoed from the nearby hills. To the south the sun-bathed horizon glimmered between gnarled trees and withered cactus hedges, and there was a steamy haze. When we switched off, Sicily's midday heat enveloped us like a furnace and reduced us to silence ... our clothes hung like glue ... We waited and no one paid the slightest attention to us on that first day on Sicilian soil."[10]

Such was the secrecy of the Luftwaffe plans that the arrival of the new units came as a shock even to Axis forces on Sicily. The aerodrome commander, Major Hans Rose, had no idea that reinforcements were on the way until Baumbach marched into his office. Needless to say, no one had prepared extra bunks, food, clothing, spare parts or other necessities for the new men and machines. It was only by bending every rule in the book that Baumbach was able to get his bomber wing made ready for action, he said later.

Despite the logistical problems, the Luftwaffe airmen were in high spirits. They were winning the war and they knew it. "Morale was very good," Heinkel bomber pilot Helmut Zlitz told the author more than half a century later. "Sure we had taken some casualties since the beginning of the war, but it wasn't like it's portrayed in the American movies. In the American movies the Allies always win." The young Germans had been raised in a society that was still bitter about its First World War defeat. They were proud individuals, many of whom supported the Nazis without question. They believed Hitler had restored the nation's honour after the Allies had forced a humiliating peace on it in 1918. Still, it's safe to say few of them were goose-stepping fanatics. "Politics was not our business," Zlitz recalled. "We were airmen, people who flew in the airforce, that was it. Nobody told us anything."[11]

Hajo Herrmann described his men as little more than civilians wearing uniforms. They seldom stood at attention, only clicked their heels on the most ceremonial of occasions and often poked fun at the Nazis while relaxing in the mess. Once, a pilot named Paul Hecking "hobbled into the room that we called the Officers' Mess, impersonating Josef Goebbels. He sat down on a chair, giving a slovenly Nazi salute, and proceeded to deliver a propaganda speech in a Rhineland dialect that made us split our sides with laughter." On another occasion, an Austrian pilot waltzed in to the sounds of an accordion with his hair combed across one eye to make himself look like Hitler. "We were not rebelling against the state," Herrmann insisted. "We stood apart from the politicians, and even from our own opinions. For us one thing came before all criticism, all joking, all personalities: to win the war, or at least not to lose it."[12]

Once the Germans had settled in, they found Sicily strikingly beautiful. Fighter pilot Johannes Steinhoff, recalling his pink-coloured villa, wrote later, "The French windows giving onto the balcony stood wide open. Beyond, the waters of the bay were illuminated by the last of the evening light while houses, slopes and rocks glowed deep yellow. It was a scene of such classical beauty that it hurt when one remembered the war. I dropped on the bed to relax for a little. Smells of Rieber's cooking wafted through the house. It was a comforting, peaceful atmosphere, the silence broken only by friendly, familiar sounds — the scraping of a chair, water hissing in the pipes."[13]

If there was a drawback to this tranquil existence it was the radical change in climate. Men only days out of the Russian winter would soon have trouble coping with Italy's heat. Within weeks of his arrival, Steinhoff wrote, "It was unbearably hot. Not a breath of wind disturbed the humid air; my shirt, dripping with sweat under my harness, clung to my body. The sun made the cockpit like an oven."[14] The airmen soon found themselves seeking shelter in the shade of olive trees. Others sought relief by making their way down twisting dirt roads clogged with donkey carts to go swimming in the sparkling blue waters of the Mediterranean.

In cool evenings they lived like kings, with batmen, cooks and orderlies waiting on them hand-and-foot. Mealtime was unforgettable. Describing one of his dinners, Steinhoff wrote that "the pièce de résistance consisted of two large dishes of scrambled eggs mixed with Italian tinned meat. Besides this, there were dishes and plates piled with tunnyfish, tinned sardines and anchovies, liver sausage, tinned ham, Italian saveloys [a type of sausage] and tomatoes and fresh fish." The pilots washed it all down with litres of wine that "glowed like amber" in the gentle lamplight.[15]

At nearby Italian airforce bases, the airmen gorged themselves with fresh fish purchased from open-air markets. There was so much food available that, when flying, they often brought along hampers stuffed with wine, cheese, cake, king-sized loaves of home-made bread, sausages and a smorgasbord of fruits. Some bomber crews even had classical music pumped in over the radio and had curtains put on their side windows.

The arrival of the Germans caused widespread excitement among the Italians, even if the Luftwaffe was hogging all the best facilities. Italian fighter pilot Ronaldo Scaroni said later, "Our morale could not have been any better. We were certain we were going to crush Malta and win the war. I can remember listening to Rome radio every night, hearing about yet another Axis victory. Whether it was us, the Germans or the Japanese, we were winning everywhere. It was uncanny. And of course we could see for ourselves the large number of Luftwaffe planes flying into Sicily. They took the most comfortable and best located airfields, like Comiso and Gela, but there was no resentment. We knew these guys were good and we were glad to have their help. We'd been bombing Malta on and off since June 1940, remember. So it was nice to have some help. We were impressed with their planes too, especially the ME-109 and the Junkers-88."[16]

The Italians were willing to concede that their partners had better planes, but they did not believe the German pilots were superior to their own. The Italian air stations housed some of the best acrobatic flyers in the world. They had won numerous speed and performance trophies at air shows across Europe throughout the 1930s and they had a reputation for exceptional tenacity in combat. They also had a playful flamboyance. At one squadron, the airmen had decorated the cowlings of their planes with paintings of black cats toying with green mice. One cocky young pilot had even dropped a cartoon attached to a pink parachute over a Malta airfield. Allied aviators who retrieved it found a drawing of an Italian pilot knocking down a pair of Hurricanes with his bare hands. In the background, meanwhile, British airmen were shown lined up to greet St. Peter at the pearly gates.

Most of the Italians were committed Fascists, but it was probably unrealistic to expect young people raised in 1930s Italy to be anything else. Mussolini, after all, had filled them with pride, promising to restore the glory days of the Roman Empire. He had brought order to the country. The pilots were impressed, too, because the dictator fawned all over them, referring to them as "my young eagles."[17] Mussolini, whose own son Bruno was an aviator, often showed up at air bases to personally decorate those who had done well in battle. For all that, few of them spent much time dwelling on politics. Fighter pilot Faliero Gelli, for instance, spent much of his time daydreaming about his girlfriend. The 25-year-old even thought of her while Mussolini was pinning a medal on his chest in recognition of the victories he had won in air combat. Twenty-year-old pilot Francesco Cavalera, on the other hand, was more worried about being seen by his fellows as a coward than he was about anything else.

For some of the Italians there was no need to worry about how they would react in battle. Although not as experienced as the Germans, they had, on average, seen considerably more action than the men facing them on Malta. One of them, Sergeant Teresio Martinoli, had shot down five British planes in 1941, the total he needed to become an ace. Then there was the exceptionally talented squadron leader, Captain Furio Doglio Niclot. Big things were also expected from a rising star named Carlo Seganti. Among the bomber pilots, the Italian torpedo-plane jockeys had established sterling reputations through their daring and highly successful attacks on British shipping. Two pilots in particular, Giuseppe Cimicchi and Carlo

Buscaglia, had become national heroes by sinking several Allied ships each in 1941.

If the Italians had any cause for concern it was not the calibre of their fighting men. The real problem was their equipment. The main Regia Aeronautica fighter, the Macchi-202, was a fast, highly manoeuvrable machine capable of absorbing a lot of punishment, but it was poorly armed. Its four low-calibre machine guns gave it very little firepower. Still, the Macchi was an absolute delight compared to Italy's obsolete bomber fleet. Most Italian bombers were slow, sluggish aircraft with low-powered engines and no armoured plating. Hitler had offered Mussolini top-of-the-line German bombers, but pride prevented him from accepting.

With the aircraft at their disposal, the Germans were supremely confident they could whip anything they would encounter in the skies over Malta. Their principal fighter, the fabled Messerschmitt-109, could fly 625 kilometres per hour and had a ceiling of 11,300 metres. More impressive still, it featured a direct-fuel injection system that allowed the pilot to launch his machine into a steep dive from any angle without fear of the engine conking out. It could also zoom upward much more rapidly than either the Spitfire or the Hurricane. On the negative side, it could not turn as tightly as either British fighter and, with only one cannon and two machine guns, it packed less of a punch. Nevertheless, most German aviators thought the ME-109 was vastly superior to the Hurricane and at least marginally better than the Spitfire.

The bomber pilots had just as much faith in their Junkers-88s as the fighter jockeys had in their ME-109s. A highly versatile plane, the Ju-88 had two 1,200 horsepower engines that allowed it to reach speeds of 450 kilometres per hour even when fully loaded with 1,800 kilograms of bombs. Once it had jettisoned its payload, it could streak for home at 500 kilometres per hour, which was a good clip for a bomber of the era. Because it could also climb to 9,800 metres and was armed with four machine guns, it was a difficult plane to shoot down.

Once the new arrivals had been housed, fed and made ready for action, Kesselring drew up his plan of battle. He would step up the nuisance raids during the remainder of February, launching an all-out blitz only when March put an end to overcast skies over Malta. His first goal would be to destroy the airfields and the radar stations. After that, his bombers would pound the dockyards, shipping, harbour installations and communications facilities. Raids would be mounted day and night to deny the defenders sleep and to use up their ammunition as quickly as possible. After a few months of constant bombardment, Kesselring believed the island might even surrender without the need for an invasion.

The opening moves were over. The time for action was almost at hand.

CHAPTER 2

MALTA BATTENS DOWN
THE HATCHES

A claustrophobic feeling settled over Malta's dusty landscape as reports filtered in about the vast buildup of Axis warplanes on Sicily. All 250,000 of the island's inhabitants were acutely aware of its extreme vulnerability. For one thing, Malta was hopelessly surrounded. To the north lay Fascist Italy and Vichy France. To the south was Libya, home of Rommel's Afrika Korps. Eastward, the swastika fluttered above the ancient ruins of Crete and mainland Greece. To the west was Franco's Spain, officially neutral but, in reality, pro-Axis to the core. The waters around the little archipelago were threatened by the powerful Italian surface fleet and German U-boats. The nearest friendly faces were more than 1,600 kilometres away in Egypt. Malta is neither hospitable nor easily defended. The place is small, covering only 250 square kilometres, or 95 square miles. The ground is rugged, hilly and largely barren. There is little fertile farmland and, without steady shipments of grain from the outside world, Malta would be in grave danger of starvation. It has four sister islands, but they are even smaller — and more inhospitable — than Malta itself. Three of them are completely uninhabited. The only populated one is Gozo, a hilly, pear-shaped island a mere 50 square kilometres — 20 square miles — in size.

Furthermore, Malta stood out like a sore thumb from the air, making it an easy target for bombers. Pilot Bill Olmsted was shocked when he first saw the place from the cockpit of his fighter. "My first view of the tiny island of Malta is still a vivid memory," he recalled decades later. "Through the mid-morning haze, it looked like a small golden leaf floating on the sea. I thought it looked ridiculously small, measuring roughly seven miles by 14 miles, and our new airdrome, Takali, stood out as obvious and exposed."[1]

Air raid over Valletta, capital city of Malta. Courtesy of Eric Crist

The place was so unprotected, in fact, that Allied servicemen had to sneak in and out under the cover of darkness. Canadian fighter pilot Stan "Bull" Turner, who was destined to play a decisive role in the siege, arrived in just such clandestine fashion three days after Hitler gave the green light to Operation Hercules. The stocky Toronto airman showed up in the pearly half-light of dawn on February 16, 1942, in the midst of a German air raid. Huddled in the passenger section of a lumbering, four-engine Sutherland flying boat, he was greeted by exploding bombs, thumping anti-aircraft cannons and probing white searchlight beams as the big plane set down in Grand Harbour.

English pilot Laddie Lucas, who was also on board the Sutherland, never forgot his introduction to Malta. "The first bloody thing we saw, when we got off this flying boat at dawn, was an incoming raid. And then we saw these five clapped-out Hurricanes struggling for height. You could almost feel the ground vibrating, the aeroplanes were so old and cannibalized. Our squadron leader, the Canadian, Stan Turner, a marvelous chap, had come out with us. We saw those old Hurricanes going up and then a whole lot of [Messerschmitt] 109s came sweeping in over the top, going like the clappers in their wide-open line-abreast formation, always beautifully flown. Turner looked up, took his pipe out of his mouth and just said. 'Good God.' I've never forgotten it."[2]

What had shocked Turner was not the condition of the old Hurricanes, but rather the fact that they were on the island at all. When he left England he had been assured his pilots would be flying the hot new Spitfires. In truth, there was not a single Spit outside the United Kingdom.

If Turner was taken aback by the realization that he would have to lead his men into combat flying an obsolete aircraft, he soon regained his composure. Pilot Albert Houle remembered him as a commander who was not easily rattled. Recalling their first meeting, he said, Turner "showed up in the Empire Hotel in Valletta [Malta's capital] where we were billeted, much the worse for lack of sleep. He was dressed in an Aussie battle jacket, no rank badges, no wings, no decorations. We did not expect him to surface very early, so took our usual time to get to the aerodrome. Stan was there when we got there and he looked as fresh as a new plucked daisy. He had a long talk with me on what I had learned of the squadron ... When he gave an order, guys spun off trying to execute it promptly. We started to jell into a top-notch unit right then."[3]

It was more than just respect for a decorated ace that motivated Turner's pilots. They did what he asked of them out of fear. As one remembered later, "Turner was not precisely a man of refinement and he hardly ever uses polite language when he utters an opinion on something. It is not easy to contradict him. After he has drunk a few glasses he would scare off a regiment of Polish cavalry. When he was with the Canadians of No. 242 Squadron [in 1941] he did not hesitate to bring out his revolver in cafes and fire at glasses placed on the counter."[4] Nor was he averse to punching a pilot in the mouth, should he decide such a form of discipline was necessary. Amazingly, he treated superior officers with the same disdain he exhibited towards junior airmen who displeased him. Once, after listening to a pep talk from his new commander, the famous British ace Douglas "Tin Legs" Bader, Turner shouted out "Horseshit!" A moment later, almost as an afterthought, he added, "Sir."[5]

But if you won Turner's respect he would back you to the hilt — both in the air and on the ground. Bader soon discovered that. Not long after he had become friendly with the Canadian, the Englishman was ordered to take command of another squadron. Incensed, Turner approached the wing commander, jammed a pipe into the man's chest and shouted in his booming voice, "Look here, sir, you can't go and post our CO away, because we won't work for anyone else!"[6]

His rough-and-tumble approach to the business at hand rapidly won him the undying loyalty of the men who flew with him. That is evident by reading the diary of No. 411 Squadron, which Turner was commanding just prior to his posting to Malta. An entry for February 8, 1942, notes: "Information received that Squadron Leader Turner, DFC and bar, is to be posted overseas shortly. The squadron are feeling extremely 'blue' as a result and a rush of applications was received from the pilots to proceed overseas [with him]. The powers that be only laughed. However, one pilot, Pilot Officer McNair, is now extremely jubilant as he was elected to go along. The rest of the lads are more down at the heel than ever. Being with us for only two months, Squadron Leader Turner has managed to prove his capabilities as a Squadron Commander in every way and a great improvement in efficiency and discipline, both on the ground and in the air, has resulted."[7]

What the report did not say is that the 28-year-old Turner had a reputation as the toughest fighter pilot in the RAF. He had joined the Royal Canadian Air Force Auxiliary in the mid-1930s, but transferred to Britain's Royal Air Force just prior to the outbreak of war, because he could see little future in the tiny RCAF. He got off to a slow start, destroying his own plane by crashing it into a tree during a training flight. Weeks later, he damaged a second aircraft during a rough landing in the middle of a blinding storm.

He persevered, however, and eventually developed into a crack pilot. When war came, he was one of the first Allied airmen to see action. Transferred to France in May 1940, he was just in time to see the Nazi blitzkrieg steamroll its way through Western Europe. Turner saw combat for the first time during the British retreat from Dunkirk, shooting down a pair of ME-109s. By the time the Allies had been driven off the continent, he had shot down four German planes and probably destroyed two others. In the Battle of Britain, he sent two Luftwaffe bombers down in flames and damaged a third. When the bloody campaign ended he was awarded the Distinguished Flying Cross and put in charge of his own flight of six fighters. In the fighter sweeps over France in 1941 he kept up the good work, bringing his score to at least 10 enemy aircraft destroyed. Needless to say, by the time he arrived in Malta, Bull Turner was one of the most seasoned Allied fighter pilots living. Malta's governor, General W.G. Dobbie, had asked for a seasoned squadron leader. So Turner was smuggled into the island aboard a Sutherland flying boat to take command of No. 249 Squadron, which was stationed at Takali.

The hard-nosed ace immediately set about making the adjustments that would be needed if the Allies were to have any hope of winning. He may have been something of a maverick, but he was no fool. A university engineering student in his youth, Turner was one of the better educated pilots in the British Commonwealth. His first innovation was to ban the dangerously old-fashioned line-astern formations. These were flights in which the planes were lined up in single file, meaning only the leader had a good view of the sky in front of his pilots. The others were too busy trying to keep their place in formation to do much looking around. From now on the Allied fliers would fly in a V-formation, making it much easier for them to cover each other's blind spots. If every pilot in the flight kept his eyes peeled, they could cover a much wider area, making it difficult for the Germans and Italians to take them by surprise. He also ordered his men to wait in huts near their planes, dressed in full battle gear. That way, they could dash to the flight line and be airborne almost as soon as enemy formations were picked up on radar. Turner drilled the need for a quick takeoff into them constantly, realizing the sooner they got off the ground, the faster they would be able to gain the vital altitude needed to take the opposition by surprise. He also insisted they form up south of Malta, so Axis fliers would have to stare directly into a blazing sun to spot them.

Turner taught his pilots to attack bombers from the front instead of the rear, as had been the custom. A frontal assault greatly increased the closing speed, giving enemy gunners less time to line up a charging Hurricane in its sights. It also afforded the attacker a better shot at the enemy plane's more vulnerable spots — the cockpit, the engines and the fuel tanks. Furthermore, a head-on charge often spooked the bomber pilots, causing them to dive out of the path of the fighters in order to avoid collisions. That broke up the enemy formations, providing the Allied pilots with easier targets. A group of bombers flying closely together could cover each other with a whole array of machine guns. But a single aircraft on its own was easy meat for most fighter pilots.

The techniques were simple enough, but they were not being followed before Turner arrived, and the results were painfully obvious to anyone who could read squadron combat reports. During January's rather sporadic harassment raids, the Axis airmen had shot down 11 Hurricanes for the loss of only six of their own planes. The Allied performance during the first two weeks of February had not been any better. The truth is only poor weather conditions, which had severely restricted operations on both sides, had saved the defenders from annihilation during the first six weeks of the new year. Now, Turner was determined to give them a fighting chance before spring weather permitted continuous fighting.

As far as English pilot Laddie Lucas was concerned, Turner was one of the great unsung heroes of the siege. "He took the island's flying apart, transformed it within a month, and left his mark upon it which was never, subsequently, to be erased. I was just a pupil in the class watching his mastery ... I remember what I was able to absorb from flying with Stan Turner in Malta in the early spring days of 1942. He was then demonstrably exhausted, and greatly in need of a rest, but the hallmark of class shone brightly through his performances and lit the way for the rest of us to follow."[8]

Turner's arrival on the scene, however important, was not nearly enough to stem the tide. The situation was nothing short of desperate, with only a dozen serviceable fighter planes left on Malta. On top of that, two of the island's three airfields were temporarily out of commission because of flooding caused by heavy rains. Fortunately, a gale raged for four days shortly after he flew into the garrison, grounding the Axis forces and giving Turner time to regroup. He put his ground crews to work virtually around the clock and even ordered pilots to help service the planes. Within a few days several damaged Hurricanes had been made operational, giving the Allies close to 20 aircraft with which to defend themselves.

His inspections of the airfields revealed disturbing facts. Hal Far, located near the southern tip of Malta, had only a single, grassy runway with a steep, rocky cliff at one end and a treacherous ravine at the other. Powerful crosswinds often swept the airstrip, making take-offs and landings dangerous. Takali, in the centre of the island, was surrounded by high hills that, along with the ever-present winds, could make flying in and out hazardous. But worse than that was the mud. Takali was located at the basin of what was once a lake, and it was quickly transformed into a quagmire whenever it rained. At Luqa, located near the southwest corner of Malta, the Allied pilots had to put up with an incomplete runway. The base, which was only four years old, had an 1,100-metre-long airstrip that was only three-quarters of its intended length. British engineers had packed up their tools and gone to France in 1940, leaving the job unfinished. About the best that could be said was that Luqa, which had been designed by First World War ace Bob Leckie, had two runways that crossed each other, thus making it possible to approach the place from any direction. Hal Far and Takali, on the other hand, had only one airstrip apiece.

Despite the almost impossible conditions, Bull Turner boldly told his men they could prevail. He showed them how to beat the odds on February 22, just six days after he had arrived. It happened in almost Hollywood style, at high noon, when radar picked up a trio of Junkers-88s coming in from the north, escorted by at least a dozen Messerschmitt-109s. Turner and seven of his pilots were lounging in deck chairs only yards from their Hurricanes, enjoying the warmth of a midday Maltese winter sun, when the call to action came. A few had been playing poker, some were chatting aimlessly, and one was writing a letter home. Now the discipline Turner had instilled in them paid off. Within seconds they were strapping faded yellow Mae West lifejackets and whitish-brown parachute harnesses over their blue uniforms. As they ran to their planes, Turner found himself savouring the anticipation of impending danger. Like most fighter pilots, he found that the ritual of preparing for a combat mission was in itself enough to get his adrenaline flowing. Hauling himself onto the port wing of his machine, Turner climbed swiftly into the cockpit, fastening his brown leather helmet onto his head as he did so. Grabbing his black rubber facemask, he plugged it into an outlet in front of him, connecting it to both the radio and the oxygen system. Pulling his goggles over his eyes, he pressed the ignition button and listened with satisfaction as the

German bomber shot down on Malta. Courtesy of Eric Crist

Hurricane's 1,000-horsepower Rolls-Royce Merlin engine roared into life. A scant two minutes after the alarm sounded, he was leading his men down the runway. All eight pilots clawed their way up to 4,500 metres, in record time, taking up position in the sun. For once the Allies had the advantage of both height and surprise. Ordering his men to dive on the bombers, Turner remained above, like a mother hen guarding her chicks. When the Messerschmitts attempted to intercept, the Canadian swooped down on them, all eight of his machine guns blazing. Glowing red tracers streaked into the canopy of the nearest German fighter, shattering it into glittering shards. Seconds later, the black-crossed machine tumbled end over end, crashing straight into the Mediterranean.

Perhaps inspired by this brand of leadership, two other pilots downed German planes that day. But the victories did not come cheaply. British flyer Ron Chaffe, flying his first mission from Malta, was shot down. Although he managed to bail out, he came down in the sea and was never seen again.

Next day the defenders claimed two more kills, giving them five conquests in just two days. But if they were developing any cockiness, such feelings evaporated before February was out, after Turner himself went down in a ball of flames. It happened, the Canadian recalled later, as a result of "a fatal comedy of errors. One of my pilots and I set off to intercept four ME-109s coming in over Gozo Island. I saw them high above me, then lost them in the sun. Ground control said they would steer us."[9]

Turner strained his eyes, looking above, ahead and to both sides. Nothing.

"Where the hell are they?" he demanded.

"You should see them by now," the ground controller replied. "They're dead ahead of you."

The ace gazed forward until his eyeballs ached, but could only see a vast, empty, azure blue sky.

Oh God! The controller had mistaken Turner and his wingman, American Don Tedford, for the Germans. That had to be it. And it could only mean there were two enemy planes closing in for the kill at that very moment.

"Break!"

Turner shouted the hysterical warning to Tedford and banked hard to the right. Too late.

"The turn had just started when the cockpit exploded in a mass of oil, glycol smoke and fire," he said later.[10] He could see tracers chewing up his right wingtip and felt a stinging sensation as a cannon shell grazed his flying helmet, tearing his goggles from his face. Directly in front of him, yellow flames shot from his engine. Wind whipped through the shattered cockpit, pinning him against his seat. Turner kicked the rudder bar and dropped the crippled Hurricane into a hideous spin, hoping to persuade his attackers that he was finished. He pulled up seconds before crashing into the ground. Luckily, the steep dive had doused the flames, and his engine, although skipping badly, was still keeping him in the air.

Turner's face had been cut by flying glass and his eyebrows were singed, but he was otherwise unhurt. Still, he was so badly shaken that he remembered nothing of the picture-perfect landing he made at Luqa. The next thing he recalled, after pulling out of the death dive, was waking up in a hospital. His wingman was not so fortunate. He managed to bail out of his burning Hurricane only to drown in the Mediterranean.

Howard Coffin, one of the three remaining American pilots on Malta, was shaken by Tedford's loss, telling his diary, "Words cannot express how I feel at this moment. I've lost a buddy and the airforce has lost a wizard pilot."[11]

Back in England, meanwhile, Prime Minister Churchill knew nothing about the individual raids, but he did know he could not afford to let Malta be lost. On the day Turner was wounded and Tedford died, the prime minister fired off a telegram to General Claude Auchinleck, commander-in-chief of Britain's Middle East forces, virtually begging him to take the pressure off Malta. Specifically, Churchill wanted the extraordinarily cautious Scotsman to launch an immediate offensive against Rommel. He was hoping such action would force Hitler to redirect some of his bombers and fighters from Sicily to Libya. But the general would not be hurried, insisting he would need another four months of preparation before he could tackle the Desert Fox.

Churchill was almost beside himself when he received the reply. He wired back telling the general he had to act sooner or the island fortress would surely be lost. Once that happened, there was no doubt that Rommel would be able to get supplies much more quickly than Auchinleck.

General Auchinleck responded with a lengthy report, laced with excuses as to why he could not take the initiative. A glum Churchill noted later the document called for a complete halt to offensive operations until June or July. Boiled down, it meant Auchinleck was willing to let Malta fall.

If Churchill was concerned at the end of February, it was with good reason. The Axis fliers, who had flown 2,450 sorties against Malta in January and 3,090 in February, were about to launch an all-out offensive that would be remembered in history simply as the "March Blitz." Malta's ordeal by fire was about to get under way in earnest.

CHAPTER 3

THE MARCH BLITZ

To the Allied radar operators working inside Malta's underground bunkers that March 1, 1942, it seemed as if the entire Luftwaffe was coming straight for them. They picked up dozens, and then hundreds, of blips on their screens as wave after wave of planes roared in from Sicily. Frantic calls were placed to all three airfields, but the RAF was only able to scramble 13 Hurricanes. Despite the odds, the defenders hurled themselves into the enemy formations.

In a magnificent display of courage, Canadian Dave Howe dove straight through a swarm of escorting Messerschmitts and made for a gaggle of Junkers-88s. Lining up the nearest bomber, he shot it to pieces. Howe had no time to savour his triumph. Moments later, his own aircraft was riddled with Mauser cannon shells and he was forced to take to the silk, breaking a leg when he landed near the town of Marsaxlokk. Next, American pilot Jimmy Dew was swarmed by ME-109s and sent down in flames. Too badly wounded to get out of his crippled fighter, he died in the cockpit. Canadian Ray Harvey, meanwhile, was mixing it up with half a dozen Nazi fighters. He managed to damage one of them, but Harvey, like Howe and Dew before him, was quickly overwhelmed by superior numbers and shot down in flames. A shattering explosion tossed him clear of the wreckage, but his parachute failed to open and the 22-year-old native of Desoronto, Ontario, plunged three kilometres to his death.

Two days after the Luftwaffe launched the March Blitz, Malta's tiny bomber force struck back. Ten Wellingtons raided Palermo harbour, sinking three Italian transport ships as they were being loaded with tanks and ammunition for Rommel. Forty others were damaged, five severely. General Kesselring responded by ordering an all-out

Wellington bomber crew in an English airfield, before flight to Malta. From left: Cliff Mortimer, Reg Thackeray, Rowly Heatson, Wally Hammond, Bert Horton and Jeff Redell. Courtesy of Reg Thackeray

attack on Malta's airfields the next day. The defenders shot down three of the attackers, but no less than eight Allied machines were blasted to pieces on the ground.

One of those who survived the raid was Wellington bomber navigator Walter Nugent. "The mess got bombed all to hell," he told the author. "It was a beautiful mess and they cut it right in half. The next morning we had breakfast there and half the dining table was gone." Nugent, a 29-year-old with a wife back in Canada, survived by taking refuge in a makeshift shelter behind the mess. "We had a stone bomb shelter that was 20 feet deep, with some rubble on top of it. It took two direct hits. The bombs made one hell of a noise, like nothing I'd ever heard before. We were lucky no one was killed because most shelters were 80 feet deep. We all came out laughing like crazy — a nervous reaction to the fright."

Nor was that his only close call on the ground. "The bombing was steady. I don't think anybody realizes just how steady it was. It was 24 hours a day. Once, I came in from a flight, went to the operations room, a little, half-bombed-out-building, and was giving my report when a raid went down. I ran to a shelter and tripped on the top step like a dope. I fell down the stairs and was knocked out. I was in a hurry because a bomb was coming down."

Before long, Malta's bomber force had been reduced to a single Wellington and a handful of old Swordfish biplanes. It was not much of a strike force, but the Allies put it to surprisingly good use. Nugent, who flew in the lone Wellington several times, said his crew constantly harassed enemy convoys headed for North Africa. "We found a convoy every night we went out and we always attacked it," he recalled. "We worked in co-operation with the Stringbags [the fliers' nickname for the antiquated Swordfish]. After we picked the ships up on radar they attacked with torpedoes."

Malta's last Wellington seemed to live a charmed life. "We never encountered any night fighters," Nugent said. "We used to fly our first 20 miles from Malta at 500 feet so they couldn't detect us. We saw a lot of them, but they didn't find us, thank God." Nor was flak all that heavy, although Nugent and his mates received a hot reception one night when they came in low to bomb an Axis vessel. "One night we got quite a bit of flak from a ship that I was bombing. But I almost got it. I came within 10 feet of it. I didn't hit it, but I probably sprang a few of its plates."

Despite the good work of the few remaining fighter and bomber crews, Air Vice-Marshal Lloyd, who was in charge of air operations on Malta, realized the battle was being lost. Firing off an urgent cable to London, he declared, "Air attacks on aerodromes very serious. Much minor damage to aircraft sufficient to make them unserviceable for night operations. They are repaired next day and then hit again ... Must have more fighters as soon a possible. Delay [in receiving Spitfires] is annoying."[1]

Annoying was not the word for it. Bull Turner had already warned Lloyd that unless his pilots got Spits within days, the defenders would be finished. Prime Minister Churchill was fully aware that unless he could get modern warplanes to Malta, the battle, and the whole war, would be lost. But how to do it? The Spitfire did not have the range to fly all the way from England and it was not designed to take off from aircraft carriers. No one was even sure a Spitfire could pick up enough speed before reaching the end of the flight deck. Even if the pilots could somehow make it into the air, they would still be a long way from their destination. The Mediterranean was essentially an Axis lake, which meant no Allied carrier could hope to get any closer to Malta than about 1,000 kilometres. The Royal Navy found that out the hard way on November 12, 1941, when the Nazi submarine U-81 torpedoed the aircraft carrier *Ark Royal* 50 kilometres east of the big British base at Gibraltar. Still, 1,000 kilometres was just barely within the Spitfires' range of endurance. Churchill, realizing he had no other choice, ordered the navy to load 16 of the sleek, pointed-winged fighters onto the aircraft carrier *Eagle*.

The unsung heroes of the operation would prove to be a small band of female pilots from Britain's Air Transport Auxiliary. They were a courageous group of young women who regularly flew warplanes straight from the factory to Royal Air Force stations across the United Kingdom. Although they were strictly prohibited from going into combat, their jobs were hazardous enough. Margot Gore, who commanded a group of 50 fliers, recalled her station being raided for 90 consecutive nights by Luftwaffe bombers. On top of that, they often had to ferry planes in the most foul weather. "I did not have all that number of casualties," she recalled later. "We had a little under the average 10 per cent death rate. Very surprising really, because the weather was often peculiar, and we had no navigational aids whatsoever: we only had a compass, but no radio ... we had to fly by contact, and we had to have certain minimum weather conditions — a cloud base and a visibility which they increased for faster aircraft. But still, if the weather was bad and you were under an 800-foot cloud base, you didn't see very far. So it was surprising, really, that we didn't fly into more hillsides."

The weather and enemy raiders were not the only dangers. Just to get airborne they had to take off from "an unpleasant little east/west strip. It was quite narrow and you went through a gap in the trees. At Chattis Hill there was an old racecourse, and you took off up a hill which was part of the gallops."

Gore seemed to lead a charmed life. Unlike many of the other women, she never had an engine fail on her and never had to put one of her planes down in a meadow. This despite the fact that the mechanics assigned to her unit had previously worked for London's municipal bus company! None of them, Gore was sure, had ever seen an airplane close up in their entire lives.

Her most memorable moment came when she received orders to get 16 Spitfires to the carrier *Eagle*.

> "One day I went into the operations [room] and found on our books a page-and-a-half of Spitfires marked P1W — Priority One aircraft were urgent, you moved them before everything else. And 'W' was even worse, because it meant you had to go and sit there, wherever the plane was, and wait till you got it to wherever it was supposed to go. Of course, this coincided with the most ghastly spell of weather! The cloud was absolutely on the deck.
>
> "There was no way you could take off. So we dutifully went over by car to Chattis Hill, where they were, and sat there. Then they rang and said, 'Haven't you moved those Spitfires yet?' I said, 'Have you looked out your window?' — 'We haven't got any windows!' they said. I said, 'Well, I have got a window, and I can't see the far side of the aerodrome, which isn't very far away.' — 'Well, they are absolutely vital! You must get them off!'"

Gore flatly refused. Then, thinking better of it, she walked over to her plane and told the nearest mechanic to prepare the Spitfire for flight. The grease monkey may not have had much experience with airplanes but, knowing an overcast sky when he saw one, he all but begged her to stay on the ground.

Gore would have none of it. She figured if she could stay low enough she might be able to keep sight of the ground. She gunned her engine and roared down the soggy runway. Unfortunately, she did not get very far. Seconds after her wheels lifted off she found herself inside a cloud. Realizing it was impossible to fulfil her mission, she turned back and landed.

In the end, she had to wait four days before she could lead her women to the *Eagle*. "We eventually got a letter from Churchill thanking us for the part that we played in the delivery of these marvellous machines," she said. "They got to Malta just in time, I gather; they were down to about two Swordfish by the time they got there."[2]

Once the Spits were on board the *Eagle* the drama was only half over. Flying halfway across the Mediterranean in search of a tiny

Pilot Eric Crist and his Spitfire airplane. Courtesy of Eric Crist

speck of an island was a bold gamble. The year before, the RAF had suffered a major setback when a formation of 37 Hurricanes got lost attempting to fly to Malta. They eventually ran out of fuel and crashed into the sea. None of the pilots lived to tell the tale. Making matters even more problematic was the condition of the *Eagle*. It was the worst excuse for a carrier in the entire British fleet. Originally built at the turn of the century as a battleship to be sold to the Chilean navy, at the conclusion of the First World War it was sold back to Britain, where it was converted into an aircraft carrier designed for wood-and-fabric biplanes. Nevertheless, on March 7, 1942, 15 Spitfire pilots (the 16th had engine trouble and had to stay behind) climbed nervously into their machines and got ready to attempt what many of them thought was impossible. None of the pilots had ever even been on board a carrier before, never mind having taken off from one.

Most of the pilots quickly discovered they could not get up enough forward speed to lift off gracefully. By the time they reached the end of the deck they simply fell off the ship, plunging towards the waves below. Because the drop was nearly 20 metres, however, they had time to pick up the extra momentum necessary to stay aloft, provided they kept their noses down for a moment or two. It took a stout heart to resist the temptation to pull up, but each pilot who disappeared over the edge reappeared seconds later, clawing for altitude.

"It was pretty scary," Canadian fighter pilot Eric Crist recalled. "We'd never seen an aircraft carrier, really. And the *Eagle* had a pretty short flight deck, only 390 feet. There were no flaps to assist you on take-off. Spitfire flaps were either fully up or fully down, there was no in between. The first one off was our commanding officer. He disappeared over the bow and finally staggered into view about a half a mile ahead. That didn't inspire any confidence. I remember the flight crews on the carrier removed the chocks. There was a sailor on each wingtip and a sailor on the tailplane to hold her down. I got her revved up pretty good. She was just jumping. And I'm of slight stature. I was only about 126 pounds. I got airborne before I got to the end of the flight deck. I had a pretty fair wind off the deck. I think I caught her just right."[3]

Fellow Canadian Noel "Buzz" Ogilvie had a more hair-raising time. "I was the second one off," he told the author. "My squadron leader was a big guy and he went first. I saw him go off and drop out of sight. That didn't give me too much confidence. Our propellers were made out of metal, so they didn't give you too much acceleration. Later on we had propellers made out of laminated wood, which was a lot better. Fortunately, the squadron leader reappeared and I thought to myself, 'Maybe I can make it.' I dropped right off the end and came close to the water before eventually gaining height. The flight was close to four hours from the take-off point at Algiers to Malta."[4]

For pilots who had spent months flying in a grey English winter, the view as they approached Malta was breathtaking. The Mediterranean was a deep blue, turning pale green near the island. Whitecaps could be seen distinctly as they pounded into the dark brown cliffs. Once over Malta itself, they could make out hundreds of red and white limestone houses, greenish-brown fields divided by stone walls, majestic church spires and everywhere bright sunshine. Sicily was visible, dark and foreboding, 100 kilometres to the north.

On Malta, the whole population seemed to know they were coming. Hundreds of schoolboys ran down to the docks before they arrived, scanning the skies anxiously. Then, hugging the waves, the

Spitfire pilot Bob Taggart and his wife. Courtesy of Bob Taggart

formation suddenly appeared. As they roared over the heads of the waving people below, several pilots waggled their wings in greetings.

The arrival of the Spitfires had an enormously positive impact on the morale of everyone on the island. "They were like manna from heaven," British infantryman Harry Kennedy recalled. "It was just like a rain after a very long drought."[5]

The Spitfires may have been a sight for sore eyes, but they were too few in number to turn the tide and, when the Axis formations assaulted Malta again two days later, the old Hurricanes were still very much in evidence. In fact, 19 of them managed to get airborne in time to intercept a morning raid by three Ju-88s escorted by only nine Messerschmitts. For once the Allied pilots had the edge in numbers and five of the attackers were damaged.

The Spitfires went into action for the first time on March 10, three days after they arrived. Led by Bull Turner, seven of them bounced a formation of ME-109s, shooting three down. They fell on a pair of Ju-88s next, damaging both of them. It was not all one-sided, however. A Messerschmitt blew a Spitfire out of the sky and its pilot, 20-year-old Australian Kenny Murray, died when his parachute failed to open.

Fighting continued on a daily basis but, for a while at least, although many enemy planes were hit, few were actually destroyed. More often than not, German and Italian aircraft were only being damaged after an Allied pilot had worked himself into a favourable position to fire. Pilot Eric Crist blamed the odds against the defenders for their inability to finish off crippled opponents.

> We were always badly outnumbered. You didn't have time to stick with one aircraft for any more than a second or two. If you damaged a bomber there were always fighters on you. You'd like to take a second shot at it but you had to look after yourself. It was difficult to finish them off because you were always under attack. It was a dog-eat-dog kind of affair. I remember one time I saw enemy fighters coming in but I thought I had enough time to line up a bomber for another shot. I cut it too fine and they got a pretty good burst into my aircraft. A big chunk of one wing came off, plus I was hit myself, although not seriously. The Spitfire went into a dive and by the time I recovered I was too low to bail out. I flew into the airstrip with my wheels up. I came in at 160 miles per hour but I made a pretty successful landing. Still, the plane was a writeoff, which was unfortunate because we were under unwritten orders to bring the plane in safe at all cost. I got out and an ambulance took me to hospital, where I was to remain for the next six weeks.[6]

Another problem was that Fighter Command had placed too much emphasis on formation flying and too little on gunnery. Indeed, a scientific analysis of combat films following one particularly savage battle led to the shocking conclusion that 75 percent of the Allied pilots were poor marksmen. "The average fighter pilot was not a good shot," British ace Johnnie Johnson wrote later. "The average standard of shooting in Fighter Command was not high, for too little attention had been devoted to gunnery instructions, and the kills in any squadron always seemed to fall to the same three or four pilots, while the remainder had to be content with a probable or a damaged, because they hose-piped their machine guns from skidding aeroplanes, opened fire from absurd ranges, and could not estimate their amount of forward allowance. The average pilot in those days could usually hit an enemy aeroplane when he overhauled it from dead line astern and

Air raid in progress over Malta. Courtesy of Eric Crist

sprayed his opponents with eight machine guns, but give him a testing deflection shot at angles of more than a few degrees and he usually failed to make a kill."[7]

The Axis pilots had the same problems. German air historian Hans Ring discovered a mere 300 pilots accounted for over half of the Russian planes claimed by the Luftwaffe throughout the whole war. The top 10 German aces shot down a mind-boggling 2,500 Soviet aircraft. Another study showed that of 80 Luftwaffe airmen in one squadron, 60 had no kills to their credit. The situation was the same among the Italians, where a handful of fliers did most of the scoring.

At least the Axis fliers on Sicily could improve their marksmanship through target practice. On Malta, unfortunately, no practice shooting was possible because ammunition was always in critically short supply.

On March 28, Bull Turner knocked an ME-109 down in flames for his second confirmed kill over Malta and his 12th of the war. His wingman, a tough Nova Scotian named Buck McNair, damaged a second German fighter in the same dogfight. Turner was teaching his pilots the importance of being aggressive. One newcomer recalled a brush with a Ju-88 that shows just how quick Turner was on the draw. "All I saw of the engagement, as I dropped further and further behind, was Stan and Crow belting into the 88 with everything they'd got until the aircraft disappeared into a cloud. I never even got a squirt at it."[8]

Despite the Spitfires, and despite Turner's brilliant leadership, it was becoming increasingly evident that the Allies were losing the battle. Malta's airfields and docks were being hit hard, as were the towns and villages. During March alone, 70 churches, 18 convents, 22 schools, eight hospitals, five banks and 48 other public buildings were destroyed or seriously damaged.

As disturbing as those statistics are, they do not begin to tell us what it was like for the people caught in the open as bombs exploded all around them. To get an inkling of what that was like we must turn to the accounts of survivors. A British foot soldier has left behind perhaps the best description of what a raid looked like. He wrote: "Bombs were dropped in and around all the creeks, causing terrific clouds of dust, flying masonry and iron. A complete motor-car went sailing over the top of us. The dust and spray often blinded our view but the dive-bombers came on. As they broke through the dust they seemed like hawks looking for prey. The sight was one never to be forgotten, the bursts of the heavies, the red tracers of the Bofors and light machine guns, and the illumination made by the crashing planes."[9]

Another soldier recalled that "the dust after any air raid is terrific, but in Malta, where the soil is so light and the stones so soft, the cloud of dust that rises is as thick as any smokescreen ... Sometimes an hour later one could see the dust cloud in a compact mass miles out above the sea, driven along with the wind."[10]

Those recollections may help us visualize the attacks but they don't tell us much about what they *felt* like. For a sense of that we must turn to a chilling account written by fighter pilot Buck McNair, who was in a building that took a direct hit from a 225-kilogram bomb. McNair, an honours student in university before the war, saw five fellow pilots blown to pieces before his eyes. His story reads in part:

> When I came to I didn't know where I was. I didn't feel I was dead, but I didn't feel whole. My eyes were open, but my jaws and chest didn't seem to be there. There was no pain, I just didn't seem to have jaws or

chest. I felt for my tin hat, then I started to be able to see just as if the sun was coming up after a great darkness. I tested myself. I felt carefully with my fingers and found that I had a face and a chest, so I felt better. It started to get light. The darkness had been due to the showers of dust from the stone buildings ... As I became conscious, I found I was upstairs; but I knew I shouldn't be upstairs. I should be downstairs. Then I realized I had been blown upstairs, either through a door or through an opening at the turn of the staircase. I'd been thrown up 20 or 30 feet.

I went out on to the roof and back down the main staircase which was barely hanging in place. I saw the bodies lying at the foot of it. They were in a heap. There was no blood. The raid was still on — the All Clear hadn't sounded. But everything seemed very quiet. Heavy dust covered the bodies. I looked at them — studied them. One was headless, the head had been cut cleanly away from the top of the shoulders. I didn't see the head, but I could recognize the man by his very broad shoulders. I heard a moan, so I put my hand gently on the bodies to feel which of them was alive. One of them I noticed had a hole, more than a foot wide, right through the abdomen. Another's head was split wide open in two halves, from back to front, by a piece of shrapnel. The face had expanded to twice its size. How the man managed still to be alive I didn't know. I thought of shooting him with my revolver. As I felt for it, I heard Bud Connell's voice behind me: "Look at this mess."

I put my hand against the wall, but it slithered down it. It had seemed dry with all the dust, but when I took my hand away I found it was covered with blood with bits of meat stuck to it — like at the butcher's when they're chopping up meat and cleaning up a joint. I turned to Bud. "For God's sake," I said, "don't come in here." Then I noticed my battle dress and trousers were torn and ripped."[11]

McNair helped get a wounded man onto a stretcher, then discovered his left arm was out of its socket. He pushed it back in place, sat down on the side of the road along with another survivor and began cursing the Germans. Deciding to get drunk, the men marched over to the mess and ordered a bottle of whiskey. When the bartender refused to serve them, they jumped over the bar, broke into the liquor cabinet and made off with a bottle of White Horse each. McNair swallowed huge gulps straight out of the bottle, only stopping after the alcohol had helped him ease some of the almost unbearable tension.

Virtually every serviceman who survived the siege experienced at least one narrow escape during a bombing raid. Arthur Inch, an RAF fitter/armourer, was nearly killed by a German bomb the day after he arrived. "From Egypt we were posted to Malta and on the night before we finally went we flew half way there in a DC-3 but we had to return as Malta was being bombed," he wrote the author. "We set off again the next evening and after eight-and-a-half hours flying time we reached the island and began circling around a few times and it wasn't until we landed that we were told that the pilot could only get one of the landing wheels down, but eventually he got the other one down. The next morning we had all to go to the sick bay and we had to scramble under the tables as a bomb exploded in the next street, so a lucky escape to start with."12

If the servicemen on Malta were taking a beating, so were the civilians. At first, however, people were fascinated by what was happening around them. Indeed, some have described the raids as almost awe-inspiring events. Myriam Mifsud, who was a teenage girl at the time, found the spectacle of German planes diving out of the sun strangely beautiful to behold. "I remember we used to make a mad dash for the roof, which was flat, with binoculars, to watch the dogfights. The mid-day sun was very bright, one big yellow ball. The Germans used to come at noon and they'd dive out of the sun, to make it harder for the gunners to hit them. It looked as if the sun had exploded as dozens of them came down out of it. The planes were all shiny with the sun reflecting off them."13

Others found the sight of Stuka divebombers hurtling down at breakneck speed unforgettable in a different sort of way. Teenager George Porter was convinced the enemy planes were in their death throes when he first saw them. "I thought they were being shot down by anti-aircraft batteries because I'd never seen divebombers before."[14]

Vincenza Desira, who was a young mother of three when the siege began, also found something bewitching about the raids, at least in the beginning. "At first it was fun. We used to go out on the roof to watch the planes. Malta is a very quiet place," and the dogfights provided people with some excitement.[15]

Before long, even the children could tell friend from foe and they cheered on the Allied pilots much like sports fans rooting for the home side at a football match. "We used to know the planes by the sounds they made," Myriam Mifsud said. "You'd yell 'Oh good, they got him.' You wouldn't think there's a man in there with a mother." Her attitude changed when she saw a pilot bail out, only to be hit by his own somersaulting aircraft. "It hit his chute and dragged him down. Then there was a big explosion."

George Porter saw more than one man die in his parachute. "I have seen German fighter planes gunning the British fighter pilots in their parachutes. I remember, it was a Sunday and there was a dogfight. The Hurricanes weren't as fast as the Messerschmitts and they got shot down. It was terrible."[16]

Eventually, it became too dangerous to go outside to watch the air battles. "When the Italian planes came over early in the war they were very high up and you couldn't see them," Mifsud said. "Bombs landed all over the place. But when the Germans came we had some very acute action going on. You couldn't go out into the streets without getting machine gunned. Some villages were completely wiped out."[17]

Vincenza Desira realized just how serious the situation was becoming when the homes of friends and relatives started to get blown up. "My brothers came to live with us because we had a shelter and they had lost their homes. Then my late husband lost seven members of his family in one air raid. They were in a shelter but they thought the air raid was over and came out. The last bomb killed them."

On many days the enemy aircraft were over Malta almost non-stop. "It became really serious," Desira remembers. "One time we were outside and we all had to lay on the ground because they were machine gunning everything."

George Scerri, who was a 12-year-old schoolboy when the war began, was also caught in the open by low-flying enemy fighters. "I was machine gunned by a Messerschmitt-109. I was on a bicycle looking at the harbour when I saw a Messerschmitt coming down fast, strafing everybody who moved. And it dropped a bomb, too. I was scared. I could see soil and dust being kicked up by the bullets. I hid behind a wall. During another raid our school was blown up by the Germans. Fortunately, it was on a Saturday and no one was there. I remember another raid destroyed the village of Zabbar. I don't know why they did that. It was about two miles away from some anti-aircraft batteries but I think they were after the buildings. They hit our parish church on the side."[18]

Milo Vassallo, who was only six when the war started, remembers his parish church being hit as well. "I was an altar boy but I left just before the raid, at 2:30 p.m., to go to a shelter. One old lady stayed behind and she was killed. She was the only person in the church."[19]

At the village of Mosta there was a much happier ending to a church bombing. It took place when a 225-kilogram projectile slammed through the roof of Malta's most splendid place of worship and landed smack in the midst of several hundred frightened worshippers. What happened next created one of the island's most enduring legends. "The church dome in Mosta is the third largest in the world and the people used to go there for safety," Myriam Mifsud recalled. "It was not a shelter, but people felt safe there. On that day a bomb hit the ceiling, which should have collapsed, but didn't. Then it fell inside the church, which was full of people, and landed by the altar. It should have exploded but never did. It was a miracle. The shell of this huge bomb, which is about five feet tall, is still there, on display in the church."[20]

At a nearby hospital on the same day people were not so fortunate. A string of bombs demolished a whole wing, killing 32 patients and two nurses.

Milo Vassallo, who lost an uncle in another raid, remembers spending night after night in bomb shelters. "Our parents even used to take us there during school days. We had our lessons in the shelters."

Lena Banavage, who was 13 when the first air raids took place, says life on Malta was one of continuous turmoil during the siege. Air raid

Lena Banavage, a 13-year-old Maltese schoolgirl at the beginning of the Second World War. Courtesy of Noel Banavage

sirens were constantly going off, and it was her responsibility to round up her younger brother and get him into a shelter. Her closest brush with death came when friends invited her to a movie theatre. She wanted to go, but her parents refused permission. As fate would have it, the cinema was bombed and all her friends were killed. On another occasion she lost a cousin, who was serving meals to sailors aboard a ship in Grand Harbour when the vessel took a direct hit. Everyone on board was killed.

Narrow escapes were so commonplace that many of the survivors talk about them almost nonchalantly. Ed Cauchi, who was 13 when the war began, told the author only one bomb struck his village throughout the siege. Later, he mentioned in passing that it had landed in the family well and that the blast had collapsed the ceiling in his father's bedroom. With prodding, he admitted he had once been caught in the middle of a raid while working in Valletta. "I was collecting money on a bus when bombs started flying all over the bus terminal, which was near the harbour. It was very frightening, but there were catacombs right under the terminal. Everybody got out of the bus and into the catacombs in a hurry. Another time when I was at the main airport I saw a German plane piloted by an Austrian take a direct hit. The pilot left the plane too late ... I could see his flesh all over the barbed wire. It was very disturbing."[21]

Myriam Mifsud had her closest call as she tried to scramble down a crowded stairway into a shelter. "Once, I was just going down into a shelter when a bomb landed really close by and the blast pushed us all down into it."

But not all the memories are bad ones. "It wasn't all terror," Mifsud says. "You were young and you forgot. You're frightened one moment and feel nothing the next. I remember in school we had to keep putting gas masks on, but they were never needed. There were funny things, too. The boys' school was near the girls' school, and whoever was in charge of the lantern would always say, 'Let's go to the boys' shelter.' We wanted to be with the boys, so there were fun times too."[22]

George Scerri felt the siege made people more innovative. "You tried to make everything yourself," he said. "And I mean everything. If you had no bike tires you stuffed your wheels with rugs."[23]

There are no such pleasant memories for the sailors who were try-ing to bring Malta some relief. The Royal Navy was having a terrible time trying to keep the garrison supplied with food, ammunition and other vital materials. Four ships had made it through the Axis block-ade in January, but all three transports that tried to get through in February had been lost. In early March, the British cruiser *Naiad* was sent to the bottom by a U-boat, and on the 20th of the month there was further disaster at sea. Four merchantmen, escorted by several British naval ships, made a mad dash for Malta, bringing with them 26,000 tonnes of badly needed provisions. The Italian navy sent one battleship, three cruisers and 10 destroyers to head them off at the Gulf of Sitre. But the British used smokescreens and aggressive tactics to drive the enemy off. In the end, three Italian vessels were sunk and the battleship was damaged. But the fight delayed the convoy long enough to allow the Luftwaffe and Regia Aeronautica to swing into action. Hundreds of enemy planes attacked the convoy with torpe-does, bombs and cannon fire. Two ships were sunk 16 kilometres from shore and a third went down right in Grand Harbour. The fourth, although badly damaged, managed to limp into port with its precious cargo still intact.

Now tragedy struck. The crippled ship sat in the harbour for three days without being unloaded. Governor Dobbie, a hopelessly indeci-sive leader, failed to take the actions necessary to ensure its supplies were brought ashore in time. The vessel simply sat at dockside because nervous Maltese workers refused to go anywhere near it. They knew it would be a prime target for any raiders. Dobbie made matters worse by refusing to set down a smokescreen to hide the ship, deciding the precaution was not necessary. When he finally realized the stevedores were not going to risk their lives to unload it, he ordered British soldiers to do the job. By then it was almost too late. German bombers struck with devastating accuracy on the fourth day, sinking the transport after only a few thousand tonnes of supplies had been unloaded. One disgusted English serviceman blamed the civilians, declaring they "ran like scared rabbits" at the sight of enemy planes.[24] But Dobbie's bungling leadership was as much to blame as Maltese cowardice. In the end it did not matter who was at fault. What really mattered was that thousands of tonnes of badly needed supplies had been lost and Malta was one step closer to ignoble surrender.

The only bright side to the débâcle was that the incredibly tough Buck McNair had managed to recover from his earlier ordeal in time to shoot down an ME-109 hovering about the convoy as it steamed towards the island. Despite this loss, the Axis fliers had clearly won the day. In addition to sinking four ships, they had knocked out Malta's submarine base, blasted Governor Dobbie's house, and hit the Takali airfield with no less than 100 tonnes of bombs. A fuel dump had been destroyed, the mess building was flattened, and the runway was so pocked with craters that the base was temporarily put out of action.

Newcomer Slim Yarra, a young Australian pilot, wrote in his diary, "The Jerries really did some spectacular bombing. The dust covered an area of at least five square miles and smoke from burning petrol and oil made black smudges against the yellow dust cloud. I was surprised and shaken to learn that this happened at least three times daily."[25]

Governor Dobbie, meanwhile, was on the verge of a nervous breakdown. Aides said he spent much of his time on his knees, praying to God for deliverance. A gentle man, he worried constantly about the safety of the Maltese civilians. He was so concerned, critics said, that he did not have the backbone to make hard decisions. As March drew to a close, he wrote to Churchill, describing the effect of lack of food on the garrison as "critical."

Frank and Lena Banavage, Maltese civilians. Courtesy of Noel Banavage

The prime minister was badly rattled. He immediately sent a directive to Major General Sir Hastings Ismay, Britain's Chief of Staff to the Minister of Defence, declaring action had to be taken. Was the island completely meatless? he asked. Were there any cows left to kill?

Churchill ruled out flying in food, pointing out the lack of available transport planes. Turning to the First Sea Lord, he suggested instead that as much as possible be sent by way of submarine. He even demanded to know how much a sub could carry in the way of vitamins and concentrates if some of its batteries were removed to create more space. Churchill, to his credit, was making every effort to salvage the situation. But he was living in a dream world if he thought submarines could keep a quarter of a million people fed for very long.

While the top military and political leaders in London and Washington were casting about for solutions to Malta's plight, Luftwaffe General Kesselring was stepping up his aerial offensive. On March 21, German planes hit Takali with another 185 tonnes of high explosives. More than 200 bombers appeared overhead, some of them diving within 135 metres of the ground before unleashing their deadly cargo. Because aerial photographs had revealed what looked like a ramp on the runway's edge, the Germans were convinced there was an underground hangar at Takali. Determined to knock it out, several Ju-88s dropped 900-kilogram armour-piercing bombs that could penetrate through nearly 15 metres of solid rock. Just for good measure, they dropped incendiary bombs so burning oil might set any fighters ablaze inside their underground shelters.

Recalling the devastation later, pilot Jack Fletcher said, "You couldn't imagine that Takali would ever be an active airfield again. It looked like the surface of the moon, there were so many craters. This was carpet bombing, pure and simple."[26]

The next day a handful of Allied fighters managed to get off the ground from Malta's other two airfields in time to intercept the enemy, with Fletcher and squadron-mate Garth Horricks each damaging a Ju-88. Fletcher actually set his victim on fire, but the German pilot flew home on one engine. Horricks, who was rapidly making a name for himself as one of the island's star defenders, was in even better form on March 25, shooting up three of the dreaded Junkers-87 Stuka divebombers.

The Stuka! This was the gull-winged two-seater that had terrorized civilians and soldiers alike during Hitler's blitz of Poland, Holland, Belgium, Norway and France. It could dive steeply at 525 kilometres per hour, delivering a pair of 225-kilogram bombs with almost surgical precision. Making it all the more fearsome was a siren attached to its underbelly that emitted an ear-splitting scream during dives. In addition to its bombs, the Stuka had a pair of front-firing cannons, operated by the pilot, and a heavy machine gun in the rear, fired by the gunner. Horricks encountered 20 Stukas 1,800 metres over Kalafrana Bay and attacked without hesitation. His first burst ripped into the engine cowling and radiator of the leader, sending him down in flames. Turning on another, Horricks fired a squirt and watched as tracers ripped into the cockpit, wounding the rear gunner so seriously that he could not return the fire. Still not finished, he peppered the starboard wing of a third divebomber, which high-tailed it back to Sicily as fast as it could go.

Horricks's performance marked the first single-day triple claim by an Allied pilot on Malta, but it was a record that would last less than 24 hours. For on March 26, Buck McNair shot up no less than four Axis planes! That day, a scant four Spitfires were available to intercept a raiding force of 30 German planes, including 15 Stukas and as many Ju-88s. McNair and Bud Connell both scored quick kills. Connell shot the tail off a Junkers-88 and McNair blasted another of the twin-engine bombers out of the sky. The two then swung around and went for the Stukas. McNair was in the lead and his first salvo sent a divebomber cartwheeling into the sea. Later that day, he was up again, damaging a pair of bombers that were silhouetted against thick cloud cover. Connell, flying constantly at his side, knocked pieces off a third. Jack Fletcher, who already had four damaged planes to his credit since arriving on Malta, shot up two more. He went after a Stuka first, scoring hits on it before it disappeared into a cloud bank, trailing a thick plume of oily black smoke. When an ME-109 tried to put a halt to this one-sided fight, Fletcher drove it off in a damaged condition.

In all, the Allied fliers had destroyed three enemy planes and damaged six others in a single day of hard fighting. Of the Axis machines that went home damaged, two crash-landed in Sicily. Another came in with a dead crewman on board. So it would be a mistake to assume that a "damage" claim was insignificant. It often meant the plane in question had to be taken out of action for several days — or even written off altogether.

As March came to a close, the Allied pilots on Malta had plenty of reason to feel good about themselves. Overall, they had shot down 31 planes during the month for the loss of only a dozen of their own aircraft in air-to-air combat. But when the shocking total of 29 Spitfires and Hurricanes destroyed on the ground was factored in, the Germans and Italians were ahead by a score of 41 planes to 31. The year 1942 was only three months old and, despite the undeniable skill and courage of the defenders, the fact remained that the outnumbered Allies had lost more aircraft than they had destroyed.

Some reinforcements had come in, of course. In addition to the 15 Spitfires that arrived on March 7, two more groups of fighters landed on Malta before the month was out. Ten Hurricanes flew in from North Africa, and nine Spitfires made it off the *Eagle* on March 15. Nevertheless, as the March Blitz ended, the Axis had the clear edge. They too had received reinforcements and still had close to 700 warplanes on Sicily.

Now was the time for the Axis powers to invade Malta. The Germans and Italians had not won absolute air superiority but they certainly controlled the skies. The island's tiny fighter force could not have provided more than token resistance had General Student's troops stormed the beaches. Why did Hitler hesitate? Perhaps because as a young man in the First World War he had been a foot soldier. He was confident he knew all there was to know about ground combat, but when it came to air warfare, sea battles and amphibious assaults, he was unsure of himself. Instead of proceeding with an invasion that would almost certainly have succeeded, he ordered General Kesselring to mount a massive series of air raids in April. Unwilling to try to take the island, he decided to blow it to pieces instead.

CHAPTER 4

THE MOST BOMBED PLACE ON EARTH

With the possible exception of the atomic bombings of Hiroshima and Nagasaki three years later, no human beings have ever been so brutally assaulted from the air as were those on Malta during the fateful month of April 1942. More than five decades later, the people who lived through it still have difficulty putting into words what it was like being pounded around the clock for days and weeks on end. Those who survived the ordeal say no one who was not there can possibly comprehend what they went through.

The Axis airforces flew 10,300 raids in just 30 days, dropping almost 7,000 tonnes of bombs on a piece of real estate only one-seventh the size of Greater London. The rain of explosives from high-flying bombers and the continuous hail of machine gun and cannon bursts from low-flying fighters made it almost suicidal to venture out-side for even a brief period. In all, German and Italian planes were over the island for 373 hours that month, or the equivalent of two full weeks. It was an unprecedented show of force that made Malta the most heavily bombed place on earth. The mournful wail of air raid sirens, the shrill screams of diving aircraft, the spine-chilling whistling of falling bombs and the shattering explosions were echoed by the never-ending thumping of the anti-aircraft guns, and sent the people scurrying underground like rats.

Pilot Jack Fletcher was surprised to find himself more afraid in the shelters than he was in the cockpit of his Hurricane, taking on five-to-one odds in a dogfight. "At least in the air you didn't feel helpless. You were fighting back. But in the shelters you could do nothing except wait. You sat there with your heart pounding, waiting for the bomb that would kill you. When you heard the whistle of the bombs your whole body would suddenly contract. Under that kind of pressure,

Bomb damage in Valletta, capital city of Malta. Courtesy of Frank Kerley

well, the nerves can't hold out forever. A lot of the boys were close to cracking."[1] At times, the Windsor, Ontario, native added, the bombardment was so awesome that the ground trembled across the whole island. Indeed, noise from some of the blasts could be heard from as far away as General Kesselring's Sicilian headquarters.

Many of the defenders went over the edge. One distraught antiaircraft gunner, seeing a whole swarm of German planes overhead for the third time in one morning, pulled out a pistol and shot himself through the head. English army officer Francis Gerard speaks of the constant pressure. "It was the incessant aspect of the attack that made it so hard to bear," he wrote. "Sleep became something to be wooed with desperation. You did sleep, after a fashion, just because you were so tired. But you didn't awake refreshed, for subconsciously you were aware of the gunfire and the whistle and crash of the bombs. I remember being blown out of bed one night. Looking back I suppose I did hear the bomb coming down, but my first conscious memory was of finding myself on the floor wrapped up like a cocoon in my sand-fly net. I was smothered in glass and plaster."[2]

For fighter pilot Buzz Ogilvie, the worst thing about the raids was that they robbed him of his rest. "When the air raids were on it was hard to sleep. Our beds were upstairs and we would run downstairs with our tin hats on and crouch under a big oak table. After a while we realized if we had a glass of Scotch before going to bed we'd sleep right through it, rather than getting up and hiding under that table. I can recall there was a ship sunk in the bay and navy divers went down and retrieved Black & White Scotch from it. They sold it to us for three dollars a bottle. On Gozo Island they made red wine, which they sold to us for a dollar per bottle. It was pretty ropey wine, but we were apt to drink anything so we could sleep."[3]

And so it went, day after day and night after night. Pilot Charles McLean recalled enduring as many as six raids in a 24-hour period. In the major attacks the airfields were always hit, along with Valletta and Grand Harbour. During lighter raids the targets could include anything from anti-aircraft guns to small villages.

Within days Valletta, the beautiful and historic capital, was all but reduced to rubble. Before the siege it had been a charming city, with narrow, twisting streets, a wonderful old opera house, palaces and churches of stunning Italian and Spanish designs, and everywhere the impressive *auberges* — the dwellings of the 16th-century knights who had saved Malta from a Turkish invasion force. Then there were the Bronze Age and neolithic temples, the high stone walls of two old forts that guarded the harbour, the ancient coats of arms carved in doorways, and other equally colourful and elaborate decorations. Now it was almost all gone, including the opera house and the *auberges* of the knights. When the government fled to the tiny hamlet of Hamrun, 32 kilometres inland, Axis fliers saturated the place with 280 tonnes of bombs in a single day, literally wiping it off the map. Across Malta, underground granaries were destroyed; fuel dumps could be seen burning from as far away as Sicily. The big submarine base at Marsaxlokk Bay was knocked out of action. At Grand Harbour the docks were pulverized. Masts and funnels poked out of the water, marking the graves of sunken ships. The bay itself was almost continuously oil-stained.

When the Germans and Italians ran out of military and industrial targets, some of them went after anything that moved. One woman recalled seeing an ME-109 strafe two boys playing in a field. Hospitals clearly marked with huge Red Cross emblems on their roofs were bombed without mercy. Even funeral processions were attacked.

Pilot Charles McLean was convinced the raids on the hospitals were deliberate. Once, he noted, nine Stukas demolished a military hospital that had Red Cross markings on it that were so large they could easily be seen from 6,000 metres. Before long every hospital on Malta had been hit and only one x-ray machine on the whole island was in working order. Governor Dobbie asked the Axis leaders to permit a British hospital ship to sail unmolested into Grand Harbour; while the Italians agreed to the request, the Germans vetoed it.

Some defended the enemy fliers, pointing out there was hardly any place on such a small island that was not located near a military or industrial target. In such circumstances, especially while dodging flak and fighters, it would be relatively easy to accidently bomb a medical facility, school or church. Still, it was hard to justify the use of some of the hideous anti-personnel bombs that were dropped after the sun went down. One, known as a "cracker bomb," exploded about 150 metres off the ground, showering hundreds of yards in every direction with thousands of tiny slivers of shrapnel. They were designed to pepper the wings, engines and fuselages of parked airplanes but, more often than not, they simply tore human flesh to shreds. Even more sinister were the small booby trapped objects, including toys, tools and even candies, that were dumped all over Malta. Despite constant warnings from the authorities, young children often picked them up, with tragic consequences. In one particularly terrible incident, a barefoot lad brought home a fountain pen that exploded when he removed the top, killing both him and his mother. "I remember once they dropped candies from the planes but everyone said, 'Don't touch them, they could be poisoned,'" George Scerri recalled. "I had an 11-year-old friend who was killed by what we called a butterfly bomb. You touched them and they'd go off in your face."[4]

Before long the whole population, military and civilian, was burrowing underground. The island is covered in limestone, which is easy to dig. Hundreds of tunnels were built. Some were huge public shelters designed by engineers, others small, impromptu caves. Some families moved all of their belongings from destroyed homes into the shelters, filling them with enough provisions so that they did not have to venture outside for days at a time.

Being in a shelter was by no means a guarantee of safety, however. During March, 122 souls died in one when a direct hit at Luqa airfield burst a waterline, drowning everyone inside. Allied pilots trying to help were haunted for years afterwards by the screams of those trapped below. Two dozen others died without a whimper in another raid, when a bomb broke a gas main, asphyxiating them inside their shelter.

Sometimes the people coming to the rescue posed a threat to survivors of the bombing. A seven-year-old Maltese boy discovered that after a direct hit caved in the roof of his bedroom. He was saved from certain death when a mattress fell on him, sheltering him from the falling debris. But he sustained a serious head injury when a frantic rescuer accidently hit him with a pickaxe.

Those who escaped the bombs, bullets and pickaxes often lived a hellish existence underground. One survivor remembered the shelters as "stinking holes, filled with rats, people praying, babies crying ... The light was poor, the ventilation was just awful and the smell could make you vomit."[5] Most were single-room, providing the inhabitants with little privacy.

Lena Banavage believes the discomfort was worse than the danger. People had to line up for bathing water, newspapers were used for toilet paper and there was often little food to be found in a shelter. Twice she sneaked out during air raids to scrounge the black market for extra provisions. When she returned she was scolded, then hugged, by her parents.

What Paul Stellini remembers most about the shelters was the feeling of safety. "We were under 100 feet of rock, so even a direct hit couldn't get us." Stellini, who was only seven in 1942, recalls missing a whole year of schooling because his father took him to live in a cave.[6]

George Porter, who was a teenager at the time, also thought the shelters were life savers. "We had good shelters, they were rocky. It would be dampish, though, similar to being in a basement."[7]

Ed Schranz remembers much the same thing. "I went all through the siege. I was in a rock shelter for three years. I was five years old and my mom used to wake us up and I'd run to the shelters." While he felt safe inside them, Schranz has never forgotten the colour of the water he had to drink while living underground. "I remember the water was yellow because of the limestone. It's better now."[8]

"Some stone shelters could trap the dead," George Scerri recalls. When someone was under the debris it was hard to pull them out. Some dead people were buried for a week. We tried to put disinfectants on the destroyed buildings but the smell in the summer was terrible."[9]

With the population huddled fearfully in shelters and caves, fierce air battles raged overhead. The first Allied pilot to encounter enemy aircraft in April 1942 was probably Canadian Skip McKay, who celebrated his 21st birthday April 1 by shooting down one Nazi bomber and damaging a second. Taking off in the early morning with three other Hurricane pilots, he dove through a curtain of his own flak to shoot down one of 15 Ju-88s bombing Grand Harbour. Landing only to refuel and reload, he scrambled to intercept a formation of 70 Luftwaffe planes. In the ensuing struggle McKay managed to damage a Stuka but had a narrow escape when a pair of ME-109s drove him almost into the Mediterranean. Diving to the wave tops, he headed home, thinking he had shaken the Germans off. One of them was still on his tail, however, and its pilot riddled McKay's wings and rudder with 14 machine gun holes before he managed to land safely. If McKay's nerves were stretched by the close call, he did not show it four days later when, along with six other Hurricane pilots, he took on 83 enemy planes over Grand Harbour. In the ensuing dogfight he sent one bomber down trailing smoke before being chased home by four Messerschmitts.

The German fighter pilots were not only numerous, they were extremely aggressive. They often followed Allied fliers to their bases, harassing them as they attempted to land. "The worst part was trying to land because the Germans would try to shoot you up while you were landing," pilot Eric Crist said. "The all-clear would sound because the bombers had gone, but the fighters would still be around. Landing was always a chore. We had a guy on the ground watching with a radio. You'd zip in quickly, sometimes even downwind. Sometimes they would chase you even when you were on the ground. If they were on our tails when we were coming in we would try to lead them over flak nests. There was a little valley over Rabat with lots of anti-aircraft guns there, if they were foolish enough to chase us that far."[10]

Even taking off could be dangerous. Once, Crist was roaring down the runway when his engine suddenly quit. He jumped out, only to see

ME-109s diving down to strafe the airfield. Undaunted, Crist drew his Smith and Wesson revolver and blazed away at the nearest Messerschmitt before being knocked off his feet by a bomb blast.

Canadian pilot Garth Horricks stunned the Luftwaffe on April 10 by shooting down ace Hermann Neuhoff. Neuhoff was the top-scoring pilot and commander of Staffel 6, with an astounding total of 40 Allied planes to his credit. He had won 21 of his victories over the Russian Front before being transferred to Sicily. Horricks, who was flying one of the oldest Hurricanes on Malta, chased Neuhoff's yellow-nosed Messerschmitt from 5,000 metres to the wave tops, clinging tenaciously to his swastika-decorated rudder. When the German had to either pull up or plunge straight into the sea, Horricks caught him with a four-second burst that set his engine ablaze. The crippled plane streaked across the sky like a runaway comet before crashing into the Mediterranean. Neuhoff, who somehow managed to bail out at the last second, landed safely in the water, inflated his rubber raft and climbed aboard. An hour later he was picked up by a British rescue launch and was on his way to a POW camp on Malta.

English ace Laddie Lucas, who visited downed enemy airmen in a Maltese hospital that night, was greeted with disbelief when he told a German pilot that Neuhoff had been captured. The incredulous flier replied that such a thing was impossible because no one was skilled enough to shoot down Neuhoff.

Despite Horricks's stunning achievement, the day was not one of celebration for the defenders. Luftwaffe pilots exacted revenge for the loss of their ace by shooting down two Hurricanes and forcing three others to crash-land. A sixth was lightly damaged and one Spitfire was also shot up, although its pilot made a safe landing. Australian flier Tony Goldsmith, writing in his diary that night, described the day's events as "Jerry's biggest effort yet. At least 100 Ju-88s and 87s and 50 or so ME-109s. Terrific odds. We couldn't do much about the bombers. Five Hurris lost, the remainder shot up, but all pilots safe. Sgt. Horricks got a 109, the best flamer I've seen yet."[11]

Horricks was at it again three days later, when he damaged an ME-109 while out looking for the four-man crew of a missing RAF twin-engine bomber. Unable to locate the downed fliers, he attacked three German fighters that were about to strafe a British rescue launch. Horricks saw his tracers striking one of the Messerschmitts in the belly before it barrel-rolled away and escaped. Jack Fletcher, who was looking for the same bomber crew, damaged a second German plane. But there were so many enemy planes in the air that the two Allied pilots could not possibly cope with them all. One ME-109 managed to shoot up the rescue launch, wounding several of its crew before forcing it to retreat without the lost airmen. As darkness fell, all hope for the missing Beaufort crew vanished. Three of them had already drowned, but a fourth, a man named MacGregor, refused to give up. Despite the loss of blood from half a dozen shrapnel wounds in his back, he swam for five hours to reach Malta. Once there, he had to climb up the side of a jagged rock cliff in the dark before finally reaching safety.

By now the RAF squadrons on Malta were down to a total of three fighters. And because the anti-aircraft gunners were running out of ammunition, they were restricted to firing 15 rounds per day. "We were strictly rationed in ammunition," gunner John Dedomenico told the author. "It was a court martial offence to use more than your ration. Ammunition was coming in by submarine. Can you imagine! A submarine doesn't have much space. Anyone breaking the rule was subject to immediate court martial."[12] Malta was, quite literally, down to its last gasp.

King George VI, realizing just how desperate the situation was, recommended the Maltese population be awarded the Victoria Cross, the Commonwealth's highest gallantry award for courage in the face of the enemy. Such a move might increase morale, giving the people the motivation to carry on despite the fearful odds against them. Government officials liked the idea but decided instead on the George Cross, which was the highest decoration available to civilians. The VC, after all, was a military medal. So it was on April 15, 1942, the King announced from Buckingham Palace he was awarding "the George Cross to the Island Fortress of Malta to bear witness to a heroism and devotion that will long be famous in history."[13] The message was greeted with contempt in Italy, where Rome Radio dismissed it as just so much British propaganda. The Maltese, Italians were told, only supported the Allies at the point of a bayonet. But the people of Malta were proud of the award and deeply impressed by the King's gesture. It was the first time such a prestigious award had been given to a whole people, and that made everyone on the island a part of history.

"The King designed the cross himself," former Maltese schoolboy George Scerri enthusiastically told the author 55 years later. "We are very proud of it. It's in our national flag now. I have the right to pin the George Cross on my chest because it was given to the whole country, and I'm very proud of that."[14] Certainly some of the young fighter pilots felt as if the award was for them, too, because they began wearing makeshift George Cross medals that they carved out of wood.

No amount of recognition, however, was going to save Malta unless it received more fighters. Seven Hurricane pilots flew in from North Africa on April 19, flying 1,600 kilometres with a blazing Mediterranean sun in their eyes the whole way. Once they got to the island fortress they found an air raid under way. Because they were carrying cumbersome long-range fuel tanks, they could not make the lightning moves needed to dodge the several ME-109s lurking in the area. Nevertheless, only one Hurricane was lost. The other six managed to land amid the shell craters at Takali, setting down with only about five minutes worth of fuel left in their tanks. Malta now had nine serviceable fighters with which to hold off at least 600 Axis aircraft on Sicily!

Fortunately, help was on the way. Prime Minister Churchill knew he had to get a large number of Spitfires to Malta fast. Sending 15 or 16 at a time from the aircraft carrier *Eagle* just was not good enough. Besides that, the *Eagle* was temporarily out of commission with a steering problem. With his own navy lacking a carrier big enough to do the job, Churchill turned to American President Franklin Roosevelt, asking him for permission to use the USS *Wasp*. U.S. Admiral Ernie King, who was bitterly opposed to placing American forces under British command, fought the idea tooth and nail. But the president overruled him, wiring back his approval to London the next day.

On April 20 — Hitler's birthday — the *Wasp* moved into position off Gibraltar and prepared to launch 47 Spitfires. Tension on board was high. Just prior to takeoff, a mechanic on deck stumbled into a whirling propeller blade and was decapitated. An American pilot named Walcott, meanwhile, was having second thoughts about his posting in Malta, where the life expectancy of a new fighter pilot was measured in days, not weeks. Just before takeoff he told a Canadian pilot he was not going to Malta under any circumstances. As soon as

Spitfire pilots Eric Crist, left, and Jack Ryckman, who was killed in action defending Malta. Courtesy of Eric Crist

they were airborne, he said, he was going to fly to Africa and defect. The Canadian did not take him seriously but, moments after he got off the flight deck, Walcott broke formation and flew to Algeria. Eventually, he made his way to the American embassy and claimed he was a lost commercial pilot. His story was believed and he was able to make his way back to the United States, avoiding a court martial.

The other 46 pilots carried on, only to be picked up by Axis radar on Sicily. General Kesselring decided against attempting to intercept such a large force in the air, opting instead to order 270 bombers and 200 fighters to attack Malta's three airfields just as the Spitfires were landing.

As the RAF fliers and the huge Luftwaffe formation converged on the island, Malta's few remaining fighters took off, hoping to provide the newcomers with at least some protection as they came in. As Eric Crist and his best friend, Jack Ryckman, scrambled into their planes, Ryckman turned to Crist and said, "I'm going to give Hitler a birthday present." Minutes later, Ryckman was shot down and killed. "He gave Hitler a present," Crist noted sadly, "but it was the wrong kind."[15]

Now there were only half a dozen defenders in the air, but the tiny force gave a good account of itself. Buck McNair led the way, shooting down a Messerschmitt that was going for his wingman. Incredibly, the burning German plane slid across the sky and collided with the

Spitfire McNair was trying to save. Almost as miraculous was the fact that the Englishman in the Spitfire was able to set his plane down with only a bent wing. McNair then turned on a Ju-88, seriously damaging it with a three-second burst. Later in the day he shot the tail off another ME-109.

Despite McNair's success, there was no way the small band of pilots could give adequate cover to such a large force of landing Spitfires. No less than seven of the newcomers were shot down as they attempted to land or were destroyed on the ground within seconds of having set down. "We lost a lot of them because we hadn't organized refuelling and rearming," anti-aircraft gunner John Dedomenico said five decades later. "They were being strafed as they came in. Later, they had organized teams to greet the fighters as they landed. They refuelled and rearmed the planes inside pens that gave them some protection."[16]

It was not just the loss of so many planes on the ground that disturbed Bull Turner. He was upset with the calibre of some of the aircraft being sent to Malta. Some had guns that did not work, others had unserviceable radios, and still others had engines that were all but worn out. Perhaps even more worrisome was the fact that few of the new pilots had any combat experience. Turner suspected that squadron commanders in England were intentionally sending their worst planes — and pilots — when they were asked by High Command to help the embattled island. He was also upset because he had been grounded. As wing commander at Takali he was considered too valuable to risk in daily combat. Unwilling to confine himself to a desk, Turner took part in several unauthorized night raids on Sicilian airfields. The attacks likely caused little in the way of damage, but they did add to the morale of the Malta pilots, who were thrilled to know the Germans and Italians were finally being given a dose of their own medicine. Eventually, Turner's nocturnal exploits came to the attention of higher authorities and he was ordered back to England.

Despite all the problems, the fact that 39 of the Spitfires had survived the trip was very good news indeed. That night the new pilots gathered in the mess at Takali to be briefed by Air Marshal Lloyd. As he spoke, air raid sirens suddenly went off. Ignoring the alarm, Lloyd told his men, "You must get in close. So close that you can see the whites of their eyes. You must kill the Germans or they'll kill you." At that very moment a bomb exploded outside the mess, sending pilots diving under billiard tables. When they re-emerged, Lloyd was still on his feet. "You see what I mean," he said.[17]

General Kesselring ordered all-out attacks on the airfields throughout the rest of the month. On April 21 there were several savage air fights, one of which resulted in the death of Canadian Stan Brooker. Poor Brooker, who had only been on Malta 24 hours, was shot down by a Messerschmitt, then killed by the enemy pilot as he dangled helplessly in his parachute. His fate was indicative of just how cruel the struggle was becoming. John Dedomenico never forgot some of the brutality he witnessed.

> I well remember an Italian pilot who came down in the sea just off the beach. People were preventing him from climbing ashore. It was a rocky beach and I don't know what happened to him. I don't know if he made it. And one German pilot was beaten to death with a shovel [by angry civilians]. That has stayed with me. There was a deep hatred for the enemy pilots, particularly in the countryside, where the people were less educated and tended to react violently. I never heard of any abuses of prisoners by the army or the police. But I know some villages treated the Germans quite roughly. The Germans seemed to bomb indiscriminately at times. Sometimes it seemed they were going after the civilian population, but that might not have been a fair assessment. It was such a small island that you couldn't help but hit civilian houses. But they did seem at times to go after things like schools and hospitals. That's the way it looked to some of us. And they dropped awful mines by parachute that had horns sticking out of them. They were very destructive. They also had sirens on their dive-bombers that scared the hell out of people.[18]

Virtually every Maltese civilian interviewed by the author has similar stories. "If an enemy pilot came down, the people would kill him for sure," George Scerri recalled. "One day my cousin hit one in the face and he was sent to jail for 14 days."[19] On more than one occasion,

Maltese anti-aircraft gunner Joe Mifsud remembered years later, the soldiers of his battery showed up just in time to prevent a mob from killing a downed German airman. Some Maltese are still bitter to this day. "I can never forgive the Germans," Ed Cauchi says. "They tried to starve us to death."

One German pilot was actually beheaded by civilians. A local bar owner collected the severed head as a trophy, keeping it in a clay pot that he delighted in showing to customers.

Italian air historian Nicola Malizia says there were several cases in which Allied pilots machine gunned Italian airmen in their parachutes. Besides that, the Italians were convinced that Canadian pilot Rocky Main had deliberately shot down one of their Red Cross rescue seaplanes, then strafed it after it hit the water. Main, for his part, denied seeing the Red Cross markings until it was too late. The Spitfire pilot who strafed four German aviators in a rubber raft after their Ju-88 went down off Malta gave no excuse beyond getting even for the slaughter of one of his friends in his parachute by Axis fliers. Before long, it was not safe for either side to bail out. Looking back from this distance, all of this murderous conduct is difficult to understand. It must be remembered, however, that both sides were taking heavy losses daily, and emotions were running high.

Of course, by no means did all the pilots succumb to such blood lust. Englishman Laddie Lucas not only would not think of killing a helpless enemy, but he often visited wounded German and Italian flyers in Malta's hospitals. Before long, he was joined by other Allied pilots, all of whom were anxious to meet the other side face-to-face. They made every effort not to appear to be pumping the enemy aviators for information. Lucas's visits came to an end, however, after he approached a young Italian gunner whose hand had been blown off by a cannon shell. The Englishman asked the poor fellow what he had done before the war, only to be told the gunner had been a violinist. Lucas left immediately, feeling sick. Long after he had left Malta for good, the incident continued to haunt his dreams.

Another pilot who felt no bitterness for the enemy was Johnny Sherlock. "Air combat was impersonal," he says now. "I'd done some skiing in Calgary before the war and a bunch of university students from Germany were in the same lodge. I met lots of them and drank a lot of beer with them. Quite often when I shot at a plane over Malta I

Fighter pilot Johnny Sherlock on the wing of his Spitfire airplane.
Courtesy of Johnny Sherlock

thought, 'I wonder if that's one of my old friends.' But I had to do it. It was a case of you or him. It wasn't like you were shooting at people who couldn't shoot back." Once enemy airmen were captured, they were treated with courtesy and respect. "We used to protect them from the civilians," Sherlock recalled. "The Maltese would wait below their parachutes with pitchforks and attack them when they landed, especially if they were Italians. We figured that wasn't quite cricket. They were just doing what they thought was right. They were no different than anyone else. They were just like you and I. Aircrew were a little different from soldiers. We didn't do hand-to-hand fighting with knives. We didn't see dirty tricks. Some pilots were shot at in their parachutes but it wasn't very prevalent."[20]

Fighter pilot Eric Crist was another who would have nothing to do with hatred. "When I was in hospital [after being wounded in a dogfight] they put all the pilots in one ward. It didn't matter whether you were German, English, Italian or Canadian. The guy next to me was a Stuka pilot. We used to play checkers. I asked him what he was going to do after the war and he told me, 'I'm going to stay in the Luftwaffe.' I said, 'I don't think so.' At that time they were winning and he probably thought he *would* stay in the Luftwaffe. He showed me pictures from his wallet of his girlfriend and his mom and dad back in Germany. He was just a kid. You were old if you were 24. I had no animosity for them. Nor do I believe any of the fighter pilots did. They were doing the same job as we were, just on different sides. I think there would have been more animosity in the trenches."[21]

The constant attacks on the airfields continued to take their toll, with no less than eight Spitfires being knocked out of action on the ground on April 21. Next day, still more bombers showed up over the fighter strips, pounding them hard for 24 hours. The runway at Takali was so badly damaged that Canadian pilot Ozzie Linton, trying to dodge the craters, ended up crashing into a boundary fence with his Spitfire tipped on its nose. An English flier had even less luck, hitting a bomb crater that caused his plane to flip over on its back. And Australian Frank Kemmet crashed into a stone wall as he attempted to land amid exploding bombs. His plane was destroyed and he died in the back of an ambulance on the way to hospital.

The Allies enjoyed some success that day, thanks to Buck McNair. He managed to get off the ground with three rookies in tow. He warned them to gain height, attack aggressively and break off combat if things got too hot to handle. Encountering a Ju-88, he led them into the attack. All four opened fire and, although it seems likely that the highly talented McNair was the victor, he insisted on sharing the kill with all three of the newcomers. The selfless move dramatically boosted the confidence of all three greenhorns.

Next day, a sandy-haired young British pilot with a firm, square jaw named Paddy Schade opened what would be a long Malta score by shooting down a pair of Stuka divebombers over Grand Harbour. Another Ju-87 was hit by another Englishman and crashed into the shallow waters of Marsaxlokk Bay, where its dead pilot remained clearly visible, still at his controls, for weeks to come. Unfortunately, a Spitfire was blasted to bits on the ground — the 13th lost in such fashion in just four days. Counting the nine Spits lost in the air over the same time period, it meant nearly half the planes that had arrived from the *Wasp* on April 20 were now gone. Several of the others were out of action with battle damage, most of which had been sustained on the ground.

Nor was it just planes and pilots that were being lost. Ground personnel, including highly skilled mechanics, were being killed or wounded almost every day. They were soon in as short supply as the aircraft they serviced. Needless to say, the pressure of such constant danger was taking its toll. Pilot Jack Fletcher, for one, was almost at the end of his rope. On April 24 he was so shaken after a harrowing dogfight with four enemy planes that he had to be helped out of his seat. Mechanics who inspected his plane a few minutes later discovered Fletcher had vomited in the cockpit. After months of combat, he was clearly in need of a rest. But with pilots in such short supply, no one could stay out of action with anything less than a physical wound, even though battle fatigue could be every bit as debilitating as a bullet wound. Fletcher managed to make one last strike at the enemy the next day when he shot down a Ju-88. The victory gave him a total of three destroyed, two probably destroyed and nine damaged over the island. Fellow Hurricane pilot Lucien Brooks shot a Stuka down over St. Paul's Bay in the same skirmish, but did not live to celebrate his victory because four ME-109s immediately jumped him, sending his Hurricane spinning down minus its port wing. Buck McNair was up that day too, fighting with his usual savage intensity, and the results were spectacular. He shot down a Stuka and a Ju-88 in quick succession, then damaged a pair of Messerschmitts. Four enemy planes had fallen before his guns in four minutes, taking six men to their deaths. On the way back to base McNair came across an Australian pilot limping home in a badly damaged Spitfire. The man's air speed indicator had been shot out, which would make landing a dicey proposition at best. Flying alongside, McNair radioed his own speed to the Aussie, successfully guiding him in for a safe landing. He was less charitable a few minutes later with another pilot who was afraid to land because an ME-109 had been spotted nearby, obviously hoping to catch an Allied plane making a slow approach to the runway. McNair, impatient to get down himself, shouted into his radio, "If you don't land off the next circuit, and if that Hun doesn't get you, I will!"[22] The chastened pilot landed immediately.

McNair was in a better mood in the mess a few hours later. Thrilled with his success in the air that day, he performed what one Australian pilot described as a "war dance." The Canadian ace made no further claims in April, but his comrades were not done scoring — or dying. Garth Horricks bagged a Messerschmitt on April 26, but still another Spitfire pilot died that day when his parachute opened partially. Before the month was out Jack Fletcher would meet the same terrible fate. He was fighting five enemies single-handedly when one of them scored a direct hit on his engine, forcing him to abandon his doomed ship. His chute opened only about halfway. Inspectors on the ground discovered that someone had removed eight silk panels from the parachute, no doubt because silk was so rare on Malta.

Fletcher would not be the only flier to lose his life in such a ghastly fashion in the days and weeks ahead. Pilot Charles McLean blamed the Mediterranean climate — and sabotage — for the failure of many parachutes to open. Recalling the death of an RAF pilot who was forced to jump from a burning fighter right over his own airfield, McLean said,

> His parachute did not open, and he dropped towards the earth like a hunk of iron. He bounced once when he hit the slope of the small rise just beyond western dispersal. His hands were bloody and some of his nails had been ripped off from struggling with the canvas and the wire-end that fitted into the key, for someone on the ground had deliberately bent the end of the wire so that it was impossible for the pilot to pull the ripcord in the air.

> Some of the pilots died like this. Others died because their parachutes, clogged up by the mixture of dust and heavy dew, came out and wilted in the air, but did not open. Even when he prechecked the wire in the key, which became a must, a pilot was never sure his parachute would work. On Takali there was no parachute section for the necessary periodic repacking. When not in use, the parachutes were stored in a small roofless hut at the back of dispersal, and covered with a sheet of corrugated tin roof-sheeting. There were so many "accidents" that after a while a parachute became nothing more than something to sit on.[23]

That there may have been saboteurs on Malta was not hard to imagine. Fifteen percent of the population spoke Italian, which had been the language of the island's upper classes for centuries. In fact, just a few years before the war began, it had been the language of the local courts. British authorities were so concerned about the pro-

Fascist leanings of some of the Maltese that they had rounded up dozens of people of Italian descent and shipped them off to Kenya at the start of the war. Later, they ordered a gallows erected at Takali as a none-too-subtle warning that anyone caught tampering with RAF equipment would be hanged.

The same day Fletcher died yet another defender was lost as a result of faulty equipment. Thomas Gordon Foley, one of Malta's most courageous pilots, died when the engine of his Hurricane failed during an air test.

Foley's loss was keenly felt, not because he had a long string of victories to his credit, but because he was always looking out for the well-being of others. One of his last letters to his mother tells us much about the calibre of the young men who were risking their lives over the island every day. Written shortly before he was posted to Malta from North Africa, it reads in part:

> Up until now I have never mentioned my flying activities in my letters solely because I did not want you to worry. However, I believe the Air Ministry has informed you I was shot down and reported missing. Now that it is all over and I am back with my squadron unharmed, I more or less regard it as a good adventure. And (I thought) you and the family would like to hear about it.
>
> On January 28, 1942 we took off on a squadron sortie to ground strafe an enemy column moving in on one of our flanks. During the engagement they managed to knock my aeroplane about a little, fortunately all their shots missed the cockpit. As I was less than 20 feet from the ground, I crash-landed with my wheels retracted. Had I been higher I would have jumped. I knew I was deep in Jerry territory so I jumped out and hid about 50 yards ahead of my plane in a bit of shrub we call "camel thorn." In less than two minutes Jerry was at my aircraft and believe me I was frightened stiff, because I thought they would start looking for me. However, they must have thought I jumped because I had taken my parachute with me.

One silly fool got in the cockpit and pressed the fire button on the control column. This sent a stream of bullets over my head. Honestly, I think I shrunk to the size of a two-year-old. I'm sure I left the imprint of my body in the sand. After a short inspection of the plane they fired some rounds in the petrol tanks and set it on fire. When they drove away one truck passed within five feet of me. If they had been the real German type I'd have been noticed but they all sat vertically upright, looking straight ahead, just as if they were on parade on the streets of Berlin. This took place about 11 a.m. I stayed hidden all day until dark and started walking towards our lines. I walked all night long guided by the stars and believe me it was a tough task walking in my loose, heavy flying boots. At dawn I crawled into a thicket and slept until 8 o'clock. I hiked until 6 o'clock that afternoon, then I came upon a little native boy with some camels. He gave me to understand I was to go with him to his father. By this time I could hardly walk, my feet were covered with blisters and I had had no food since the morning of the day before. So he made a camel kneel down and I finished the last five miles to his village on the rear of a camel. In the Bedouin village I was quite a curiosity. Little dirty-nosed, half-naked children came rushing out kissing my hands and generally making a nuisance of themselves. I spent the night in the tent with this boy's family. They offered me food, but I was too sick and only accepted sour goats milk, which I drank from a dirty communal bowl, sitting around the fire with the boy's parents and his sister. Their living conditions are very primitive and filthy beyond comprehension. I slept that night on a wicker matting wrapped in my flying suit, one huge rug over the five of us. I was between the son and father with the goat at our heads and the fire at our feet. All under one roof. What a sight that was. I didn't know whether they would slit my throat

in the night or not. I had previously promised them a
huge reward if they would take me to the English. I
was banking on that. This they did, the boy's father
led me across the desert to a unit of South Africans.
The reward I promised them was realized in the form
of bully beef, tea, sugar and cigarettes. They were
happy and so was I.

Of the Bedouins I can honestly say they were as
hospitable to me as their limited means would allow.
They have very high regard for the English, would say
little about the Germans, but the bitterness they hold
for the Italians is indescribable. Since Mussolini drove
them from the fertile coastal area back into the
desert, during his colony drive, they simply have no
use for them whatsoever.

So that is the story, I wouldn't have told you
except for the fact I feel sure H.Q. would report to
you I had been shot down. I'm not unnerved by any
means and I still think a fighter pilot has the best job
of the lot.[24]

As the worst month of the siege so far came to an end, the defenders had little reason to be optimistic. Of the 46 Spitfires that had
landed 10 days earlier, only seven were still operational. Along with
five Hurricanes, that gave Malta a grand total of 12 serviceable fighters. Worse than that was the news brought back from Sicily by a
reconnaissance plane. Its pilot had taken photos of glider strips being
set up beside several Axis airfields: the enemy was preparing for an
invasion.

CHAPTER 5

DISEASE AND FAMINE HIT MALTA HARD

A new plague descended over beleaguered Malta with the coming of May — disease.

Typhoid fever broke out soon after bombs caused raw sewage to seep into the island's drinking water. Before long, hundreds were seriously ill, including several fighter pilots. If that wasn't bad enough, polio appeared, killing 17 and crippling 400 more. Fortunately, none of the fliers were stricken with the disease, but its presence caused widespread concern at all three airfields. Scabies, a tick-like parasite, did not discriminate between civilians and servicemen. It seemed everyone on the island came down with it at the same time, with thousands suffering from painful skin rashes, lesions and terrible itches. Many scratched themselves until they bled. In all, 4,000 people had infectious diseases of one sort or another that required hospital treatments and a full one-third of all newborns died in infancy.

Sadly, there was little in the way of medical supplies available to relieve the suffering. Even basics such as aspirins were in short supply. As a result, illnesses such as tuberculosis, pneumonia, pellagra, dysentery and the strange stomach flu known only as the Malta Dog sprang up everywhere. At times, as many as half the pilots had "the Dog." The pain was almost unbearable. "It was like someone had reached into your guts and crushed all your internal organs,"[1] British pilot Paddy Schade recalled. "I had it all the time," pilot Johnny Sherlock told the author. "I lost 40 pounds the hard way but the quick way."[2] Fellow pilot Eric Crist added, "Everybody was hit by Malta Dog, or sandfly fever. Everybody, without exception. It was endemic to the place. I weighed about 126 pounds when I went to Malta in March and I was 116 when I left in September. I'm sure the Malta Dog had something to do with it."

RAF pilots augment their diet hunting rabbit. From left: Eric Crist, Larry Robilliard and Jack Morris. Courtesy of Eric Crist

Scores of people died of various ailments but the deaths were never reported because families were fearful of having their meagre rations cut, should the authorities find out they had one less mouth to feed. With starvation a looming threat, strict rationing had been imposed. Bread consumption was slashed, first by a quarter, then by 33 percent. But even with that there was not enough food to last beyond mid-June. Even water reserves were down to a scant five weeks, so lice and fleas proliferated on unwashed bodies.

Gaunt civilians and servicemen began eating the hundreds of orange and black cats that roamed the streets of every city, town and hamlet. As a result, there was soon a plague of rats. Pilot James Ballantyne once awoke in his bunk in the middle of the night to find a huge black rat perched on his chest, staring him right in the eye. The sight gave him a bigger fright than anything he had ever experienced in aerial combat. Eventually, the rodent menace was brought under control when Governor Dobbie offered Maltese schoolboys a reward for every rat they killed. The frugal Dobbie would only pay a penny for each one, but the lads went on the rampage, slaughtering them by the thousands.

Killing rats, however, was not going to feed the population. The grim fact was that Malta had too many people to be self-sufficient in food. In all history there had seldom been so many souls trapped inside one besieged fortress. At the beginning of the year there had been 20,000 cows on the island, but they had all been devoured by the end of April. Most of Malta's goats had been eaten too, creating a severe shortage of milk. Even canned milk grew scarce, along with fish, coffee, butter and sugar. The situation was so serious that no meat was distributed on three days of every week. It is tempting to accuse the Maltese of being reckless by eating virtually all of their livestock so quickly, but the truth is there was no choice. The farmers did not have any extra food, so the cows and goats would have starved to death if they had not been slaughtered.

Before long, egg vendors needed police protection from hungry mobs. People were even digging up flower gardens to plant vegetables. A few went so far as to steal goldfish from ornamental ponds in front of Valletta's few remaining palaces. Jobs in flour mills were cherished because workers could eat the sweepings from the floors, where some flour was often mixed in with the dirt. People sold jewellery, watches, even wedding rings, to buy a few eggs on the black market. Still it was not enough. Teenagers who should have been pictures of perfect health occasionally had to be carried into air raid shelters because they were too feeble to walk. Before the month was out, adult males would be restricted to 56 ounces — about 1.5 kilograms — of rice, fish, cheese, fats and meat (if it was available) a day, along with 13 ounces of bread — slightly more than one-third of a kilogram.

"You had no strength in your body," recalled George Scerri, who was a 12-year-old schoolboy at the time. "I don't know how we carried on. One day I was sick and dying from hunger. I remember being at home and my mom nearly crying. I was in a lot of pain in my stomach. I had scabies because of malnutrition. We prayed and prayed and prayed. Then I saw a big brown dog coming with a piece of bread in its mouth. I don't know where it came from because anything good for cooking, including dogs, they'd already cooked it. The dog left the bread for me and I never saw it again. It was about a quarter of a pound of bread. We ate the bread and were happy. We praised the Lord because it was miraculous. It was written up in the *Times of Malta.*"

Before the siege lifted the people of Malta would rely on more than just divine intervention to stave off hunger. Once he had recovered from his brush with death, Scerri made regular trips to the black market with his mother. "I used to go with my mom after midnight. The farmers said, 'Come late because we're supposed to give everything to the government.' I remember once we had to go past the St. Mary's fortress and the soldiers challenged us. There was a curfew after 9 p.m. We begged them to let us go and they did. People used to give gold for flour. I remember once when the oil tanker *Ohio* limped into Grand Harbour the captain gave a bag of flour to civilians who helped the wounded off. It was the first time I ate flour in two years. It was mixed with petrol. My father brought it home and it had a taste of gas. It stunk, but we made two loaves of bread out of it."[3]

Vincenza Desira, a young Maltese housewife trying to keep food on the table for three children, said, "We had a lack of food. We couldn't even find any dogs or cats around. I was caught twice getting food from the black market. It was so very scarce. Once, when the government opened a large storage place where food was kept, they found nothing because the rats had eaten all the food."[4]

Many small children only survived because their mothers went without eating for days at a time. "Bless my mother," Carmel Portelli said decades later. "There was hardly any food but I didn't lose too much weight because she often gave me her bread. She'd say, 'I'm not hungry, you eat it.' You were young, you didn't realize she really was hungry. It was not just my mother that did it. Lots of mothers did the same thing. There was very little food. I remember when a ship was sunk in the harbour, people used to dive down to get the flour out to sell it on the black market."[5]

The lack of adequate rations made such an impression on British aircraft mechanic Arthur Inch that he spent the best part of a two-page letter to the author talking about his meals. "The first month I was in Malta I lost a stone [14 pounds] in weight," he recalled. "We all had ration cards and each time we had a meal the card was punched, so there were no double runs!" His first breakfast on the island consisted of half a soya bean sausage. Shortly after that, he received a single strip of bacon as his first meal of the day. Because he was still new to Malta, he cut the fat from his meat. "The chap next to me asked if he could have it! It wasn't long before I did the same."

> We were weighed out nine ounces of bread each morning and that had to last you the whole day. Sometimes it was backed up by a hard biscuit. Meat was often tinned bully beef or Spam and only one

thin slice of each. Sometimes we got goat's meat stew with a few local vegetables floating around and a tiny spoonful of mashed potatoes. For pudding it might be a couple of chunks of tinned pineapples or fresh figs and grapes which were fairly plentiful and we could often buy them from the street market. Once a week we might get four small squares of chocolate and we broke up the hard biscuit, added bits and stirred in the melted chocolate and heated this up in our mess tins. We called this chock duff! This was a good stomach filler and we waffed it down with gusto. On the black market we could get a small, round loaf of bread for 40 fags so we bartered for one and divided it into quarters and sat eating it like a piece of cake. Then to cap it all we got what we called Malta Dog, an upset stomach which entailed many visits to the latrines. Treatment prescribed was to eat nothing for 24 hours, plus a cupful of castor oil, so we then collected our food rations until we could eat again. That was the first and only time I was definitely starving and I wonder how we survived.[6]

Hopes that local farmers could salvage the situation were dashed when a lack of fertilizers caused a disappointingly low crop yield that year. Nevertheless, there were still plenty of potatoes, which the Allied propaganda machine tried to sell to the population as some sort of miracle food.

"There were very severe shortages of food," anti-aircraft gunner John Dedomenico said later. "I remember dinner consisted of two pieces of bread and a couple of sardines. Occasionally, you got a bar of chocolate, but that was a very big occasion. There was no sugar, you used jam in your tea. There was a black market ... I remember my mother used to buy a loaf of bread for $5, or the equivalent of 20 Canadian dollars. There was also some hoarding that went on. I remember we had a couple of cases of condensed milk sitting in the basement. Maltese are very heavy users of bread. Bread and pasta are staples of the working man, not so much meat. And of course we were short of flour."[7]

To make supplies last as long as possible, Governor Dobbie set up so-called Victory Kitchens, providing people with a watery stew that was sometimes fortified with chunks of cat, dog, donkey and goat meat, with a little horseflesh thrown in for good measure. The smell was almost enough to turn half-starved folks off eating. Almost, but not quite. At first, 10,000 meals were served a day but, within weeks, 200,000 people were lining up for the daily handouts.

"Only God knows what was in those stews," John Dedomenico says now. "It was a makeshift, mobile sort of arrangement that they set up in the village square. People came with ration cards and a pot. The guy in charge doled out a certain number of spoonfuls for every ration card. I remember my mother going out at 5 a.m. to line up for the soup kitchen that would open at 11 a.m. She'd come home at 2 p.m. with a horrible-looking stew." As bad as they were, however, the Victory Kitchens were essential to survival because the island was running out of fuel with which to cook meals. "Very few people had gas for cooking," Dedomenico recalled. "Most cooking was done by kerosene and there wasn't a lot of it left. The Victory Kitchens were an attempt to overcome that problem."[8]

On the airfields the pilots escaped the Victory Kitchens, but their diet was no better. At most squadrons the men were expected to live on a daily meal consisting of a plate of corned beef, a few dates and olives, and a skimpy ration of carrots dipped in revolting cod liver oil.

Kerosene, the island's main fuel, was also needed to provide light in the evenings and warmth at night. Malta could be swelteringly hot by day, but uncomfortably cold during winter and early spring nights. People got around the shortage for a time by burning their own furniture and the wood from their chicken coops.

It was not just the lack of essentials such as food, water and fuel that sapped the spirit. Pilots who went browsing through the shops during off hours found that shelves were all but empty. There was no soap, toothpaste, razor blades or pens, and little in the way of clothing. Indeed, Governor Dobbie, who had described the situation as "critical" earlier in the siege, was now saying that this description was too mild. In a brutally frank telegram to Prime Minister Churchill, he warned that the island would soon have to surrender unless it received more flour and ammunition.

Most people on the island, including the fighter pilots, were too tired to do much more than sleep whenever they were not busy with more pressing tasks. The situation was so bad, pilot Charles McLean believed, that morale was in grave danger of cracking. "Listlessness was spreading as the initial drive of the pilots slowly receded, and silent despair and hopelessness slowly but surely ate into everyone."[9]

This would have been another opportune time to finish off Malta through invasion. The defenders were down to a dozen serviceable fighters, including several old Hurricanes, and the anti-aircraft gunners were running so short of ammunition that they were being restricted to six rounds per day. The situation was so serious that when swarms of German and Italian raiders pounded all three airfields on May 8, most of the Allied pilots could do nothing more than fire away at them from the ground with ancient bolt-action rifles. In one such lop-sided fight at Takali, Bud Connell was wounded by a Stuka divebomber. Wilbert Dodd, who was one of the few defenders to get airborne, attacked an Italian Macchi-202 just south of Malta. He closed to within 100 metres before riddling the enemy ship with machine gun and cannon fire from a three-second burst. The Macchi spun down out of control trailing smoke, and Dodd was credited with a probable kill.

Two other enemy planes were destroyed for certain, and both in extraordinary fashion. It happened when a British radio operator came up with an ingenious plan to lure Axis pilots into a trap. He suspected the Germans and Italians were monitoring the radio signals of the Allied fliers. In fact, he was convinced the voices of several of the RAF flight commanders were well known to the enemy. So he ordered an imaginary "flight" of Spitfires into the air that afternoon. "The Hun bombers came over in force with quite a large fighter escort," he recalled later. "It happened there were several fighter pilots with me in the operations room, one of whom was a Canadian with an unmistakable voice. I put him at the microphone at a stand-by radio set and proceeded to give him dummy orders as if he were flying his fighter. This, we suspected, caused a cry of 'Spitfeuer Achtung!' to go over the German radio. In any case, two 109s enthusiastically shot each other down, without any British aircraft being airborne ... We claimed that Pilot Officer 'Humgufery' shot down the two Huns!"[10]

The incident raised morale all over the island. It also gave the Allies proof that the enemy was intercepting their radio messages. That information would be put to good use in coming weeks. Interestingly enough, the Germans were employing the services of a Canadian-born radio operator on Sicily, who monitored Allied conversations. Luftwaffe fighter pilot Johannes Steinhoff noted in his memoirs the Germans had a monitoring crew that "listened in to the enemy's radio messages both in speech and Morse. Through being in direct contact with these specialists and their evaluations, my group was informed in good time of the matters that most concerned them. Sergeant Henrich, who was in charge of the monitoring section, had been born in Canada and English was his mother tongue."[11]

Unknown to the radio operators on either side was the fact that the Allies were about to get two major boosts. The first came on May 8, when the speedy supply ship HMS *Welshman* slipped out of Gibraltar and steamed eastward carrying a cargo of dehydrated foodstuffs, canned meat, ammunition, powered milk, smoke-making canisters, aircraft engines and 100 airplane mechanics. The vessel, which could sail at 40 knots, had been disguised to look like a destroyer from the German puppet government of Vichy France. It even flew the French flag, and its British officers wore French uniforms whenever they were above deck. The modifications proved invaluable when a pair of Ju-88s buzzed over *Welshman's* bow near Tunisia on May 10. The enemy pilots were completely fooled by the deception and the ship continued on its merry way, pulling into Grand Harbour on May 11. Luftwaffe bombers immediately tried to sink it in port but the smoke canisters provided a protective screen that made an accurate attack all but impossible. The entire cargo was safely unloaded and *Welshman* slipped out of Malta that night, racing safely back to Gibraltar.

The other big break came May 9, when the aircraft carriers *Wasp* and *Eagle* sent a combined total of 63 Spitfires winging their way towards Malta. This was by far the largest and boldest reinforcement operation mounted to date, and it is no exaggeration to say the island's fate depended on the outcome. *Welshman's* gallant crew had given Malta enough food to last a few more weeks but, without a decent-sized fighter force, the garrison was going to be bombed into oblivion. Bull Turner, who had left Malta a few nights earlier aboard a

Spitfire pilots on Malta. Seated from left: South African Bob Sims, Canadians Eric Crist and Jack Ryckman, and an unidentified British airman. Courtesy of Eric Crist

transport plane, had been chosen to co-ordinate the operation. It was his job to brief the pilots on what course they should take and to fill them in on the conditions they would face once they got to their destination.

Just before dawn the planes began taking off. Almost immediately tragedy struck. It happened when Toronto pilot Bob Sherrington failed to pick up enough speed before lifting off the deck of the *Wasp*. His fighter plunged into the sea and the big carrier ran right over it, slicing the plane in half, killing the 20-year-old Sherrington instantly. Regina pilot Jerry Smith almost suffered a similar fate. He managed to get airborne only to discover a problem with his gas tank. There was no way he would be able to make it all the way to Malta, so he was instructed to ditch his plane alongside the carrier. It was an order the 21-year-old Prairie boy was not anxious to swallow. He knew the Spitfire was notorious for sinking like a stone. No less an expert than Brendan "Paddy" Finucane, the fabled Irish ace with 32 German planes to his credit, had already drowned while attempting to ditch in the English Channel. If a man with his experience could not get out of his cockpit in time, what chance did a rookie like Smith have? He

Officer Corps of the Royal Malta Artillery (anti-aircraft gunners). Courtesy of Peter Mifsud

was not about to find out. While the astonished crew of the *Wasp* looked on, Smith did what the experts said could not be done — he landed a Spitfire on a carrier. It was not a pretty sight, but after bouncing off the deck and jamming on the brakes for all he was worth, the young pilot was able to bring his plane to a halt a scant two metres from the bow of the ship. American pilot Douglas Fairbanks, Jr. was so impressed with the feat that he presented Smith with a pair of U.S. Navy wings. Smith stayed behind on board *Wasp* while his Spitfire's fuel tank was repaired.

Sixty-two other fighters made it safely into the air and headed east. But death was not done with them yet. As they neared Malta in groups of twos and threes, Canadian pilots Charles Valiquet and Johnny Rounsefell spotted an Italian seaplane lumbering along a few thousand feet below. Their instructions were to ignore the enemy if at all possible and head straight to Takali. They simply did not have enough fuel for a dogfight. A great deal of petrol was used up in combat flying, and even a battle lasting as little as five minutes could make it impossible for them to make land. But this looked like such easy pickings that the two RCAF fliers could not let it go. One quick pass would likely be enough to give them their first taste of blood. Then they could fly on to Malta in triumph.

The Italian rear gunner's heart must have been in his throat as he saw the two Spitfires sweeping down on him. He had only one machine gun against eight cannons and eight machine guns. He let go with a long-range burst, aimed directly at the lead Spitfire. His tracers shattered the cockpit of Valiquet's fighter. The 21- year-old Montreal native was fatally wounded and his Spitfire veered uncontrollably into the path of Rounsefell's onrushing aircraft. Before he could react, the 20-year-old Vancouver pilot collided with his dead wingman. The two Spitfires crashed into the sea. Neither pilot was ever seen again.

As the remaining 59 Spitfires came in to land, the Axis fliers were waiting for them. In the next few minutes utter chaos reigned. Johnny Sherlock remembered seeing flak bursting all over the island as he made his final approach. Dozens of pilots were yelling frantic warnings over the radio as they spotted Macchis and Messerschmitts swooping in from the north. Sherlock actually saw one ME-109 in the landing circuit above Takali with its wheels and flaps down. The exceptionally bold German was attempting to fool the anti-aircraft gunners into thinking he was an Allied pilot coming in to land. Fortunately, he was driven off by pilot Cy King before he could cause any damage. A few Spitfire jockeys could not take evasive action because they were out of fuel and were gliding in on dead engines. As Sherlock looked on in horror, one of them ploughed headlong into a building below. An ME-109 was firing at Sherlock, making it impossible for him to concentrate on his own landing. But there were only a few drops of fuel left in his tank. He had to get down immediately or not at all. Ignoring the German on his tail, Sherlock dropped his nose and made a perfect three-point landing.

Another pilot, M. W. Vineyard, was more concerned about the dozens of bottles of Coca-Cola that he had stored inside the fuselage of his Spitfire than he was about the Germans or the state of his fuel supply. As soon as he landed he scrambled into a nearby slit trench to take cover. Then, remembering the soft drinks, he dashed through exploding bombs, leapt back into the cockpit and guided his plane — and its precious cargo — into the safety of a blast pen.

Yet another pilot who had a narrow escape this day was 20-year-old John "Willie-the-Kid" Williams. The Chilliwack, British Columbia, native found four Messerschmitts on his tail as he approached Grand

Harbour. Williams, who was experiencing his first combat, quickly demonstrated the coolness and cunning that he would soon be famous for throughout Malta. Diving for the waves, he pulled up at the last possible moment and made straight for an Allied flak crew on shore. The wily Canadian opened fire, purposely spraying bullets into the water in front of the anti-aircraft gunners. By now the four ME-109s had pulled out of their dives and were hard on his tail, firing relentlessly. Williams, who had taken care to ensure his shells missed the shore gunners, was nevertheless hoping they would mistake him for the leader of an attacking formation of five German planes. They did. And just as he had calculated, they could not spin their big Bofors guns around in time to get a bead on him. But as he flashed over their heads, the ack-ack crew let fly at the four Germans, scattering them in every direction. One was seen retreating with a trail of black smoke gushing from its engine.

There was still more drama to be played out on that unforgettable day, both in the air and on the ground. The air action came when a large formation of Italian Cant bombers tried to destroy the newly arrived Spitfires on the ground. Englishman Paddy Schade, one of the few Allied pilots still circling Malta, dove into a gaggle of five Cants, shooting two of the tri-motor bombers down in flames. When a flight of Macchis tried to intervene, he damaged one of them with a burst fired from a range of 275 metres. An exhausted Cy King, meanwhile, landed his Spitfire only to be greeted by Australian ace Gordon Tweedale. Tweedale, one of Malta's most distinguished defenders with seven planes to his credit, was a Hurricane pilot who had never flown a Spitfire. Nevertheless, he was under orders to take King's plane up as soon as it could be refuelled. King quickly gave him a few pointers on how to handle the fighter, and the Aussie took off just in time to greet a flight of ME-109s. Moments later, he was shot down and killed.

Despite this tragedy, the system of having fresh pilots standing by to take off as soon as the planes could be made ready to get back into the air undoubtedly saved many of the new Spitfires from being demolished on the ground. The Allies had learned their lesson from the ill-fated March reinforcement débâcle. This time, five ground crews were assigned to each aircraft pen, along with a rested Malta pilot who would take over from an aviator who had just landed after a 975-kilometre flight. Anti-aircraft gunner John Dedomenico is convinced the system took the enemy by surprise. "It was an incredible thing," he recalled. "That was a surprise to the Germans. We'd lost a lot of planes earlier because we hadn't been organized. But this time the refuelling and rearming was done before the planes could be strafed. As the Spitfires landed, the teams refuelled and reloaded. If for some reason a fresh pilot wasn't available, the man who had just landed had a pee and off he went again."[12]

As night fell the defenders had been bolstered by close to 60 Spitfires. For the first time the Allies would have a formidable force with which to defend the island. The Axis forces still had overwhelmingly superior numbers, but at least the Allies would now be able to offer more than just token resistance.

If there was a disturbing aspect to the reinforcement operation, it was that once again most of the new pilots had no combat experience. When RAF commanders on Malta went over the log books of the new arrivals they were shocked to discover some were fresh out of flight school, with only a few dozen hours' flying time since graduation. At least three pilots were considered so green they were loaded onto a Sutherland flying boat and sent back to Gibraltar that very night.

Luftwaffe General Kesselring, meanwhile, did not grasp how many Spitfires had been ferried in on May 10, because the next morning he sent over 20 Stukas and 10 Ju-88s with only a small fighter escort to bomb Grand Harbour. No less than 50 RAF planes — 37 Spitfires and 13 Hurricanes — rose to greet them. Within minutes one of the most important air battles of the siege was under way. This was Malta's chance to lay a beating on Kesselring, and her pilots took full advantage of it, tearing into the enemy formations with reckless abandon. Within minutes German bombers were going down like bowling pins. Englishman Archie Bartleman had a field day, shooting down three Stukas in as many minutes. Australian Paul Brennan reported that the Ju-87 he shot down disintegrated, with huge chunks flying off in every direction. Before the smoke cleared at least 12 Nazi bombers had been shot down. German fighters that tried to intervene were overwhelmed by superior numbers. Australian Tim Goldsmith reported his section of four Spitfires took on two ME-109s. Goldsmith took advantage of the situation, shooting down one of two Messerschmitts destroyed that unforgettable morning. In all, 14 enemy planes were shot down and many others damaged for the loss of just two Spitfires, one of which was accidently destroyed by Maltese anti-aircraft gunners.

After lunch the Germans were back, but so were the Spitfires. Another wild dogfight erupted, with several more enemy aircraft being seen to crash into the sea. One of the kills was registered by the rising British ace Paddy Schade, giving him three victories in just two days and six since his arrival on Malta.

The final raid of the day was mounted by the Regia Aeronautica. Thirty fighters were riding shotgun for half a dozen Cants when they ran headlong into more Spitfires than any of them had ever seen before.

"I'll never forget that mission," Cant crewman Tony Ferri said more than half a century later. "We were told at briefing to expect trouble, that the Germans had run into heavy opposition earlier in the day. There was anxiety as we put on our flying gear. None of the crew said much, but you could cut the tension with a knife. The squadron commander tried to relax us, pointing out we'd have dozens of fighters escorting us, but it did little good. I remember sitting on the grass under the wing of our plane, waiting for the signal to take off. It was so peaceful. The three engines had been tested, then turned off. The only sound was of the birds. You could see a donkey grazing nearby and you could smell the blossoms. It was about 5 p.m. so it wasn't terribly hot. The tranquillity of the scene, and the knowledge of what lay ahead, made me ache for life, if I can put it that way."

Ferri noticed that the tension eased up a little as the crew climbed into their Cant and began preparing for takeoff. "We snapped on our parachutes and life jackets, the guns were checked, oxygen masks were hooked up and our pilot glanced over at Mount Etna to see which way the wind was blowing its smoke plume. At this point there was a nervous energy that was almost intoxicating. Then the engines roared into life and we taxied into position for takeoff. You could see the grass being beaten down by the whirling propeller blades. Then we were off, with five other Cants coming just behind us. As we neared Malta we could see dust in the distance, where the British planes were taking off to intercept us. We looked around and could see our own fighters high above us in the sun. Flying over enemy territory always gave me a queer feeling. You knew they could see you, that people who hated you were running to their flak guns and planes, getting ready to try to kill you. Somebody suddenly shouted, 'There they are!' It never ceased to amaze me how quickly the Spitfires and Hurricanes would appear. One moment you were alone in the sky and the next second there they were, coming at you head on, with guns blazing. When I first saw the guns winking on British fighters I thought they were turning their landing lights on. But by this time I was experienced enough to know better."

Ferri saw a Cant about 100 metres ahead of him suddenly explode in an orange fireball. "It went straight down; I didn't see anyone get out. That got your attention very quickly. Another Cant was hit and fell away, but the rest of us pressed on. By this time our fighters were mixing it up with the English so we were left alone for the moment. That's when the flak came up at us. You could see muzzle flashes all over Malta, or at least it seemed that way to me. Our plane was hit in the starboard wing and in the fuselage but none of the crew was hurt. We dropped our bombs and, as always, you could feel the old Cant rise up involuntarily as the extra weight of the bombs fell away. We turned for home, but half a dozen Spitfires were after us. I think there were so many that they got in each other's way, because they only put one cannon shell into our rudder. Our rear gunner was firing back for all he was worth. You could smell the gun powder all over the plane. Somehow, we got the hell out of there. I was OK while we were airborne but after I got into my quarters I was shaking like a leaf and I'm not ashamed to tell you I started to cry. I swore I wouldn't go to Malta again, but of course I did. None of us had any choice in the matter. If you refused to fly you could be shot."[13]

That evening the page-one headline in the *Times of Malta* screamed:

SPITFIRES SLAUGHTER STUKAS

For once this was not just so much wartime propaganda. During the day's three raids a combined total of 23 Axis planes had been shot down and 40 more returned to Sicily sporting battle damage. It was a resounding victory that lifted morale all over the island. The defenders were still seriously outnumbered, but they had given Kesselring a bloody nose and they knew it. An alarmed Kesselring pulled in his horns the next day, sending only a few bombers over with a heavy fighter escort. Nevertheless, Willie-the-Kid Williams managed to open his Malta account by blasting a Ju-88 out of the air. He would damage two more enemy machines over the next few days. As always, there was a price to be paid. British ace Peter Nash, who had 10 victories to his credit, was killed by a Messerschmitt pilot before the week was out.

Amid all this violence and bloodshed came a touching face-to-face encounter between a Canadian pilot and a German flier. It happened on May 18 when Nova Scotian Norm Fowlow and Bavarian Johannes Lompa were both forced to bail out of their burning fighters. Both came down in the sea off Hal Far. The German, a poor swimmer, could not get his life belt to inflate, and his rubber raft was nowhere to be seen. Fowlow, who had spent many happy hours of his youth frolicking in Trinity Bay, was a strong swimmer. Fortunately for Lompa, Fowlow was also the son of a Church of England clergyman who had been taught since boyhood to show concern for those less fortunate than himself. Indeed, his father, who was a pacifist, had been deeply disappointed by young Norm's decision to become a fighter pilot. But the Reverend Fowlow would have been proud had he been able to watch as his son kept Lompa afloat until an Allied rescue launch appeared on the scene. The German, who was the first aboard, immediately turned and helped Fowlow into the vessel. The two shook hands and slapped one another heartily on the back. Pilot Johnny Sherlock, who was on board the launch, said later, "Lompa was as friendly as all get out, and happy to have been picked up. He knew the war was over [for him] and he'd survived it."[14] During the 20-minute ride into shore, both Lompa and Fowlow fell fast asleep. When the Canadian got back to Luqa airfield he was pleased to find out he had been credited with shooting down an ME-109 before he was forced to take to the silk. Possibly his victim had been Lompa. It is even possible the two shot each other down.

The loss of Fowlow's Spitfire was made up in spades later that day when another 17 of the pointed-winged fighters flew in from the carrier *Eagle*. Like all their predecessors, they arrived in the middle of an air raid. This time, however, they all made it down in one piece. Bit by bit, Malta was gaining strength.

The newcomers were immediately thrown into the fray. One of them, Buzz Ogilvie, shot down a Ju-88 in his first action over the island. "A fellow named Halford and I were scrambled after they picked up a blip on radar," he recalled in a 1997 interview. "We picked up a Ju-88 and Halford indicated he was making the first attack. Well, the rear gunners on those Junkers were really fine marksmen, and Halford was hit. He had to pull up. I made my attack low over the water, about 1,000 feet up. I had to allow a lot of deflection, just like when you're duck shooting. I fired and then tilted my wing to bank away. As I did so, the Ju-88 disappeared and I couldn't see it anywhere. We didn't make a claim, but the operations officer said it went into the drink. He'd been monitoring the Germans' conversations, that's how he knew."

Ogilvie had no time to celebrate his first kill. "I scrambled right after that, because my aircraft was the only one that was serviceable and they'd picked up another blip. I took off and ran into a Cant three-engine plane painted white with red crosses on it. It had obviously been sent over to pick up the crew of the Ju-88 we'd shot down. I was hesitant to shoot it down, called operations and said, 'It's got red crosses on it.' They radioed back, 'Shoot it down.' I couldn't do that, so I pulled up alongside the Cant and motioned to the pilot to head for Malta. When he turned for Sicily I fired a broadside in front of him. I indicated I'd shoot him down if he didn't return with me to Malta. Just when he was banking to return, somebody else came up behind us and blew him out of the sky. It was the biggest explosion I'd ever seen."[15]

As we have already seen, this was not the first time an Axis hospital plane had been ruthlessly shot down. The truth is that while most pilots were loath to fire on such machines, the High Command insisted they be attacked on sight. The authorities feared that in addition to performing their mercy missions, the crews of the Red Cross planes were spying on Allied shipping. Besides that, any German or Italian fliers plucked from the water by an Axis seaplane might be back over Malta dropping bombs within 24 hours. From a strictly military point of view, it made perfect sense to make sure downed enemy aviators were either captured or left to die in the Mediterranean.

Fighting continued at a feverish pace, with Buck McNair destroying two ME-109s in the last days of May. Shortly afterwards he was awarded the Distinguished Flying Cross. The citation reads: "This officer is a skillful and courageous pilot. He invariably presses home his attack with the greatest determination irrespective of odds. He has destroyed at least five and damaged seven enemy aircraft. Four of these he damaged in one combat." In that particular fight, he had chased a German bomber halfway back to Sicily, scoring several hits on it. But the German rear gunner knew his stuff and kept McNair at bay until, low on fuel and ammunition, McNair was forced to break off and return to base. As far as Eric Crist is concerned, no pilot deserved the DFC more than McNair. "If you imagine the stereotypical fighter pilot, Buck was it. He looked the part. He had it all, the Robert Redford look" — and the courage to go with it.[16]

Another pilot who rose to the forefront at this time was an eccentric Englishman named Ronnie West. A scrawny fellow with a deep brown tan, he delighted in showing up bare-chested in the mess, wearing a towel on his head and playing the clarinet. Some newcomers mistook him for an Arab civilian and were stunned when they saw him the next day on the flight line in full uniform. Like every Malta veteran, he had more than his share of close calls. Once, he was shot down by an ME-109 as he attempted to land. Fortunately, he walked away from the wreck without a scratch. On another occasion, he mistook a flight of Messerschmitts for a British formation and happily joined up, only to be shot down by Maltese anti-aircraft gunners. Once again, however, he emerged unscathed. Before long he proved himself rather handy in a dogfight, destroying eight Axis planes and damaging eight others before being posted home.

Mercifully, fighting tapered off a little before the end of the month. The Allies did suffer another loss, however, when a dozen Hurricanes attempted to fly to Malta from North Africa. Three failed to arrive after their pilots got lost, ran out of fuel and came down in the sea. Two English fliers were killed, but Canadian Norm Ganes was picked up by a German ship and spent the next three years in a prisoner of war camp. The decision to send a flight of old Hurricanes to Malta at this late date was almost criminal. But it does show that the Allies, despite their growing strength, still felt they needed every plane they could get their hands on.

As May 1942 came to a close, the island's defences had never been stronger. Still, the food situation remained desperate. Unless a convoy could get through in June, Malta was going to have to run up the white flag.

CHAPTER 6

THE LOST CONVOY

Defeatism gripped Malta as June opened.

In this, the fifth month since Hitler had given the green light to Operation Hercules, everyone on the island was losing hope. Even senior officers were talking about surrender. Bombings had already killed 1,200 people, wounded thousands more, and destroyed virtually every building of any consequence. Tens of thousands were sick, and everyone was hungry. The food supply would be exhausted in a matter of weeks. Some fighter pilots had already approached their squadron commanders to discuss means of escape. Flying back to Gibraltar was not a realistic option because the Spitfire didn't have the range to make it. That meant the pilots would have to land on aircraft carriers stationed east of Gibraltar and the Spit, despite Jerry Smith's remarkable feat, was not designed for landing on a carrier. Not one in a hundred could be expected to set down safely. Some pilots wanted to fly south as far as they could go into Africa before they ran out of fuel. That would take them out of the range of Rommel's Afrika Korps, but it would also leave them lost in the middle of a vast wilderness with little hope of rescue. A few suggested flying to Tunisia or Algeria to be interned by the Vichy government. That was hardly an ideal solution, but it was better than an Axis POW camp.

What the pilots did not know was that their new commander, Lord Gort, was not interested in escape. He was contemplating a suicide mission for them. "I resolved that rather than capitulate by formal surrender, if the crisis came, I would lead what remained of the garrison in an invasion of the coast of Italy and go down fighting," he admitted later.[1] Nor was this the idle boast of some desk-bound blowhard. Gort, who had replaced Dobbie as Governor of Malta the month before, had won the Victoria Cross, the Commonwealth's highest gallantry award, for his courage under fire during the 1940 Battle of France. This was a man who was willing to throw his life away rather than accept defeat, and he expected everyone under his command to do the same thing.

There seemed little hope of receiving any outside help. On every front the Allies were in disarray. In mid-May Japanese troops had run the British out of Burma, and now they were almost at the gates of India. At the same time, on the Russian Front German forces had captured Crimea's Kerch Peninsula after a fierce battle in which they destroyed several hundred Soviet tanks. In North Africa, Rommel had launched a surprise offensive that set the British Eighth Army back on its heels. Within weeks he had driven the English all the way to El Alamein, deep inside Egyptian territory, a mere 100 kilometres from Alexandria and only 475 kilometres from the coveted Suez Canal. Four-fifths of the tank force Britain sent into the desert had been lost.

Fortunately, despite all the troubles the Allies were facing around the globe, Winston Churchill was not prepared to throw Malta to the wolves. He knew the island had to be held if the Allies were to have any hope of winning the war. In his memoirs, he admitted he was prepared to risk every aircraft carrier in the Royal Navy, if that is what it would take to run a convoy through to Malta. Something had to be done, he added, because the island "cried aloud for help. The strain was at many points more than could be borne."[2]

In East Prussia, meanwhile, General Student was meeting with Hitler in a bid to have the invasion of Malta moved up. He believed the island was getting stronger — at least in terms of fighter defences — and he felt it would be unwise to wait until late summer to launch an all-out assault. The attack, he proposed, should be undertaken immediately. The Führer agreed that a Malta bridgehead was possible. But after that, he warned, the British would send several squadrons of warships converging on the island from both Gibraltar and Alexandria. And as soon as the Italians got word that the English fleet was on its way, he added contemptuously, they would go scurrying back to their Sicilian ports. Student and his paratroopers would be left facing the Royal Navy on their own. When Student protested, insisting the Italians were better than Hitler was giving them credit for, the Nazi dictator curtly cut him off. "I forbid you to return to Italy!" he raged. "You will stay in Berlin."[3]

Later in the month, Mussolini wrote to Hitler all but begging him to invade the island. The conquest of Malta would free up 700 warplanes for use in North Africa and Russia, save scores of Axis ships from being sunk, and dramatically shorten the time it took to get supplies to Rommel, he pointed out. Mussolini had statistics to prove his point: Allied forces on Malta were still managing to sink an average of one Italian transport a day, despite almost five months of continuous air raids by Axis planes. Unless that was stopped, he said, the Afrika Korps would soon run out of supplies.

Hitler, however, would not be budged. He wrote back announcing Operation Hercules was being postponed until September. In some ways, Hitler's reluctance was understandable. The Italian army had been performing poorly in North Africa, and there was no guarantee that Italy's navy would do any better in the waters off Malta, where a pitched battle with the British fleet would probably accompany an invasion attempt. Besides, Hitler had been assured by General Kesselring that Malta was no longer a force to be reckoned with. As recently as May 10 the general had wired Hitler declaring triumphantly that every military and industrial target on the island had been destroyed. Even if that was an exaggeration, Hitler knew he could starve the garrison into surrender within weeks.

If the Germans were hesitant about what to do next, the Italians were not. On June 2 the Regia Aeronautica sent a huge force of fighters over Malta in a bid to draw the Allied pilots into a shootout. Three lumbering Cant bombers provided the bait while 60 Macchis and Reggianes hovered several hundred metres overhead. Don "Shorty" Reid, a baby-faced flier who was scarcely five feet tall, was one of 20 Spitfire pilots to accept the challenge, penetrating the fighter screen to attack the bombers head on. He damaged a Cant with a two-second burst, then turned to meet a Reggiane coming up behind him. Coming around sharply, he got onto the Italian's tail and unleashed a salvo that sent the enemy ship plunging down, apparently out of control. Reid, in his first combat, was credited with one plane damaged and a second probably destroyed. Two other pilots were credited with damaging enemy machines as well, but the Italians had a success of their own, shooting a Spitfire down in flames. The doomed fighter was seen to fall in Kalafrana Bay, coming to rest almost on top of a sunken Stuka that had been destroyed a few days earlier. So many planes had been lost in the siege that those being shot down now were falling onto the wrecks of other aircraft!

The next day there was little fighting over Malta itself, but a bitter clash erupted above the Mediterranean when 31 Spitfires took off from the carrier *Eagle* and headed for the island. This time, the Luftwaffe made a serious bid to intercept the formation long before it reached its destination. Shooting down the new Spitfires as they attempted to land was not working. Instead, Kesselring decided the best thing to do was to force the Allied pilots into a prolonged dog-fight on the way in. With any luck, a large number of them would use up all their remaining fuel and be forced to ditch into the sea.

"Twelve 109s attacked out of the sun when we were about half way to Malta," pilot Wally McLeod recalled later. "It was a perfect bounce. I didn't even know they were there until tracers started streaking over my starboard wing. One got on my tail, but thank God he was a poor marksman ... I was able to get away before he could nail me."[4] McLeod climbed directly into the sun, losing the Messerschmitt pilot in the glare. Some of the others were not so lucky. No one ran out of fuel, but four Spitfires were shot down. Not one German plane was lost.

As the survivors got closer to Malta they were in for another sur-prise. McLeod radioed Valletta for directions and, moments later, a German speaking perfect English gave him co-ordinates that would have taken him straight to Italy, had he followed them. But McLeod recognized the deception and continued on his course, depending on his compass to guide him in for a safe landing.

Overall, despite the losses, the operation had been a success for the defenders, if only because there were now 27 more Spitfires inside the embattled little fortress. What's more, although no one knew it at the time, Wally McLeod's arrival gave Malta one of the finest fighter pilots the war would produce.

Born in Regina, Saskatchewan, a week before Christmas 1915, the 26-year-old McLeod was several years older than most of the other aviators on Malta. He was also less personable. He had lost his mother at an early age. His experiences during the Great Depression had also left their mark. Western Canada was hit harder by the Dirty Thirties than most other places and Wally, despite a good education, was unable to find work. He soon became a bitter young man with a chip on his shoulder. For a time he travelled across the Prairies, showing Hollywood movies in school gymnasiums, church basements and town halls. It provided him with enough money to get by, but it was not the teaching career he had worked for. So when war came in 1939, he sold his film projector and joined the RCAF.

In many ways he was luckier than the other newcomers to the island. Certainly his training had been more extensive. After stints at flight schools in Brandon, Manitoba, Camp Borden, Ontario, and at Saskatoon and Prince Albert in Saskatchewan, he received still further training in the United Kingdom. After more than a year of preparation he was finally posted to an operational fighter squadron in southern England. Before being sent to Malta he took part in several combats over Nazi-occupied Europe, destroying one German plane and damaging three others. It was not an outstanding score, but at least he arrived on the besieged island with some actual combat experience. More than that, he arrived with an attitude. For Wally McLeod was a blood-thirsty killer out to make a name for himself. He had a burning ambition to become the leading Canadian ace. At Takali, he would get every opportunity to fulfil his dream.

McLeod's first taste of action over the island came on June 4. His desire to score kills very nearly cost him his life. He attacked an Italian Cant, setting one of its three engines on fire and causing a second to sputter.

Throttling back to finish off the slower flying machine, he failed to keep a close watch behind. A Macchi came out of nowhere and put a dozen holes in his Spitfire. Had the Italian pilot been armed with cannons instead of machine guns, it is likely that McLeod's carelessness would have been fatal. As it was, the Canadian was barely able to coax his damaged ship home. As he flew back to base he got a glimpse of the fate he had so narrowly escaped when he saw a Spitfire shoot down a Macchi. The enemy flier was hurled into space when his aircraft exploded; with his parachute on fire, he plunged nearly five kilometres to his death.

On June 6, General Kesselring ordered massive attacks on Malta. With Hitler refusing to sanction an invasion, Kesselring decided he had no choice but to wage a brutal war of attrition and wear the defenders down, no matter how long it took. Fighting began in earnest at dawn and raged almost without letup until after the sun had gone down. Englishmen Laddie Lucas and Canadian Frank Jones were the first to draw blood, teaming up to shoot down one of three Ju-88s spotted flying low over the water. Canadians Ozzie Linton and Basil Butler joined the fray moments later, jointly sending a second Nazi bomber cartwheeling into the sea.

It was a good start, but it was only the beginning of what would be one of the best days yet for the defenders. Shortly after the first skirmish a huge formation of Italian planes showed up on Allied radar screens. Five Cant bombers escorted by nearly 40 Macchi and Reggiane fighters were making straight for Grand Harbour. Two Italian aircraft were blown out of the sky. The only damage sustained by the Allies came when Wally McLeod's engine was knocked out by a burst of fire from a gunner aboard one of the Cants. Keeping cool, McLeod glided out of the fight and landed without further incident. It was the second time in three days that Italians had shot his Spitfire to ribbons.

The third alert of the day came before 10 a.m, but this time it was a mercy mission. Two dozen Italian fighters came in low, combing the sea in a bid to locate the Reggiane pilots lost earlier in the morning. The Axis fliers were sitting ducks. The Spitfires dove out of the sun with unexpected suddenness. Canadian Frank Jones sent one enemy plane down in flames, and Englishman Raoul Daddo-Langlois bagged a second. The demoralized Italians made a hasty retreat back to Sicily. Still, the Regia Aeronautica was not finished for the day. Just after lunch it was back, with 19 fighters being sent out to look for missing comrades who might be down in the sea aboard life rafts. Once again the Spitfires waded into their ranks, shooting three more down. Johnny Sherlock's plane was hit, however, and he was forced to execute a crude belly landing at Hal Far. "I had two or three crash landings," he says now. "One time my tail was shot off a little, and I landed with my wheels up. I couldn't come in slow enough. Every time I slowed down I lost control because the elevators and part of the rudder were missing. I was running out of airdrome so I put the wheels up and skidded in."[5]

If the Allies were feeling smug after shooting down nine enemy planes without loss, they were reminded just how dangerous the Axis fliers could be two days later when a pack of Messerschmitts shot down two Spitfires without loss. More help was on the way, however.

For on June 9 a young Canadian fighter pilot destined to change the course of the siege landed on Malta. His name was George "Screwball" Beurling.

Beurling! Here was a man with a reputation as the bad boy of the Royal Air Force. Born in Verdun, Quebec, in the middle of a snow-storm, the 22-year-old had been a rebel all his life. As a boy he had shown little interest in his schoolwork, mainly because all he could think about was flying. "Every since I can remember, airplanes and to get up in them into the free sky had been the beginning and end of my thoughts," he wrote later.[6] George took his first flight at age nine. He would go up with any pilot who agreed to take him for a ride. He spent every spare moment at LaSalle Road airport, five kilometres outside Verdun, watching in fascination for hours at a time as air-planes took off and landed. And when he discovered there were not enough spare moments in the day to satisfy him, he simply played hookey. This, he noted, meant two spankings — one when he got to school and a second when he arrived home at night. But to George, the beatings were more than worth it. When his parents banished him to his room instead of strapping him, the boy spent hours building model planes. He then sold them, using the money to buy flying lessons.

The young enthusiast took the controls of a plane for the first time at age 12. He soloed in the mid-winter of 1938 and, from then on, there was no stopping him. After getting his pilot's certificate, he headed west, hoping to obtain a commercial licence in Vancouver. After that, he planned to go to China to fight in the Chinese Air Force against the Japanese. But try as he might, Beurling could not get to China. Crossing into the United States with hopes of boarding a ship at Seattle, he was charged with illegal entry and tossed in jail. Sent home, he drifted aimlessly eastward. By this time, war had bro-ken out in Europe, and George marched into the nearest airforce recruiting station. The RCAF took one look at his poor academic record and sent him packing. Bitterly disappointed, George decided to go to Europe and fight for the Finnish Air Force against the Russians. The Finns, he understood, would take anyone with a pilot's licence. They were fighting a desperate battle with the Communists and they did not care how a man had done in Grade 12 algebra, provided he could fly and shoot. But because he was still only 18, the Finnish embassy insisted that he get written permission from his parents. And they refused to give it.

Determined not to give up, he signed onto a munitions ship and headed to England, where he hoped to join the RAF. The crossing was harrowing. Seven ships in the convoy were sunk by German U-boats, but Beurling's got through. Once in the U.K., he went to a Royal Air Force office and offered his services. The recruiting officer was impressed, but told the young Canadian he could not sign up without a birth certificate. Undaunted, Beurling returned to his ship and sailed back across the Atlantic to get the missing document!

The British took due note of Beurling's extraordinary tenacity and sent him to flight school. Here, he came close to getting drummed out of the RAF after he buzzed a control tower, knocking a sentry over the railing with the force of the wind from his propellor. Fortunately for the people of Malta, the authorities decided to give him another chance. Posted to No. 403 Squadron early in 1942, he flew several missions over France, shooting down two Focke Wulf-190 fighters. At the same time, he managed to alienate his superiors by frequently leaving formation to go off looking for trouble on his own. So when he asked permission to replace a married pilot who did not want to report to such a hot spot as Malta, his commanding officer gladly let him go.

Beurling never forgot his arrival on the island. Minutes after he landed at Takali, a pair of Messerschmitt pilots brazenly flew in at tree-top level, strafing the buildings and ground crews as they worked to patch up bomb craters. The Canadian was both shocked and excited. He loved the thrill of combat and he was happy at the thought of being able to engage the enemy without having to fly very far to find him. Describing his arrival later, he wrote enthusiastically that

> Bombs were liable to come whistling around your ears at any minute. If you looked up you'd see Spits and MEs split-assing all over the sky and every once in a while some poor devil who hadn't kept his tail clean would come spinning down in flames. Flak went up in flowerbeds and parachutes came drifting down. From the ground the constant din of ack ack batteries ... Up high the clatter of machine guns and cannon

bursts and the roar of full-engined Spitfires, MEs and Macchis diving ... erks [ground crews] scurrying about the drome patching bomb craters ... engineers detonating time bombs ... rescue launches rushing to sea to pick up floating parachutes ... the Maltese population trying to carry on the day's chores between headlong dives for shelter and protection of walls, cracked up houses or wrinkles in the rocks ... cats and dogs fighting in the streets in keeping with the temper of the place ... Never a dull moment. That was Malta in the blitzes. Before you had been there a day you got the idea Jerry had decided to either sink the damned island or blow it away — and you weren't far wrong.[7]

Beurling's squadron commander, Laddie Lucas, instantly recognized that the newcomer, despite his reputation as a troublemaker, was a man with the temperament and ability to be a splendid fighter pilot. Recalling their initial meeting, he wrote, "Beurling was untidy, with a shock of fair, tousled hair above penetrating blue eyes. He smiled a lot and the smile came straight out of those striking eyes. His sallow complexion was in keeping with his part Scandinavian ancestry. He was high strung, brash and outspoken. He was a rebel, yes; but I suspected his rebelliousness came from some mistaken feeling of inferiority. I judged that what Beurling needed most was not to be smacked down but to be encouraged. His ego mattered very much to him."[8] Lucas clearly liked what he saw, but he warned the newcomer he would be shipped out on the next transport plane leaving the island if he did not learn to obey orders.

Beurling justified Lucas's faith in him on June 12 when four Spitfires scrambled to intercept a dozen ME-109s. The Canadian blew the tail off one of them in a ten-minute fight, but — although it is impossible to imagine that the enemy plane could have flown back to base without its rudder — he only received credit for a "probable" kill because no one saw it crash.

At about the same time that Beurling was demonstrating his brilliant marksmanship against the ME-109s, Canadian pilot Ozzie Linton was experiencing a bizarre encounter with a flight of Stuka divebombers. Linton was moving in for a frontal assault when his propeller oil seal suddenly broke, smearing the Spitfire's windscreen with a heavy coat of black liquid. Unable to see forward, Linton broke off and headed for home. Moments later, like a bear cub blundering into a hornets' nest, he stumbled headlong into a huge formation of enemy planes. "As I was returning to base, wondering what had happened to my No. 2, I suddenly saw the Ju-87s on either side of me, and only a few yards away, going in the opposite direction!" he wrote later. "I then realized I was in the final moments of flying straight through the flight path of the returning bombers, with their gunners loosing off at me for all they were worth." Fortunately, the Germans were almost as startled as Linton, and their aim was not lethal. He managed to survive the hail of lead and, perhaps almost as amazingly, to make a safe landing without any forward visibility. Once on the ground, he shuddered as he examined what was left of his Spitfire. "Several shells had entered the fuselage behind me, and one had passed through the small space between the upper and lower petrol tanks, immediately in front of the cockpit ... I wondered then — and still do — what must have been the thoughts of the German crews as they saw a 'respected' Spitfire closing on their flight path, flying straight through it, and neither firing nor turning to engage."[9]

While Linton's plane was being repaired, the Axis fliers showed up again, sparking a spectacular early evening battle involving close to 100 aircraft. Buck McNair destroyed an ME-109 whose pilot managed to bail out. The German was rescued by a Luftwaffe flying boat, but two Italian pilots perished in other actions. One Spitfire was shot down, but its pilot parachuted to safety.

Back in London, Prime Minister Churchill was giving the green light to a dramatic plan to send two convoys steaming towards Malta simultaneously from east and west. Six transport ships — including a desperately needed oil tanker — were to make the run from Gibraltar escorted by no less than 10 Royal Navy warships. Following a little further behind were to be two aircraft carriers with their own escort of 11 destroyers and one battleship. At almost the same moment, an eastern convoy was leaving Alexandria with 11 transports guarded by 20 naval vessels. In all, the two convoys were carrying close to 120,000 tonnes of food, fuel and ammunition. It was enough to last Malta until well into the autumn, provided all the ships could get

British sailor Frank Kerley. Courtesy of Frank Kerley

through the gauntlet of enemy planes, ships, torpedo boats and U-boats that would surely be sent out to destroy them.

In addition to sending a powerful escort of surface ships, Churchill had two more tricks up his sleeve. First, he sent nine British subs into the Mediterranean to seek out enemy ships. Secondly, he ordered a daring commando raid on German airfields on Crete and mainland Greece. Seventeen Ju-88s were destroyed or seriously damaged on the ground by elite soldiers who sneaked onto tarmacs and placed time-bombs right on their wings! The blasts also destroyed several fuel dumps, a number of trucks and a few nearby buildings. By the time the smoke cleared, there were more than 100 German casualties. Several of the commandos were killed, however, including a 14-year-old boy who had been allowed to go on the mission after convincing his superiors that he was 18. There was one more victory when a small British bomber force attacked a German airfield in Greece, destroying one Ju-88 on the ground.

Despite these successes, the convoys were in for a terrible ordeal. Frank Kerley, a sailor aboard the Royal Navy destroyer HMS *Matchless*, described the ill-fated journey vividly in his unpublished

memoirs. "Passage to the Mediterranean takes one through the Bay of
Biscay, which has to be the roughest and most treacherous of any of
the seas," he wrote. "Forty foot waves and howling gales, troughs so
deep one moment a ship was in full view, the next minute it was gone
out of sight, only to reappear as the next wave rolled by. This time we
knew where we were headed, for our captain told us we had to be alert
at all times as we could expect trouble."[10]

That may have been the greatest understatement in naval history.
The eastern convoy got hit first, encountering savage opposition from
the word go. There were still enough Luftwaffe planes left on Crete to
sink two transports and three destroyers. Following that, a Nazi U-
boat sank a British cruiser with the loss of all hands. The Italian fleet
moved in next, but pulled back after one of its warships was destroyed
by an English submarine. Nevertheless, the enemy ships were still
lurking nearby and the convoy's escorts were rapidly running out of
ammunition. Reluctantly, the British Admiralty ordered it to turn
back for Egypt.

The Gibraltar convoy was now Malta's last hope. Unless at least
some of its ships could make Grand Harbour, the island would have to
capitulate. Speedy Italian torpedo boats and Regia Aeronautica aircraft launched aggressive attacks off Sardinia, sinking one destroyer
and badly damaging a second. But the transports were still intact and
the convoy pressed on. An Italian cruiser challenged them next, but
was driven off by *Matchless*. Next day, June 16, Stukas and Cants
blasted the ships with bombs, torpedoes, and machine gun and cannon fire from dawn until dusk, sinking three of the merchantmen.
They would have got them all, except for the fact that Malta's fighter
pilots had been equipped with long-range fuel tanks and were able to
provide some air cover as the embattled survivors moved closer to the
island. Just how hard the fighting was that day is best captured by
examining the experiences of a single pilot — Canadian Jerry Smith.
During the morning's actions the Regina aviator was credited with a
Stuka probably destroyed and an ME-109 damaged before flak from an
Italian ship damaged his Spitfire, forcing him to return to Malta. Buck
McNair covered his retreat, spraying the enemy vessel with a prolonged burst that killed several sailors caught above deck. Smith,
undeterred by his brush with death, returned to action that evening,

Valletta seen from the sea. Courtesy of Frank Kerley

shooting a Junkers-88 down in flames before damaging a second German bomber. His machine was hit again, however, and this time he was forced to bail out, coming down in the sea just as the sun was setting. Fortunately, a British destroyer happened by and plucked him from the waves before night fell. Once on board, Smith noted in his diary, he found the deck jammed with sailors who had been rescued after their ships had been sunk.

The fighting continued to rage overhead until daylight had completely disappeared. One of the last kills of the day occurred when three British pilots and a Canadian teamed up to force an Italian seaplane to land on the water. All four Allied fliers then strafed it until it burned and sank. Somehow, the Axis crew escaped unscathed and was rescued. An ME-109 attempted to drive off the Spitfires, but Willie-the-Kid Williams arrived on the scene and chased it off trailing black smoke. During the final dogfight of the day four Spitfires mauled a dozen Ju-88s before they could bomb the two surviving transports. The Germans had no fighter escort, possibly because they thought they could sneak in under the cover of the fading light. In any case, two were shot down and a third was badly damaged. The surviving Germans scattered and fled.

As dawn came the next day the two transports were within sight of Grand Harbour when one of their escorting destroyers hit a mine and capsized. Moments later, *Matchless* nearly suffered the same fate. "*Matchless* was leading the way into harbour when we struck a mine which blew the bow off," Kerley wrote. Fortunately, there were no casualties and "we managed to crawl in, as did one of the merchant ships, which had also been mined. Of the original convoy we arrived with two destroyers and two merchantmen. Were the people of the island glad to see us! They had been through deprivation for quite a while, certain things had long been consumed and strict rationing was the order of the day. It was said that cats, dogs and even rats had been reduced!"[11]

This time, Lord Gort saw to it that the ships did not sit around for hours on end waiting for workers to unload the precious cargo. He had 2,500 soldiers and civilians down at the docks, and they toiled throughout the night, unloading 15,000 tonnes of food and fuel.

The outcome of the convoy battle was a bitter pill for the defenders to swallow. Eleven ships had been lost, along with hundreds of Allied sailors. Lord Gort, to his credit, did not try to conceal the seriousness of the situation, frankly telling the population there would have to be more sacrifices, more rationing and more hunger. With strict rationing, the new supplies might allow Malta to hold out until mid-August. But after that another crisis would be at hand.

Meals in the Victory Kitchens declined in both quantity and quality at this stage of the siege. Many desperate people took to looting stores and private homes during raids, when most of the population was huddled underground. The authorities reacted harshly. One Maltese man received 18 months' hard labour for stealing three cases of powdered milk. A woman working in a Victory Kitchen was jailed for a year and a half for forging meal tickets, and a serviceman was fined $100 for stealing two chocolate bars. With gasoline running dangerously low, private cars were banned from the roadways, and buses were only allowed to run for a few hours in the mornings and evenings. Bicycles became the standard means of transportation for both civilians and military personnel. Lord Gort helped set the tone himself by turning in his staff car for a bike. He also called on Archbishop

Pilot Eric Crist in front of pilots' mess at Mdina, Malta. Courtesy of Eric Crist

Caruana, Malta's leading churchman, persuading him to publicly declare hoarding of food a mortal sin. In addition, he instituted a careful biweekly check of all supplies, thus dramatically reducing pilferage. And he put a halt to the five-course meals that were still being served to senior administrators and the Maltese upper classes in some restaurants. His actions were widely applauded, although more than a few people thought he had gone too far when he ordered the prize racehorses of the rich slaughtered and their carcasses donated to the Victory Kitchens. Finally, he decreed that concentrations of vitamin tablets must be flown in from England at night because he feared a lack of Vitamin E would diminish the reproductive powers of those on the island. Everyone was now eating less than half the small ration available to civilians in England, and water was so scarce that people were constantly dirty and often went thirsty.

A lull in the fighting followed the convoy battles, lasting an astonishing six days. The Axis aviators may have inflicted punishing losses on the Allied ships, but their own casualties were also serious. Furthermore, many of their planes were badly in need of an overhaul. The Allied pilots, too, needed a rest. The island had suffered through some 2,000 raids since the year had begun, and people were reaching the limit of their endurance. On several occasions, weary pilots nearly came to blows in the mess over the most trivial arguments. As Lord Gort observed, "In places like Malta, mountains are made of molehills because so many people become temperamental under bombing."[12]

The aviators spent their idle hours playing cards, listening to records, writing letters and sleeping. The Glenn Miller smash hit "In the Mood" was remembered by many of the fliers as their favourite, although it was played so much that almost everyone became thoroughly sick of it. Pilots at Takali were better off than those stationed at the other two airfields, because there were private homeowners nearby who took them in. George Beurling later wrote, "The Sergeant pilots lived comfortably enough in a huge private home. We ate in another house near by, with bar and lounge in the same building. The food was siege grub: bully beef, bully beef and more bully beef in innumerable disguises, but still bully beef."[13]

Kenneth Boyle, who flew aboard one of Malta's Wellington bombers, also remembered the sergeants' messes as comfortable places. "Personally, I did not want to be commissioned because when you went into the sergeants' mess you were the top dog. The drinks were sent to your table. If you got a commission as a pilot-officer you were the lowest officer in the officers' mess. You were nothing."[14]

When they ventured off base, the pilots found they were adored by the civilians. One RAF senior officer noted years later that his men were mobbed almost as movie or rock stars are today, with civilians often lifting them on their shoulders and carrying them through the streets. On the negative side, there was little to do, even in Valletta. "There was no entertainment," Johnny Sherlock said. "There were no taxis, so if you wanted to go to Valletta you had to walk five or six miles from the aerodrome."[15]

The most lively entertainment may have been provided by Minnie, a drunken pet monkey that followed British radar operator John Booth everywhere he went.

"Minnie was really weird," Canadian pilot Carl "Moose" Fumerton recalled. "I first met that monkey in England at an RAF station. He was sitting on a pile of boxes, wearing a red jacket and pillbox hat. It could be cold in England in October, you know. Then when I went to Gibraltar I saw that monkey again. And when I got to Malta there it was again. He was constantly with John Booth. He even went into bars with him and got to like the liquor. He'd fly over to the bar when he saw a drink and down it. The pilots were too surprised to do any-thing about it. Finally, he got so drunk he messed up the bar."

Fumerton, a night fighter pilot who flew a two-seater Beaufighter, even went on a combat mission with Minnie and Booth. "The mon-key used to share oxygen with John," he said. "When I opened fire I could hear that monkey's chatter above the roar of the guns."[16]

Booth was by no means the only "character" on Malta. The most eccentric of them all may have been British Spitfire pilot Tony Bruce. Bruce was an animal lover who was forever bringing lizards and snakes into his quarters and even the mess, much to the displeasure of his fel-low pilots. Later in the war, while serving on Sicily, he adopted three huge, poisonous snakes, which he kept in a little cardboard box. Inevitably, the snakes escaped, forcing everyone on the base to check their beds very carefully before retiring for the night. Perhaps just as inevitably, one of the snakes crawled into the cockpit of a Spitfire and hid behind the instrument panel, only emerging when its startled pilot, an Australian named Jocko, was flying a combat mission.

"One of the Spitfires in the formation began to act strangely," pilot Rex Probert recalled later. "It was dipsy-doodling all over the sky; nip-ping in and out of the formation, while at the same time neglecting to answer our calls. We thought at first he was being attacked by some-one we couldn't see, but after some time he returned to the formation and we all completed the sweep. Naturally, when we landed we all went over to Jocko, and quizzed him about his strange behaviour. It was then that we discovered where one of Tony's snakes was — in Jocko's cockpit — stabbed through the head. It had emerged from under the instrument panel when Jocko had gone through 10,000 feet during the climb ... When it emerged there was a fight between Jocko and the snake. Fortunately, Jocko won."[17]

Despite his antics, Bruce was a popular pilot, possibly because he was a man of uncommon courage. Once, after being shot down off Malta, he survived 15 hours in his dinghy before paddling to shore. In fact, he arrived back in the mess just in time to join his friends in drinking a toast to his departed soul!

The exotic pets and outlandish personalities were not confined to the Allied side. On Sicily, German pilot Heinz Baer kept a pet lion cub, which roamed through the mess and around the living quarters of the fliers at will. At a nearby Italian airfield, Sergeant Luigi Valcano bought some fish in an open-air market and planned a gourmet meal for the pilots of 360 Squadron. But when he got back to the mess, he was mortified to discover there was no cooking oil. Valcano improvised by using airplane motor oil! No one noticed the difference at the dinner table. Indeed, several pilots complimented him on his cooking. But, next morning, the entire squadron reported sick with severe stomach cramps and diarrhoea. All operations over Malta had to be scrubbed for 24 hours.

Such antics provided some diversion from the war, but there was no getting away from it for very long. More bad news struck the Allies on June 20. This time it sent shock waves around the world. Rommel had captured Tobruk, taking 25,000 British soldiers prisoner. Hundreds of tonnes of supplies, including 100 British tanks, fell into his hands. The Desert Fox was now convinced he had enough fuel and ammunition to head straight for the Suez Canal. General Kesselring disagreed, warning Rommel to halt his offensive until Malta was captured. Fortunately for the Allies, Rommel insisted there was no need for delay, and Hitler agreed with him.

Churchill, who was in Washington meeting with President Roosevelt, was beginning to fear that Rommel was unstoppable. In his memoirs he described the loss of Tobruk as one of the worst setbacks of the war. "Not only were the military effects grim, but it affected the reputation of British arms ... Defeat is one thing; disgrace is another," he wrote.[18]

On Malta, there was nothing anyone could do except carry on. Fighting resumed on June 22 when a small German force bombed Hal Far. "Shorty" Reid drew the only blood for the Allies, shooting down an ME-109 for his first victory. Reid, an 18-year-old who looked no older than 14, was a favourite among the Spitfire pilots because of his aggressive spirit. "He looked like an angel, but once he got airborne he was a real fighter," one pilot remembered later.[19]

Another pilot, Wally McLeod, was gaining a reputation as not only a fighter, but also a bloodthirsty killer. On June 23, flying with a British wingman, he spotted a dozen Macchis and a lone Ju-88 flying 600 metres below. Despite the odds, he attacked immediately, going straight for the bomber. Two of the Italian fighters quickly came to the rescue, using the classic pincer to box McLeod in. Slowing down almost to stalling speed, McLeod watched the Macchis overshoot his

Spitfire and dash out in front of his guns. McLeod flung himself at the nearest Axis machine, opening fire from a scant 25 metres' range. His aim was off, but the terrified enemy pilot dove so steeply in his bid to escape that he slammed straight into the sea. "He went into the drink from sheer fright," McLeod gloated later.[20] Amazingly, the Italian lived to tell his side of the story. Aldo Buvoli, a six-kill ace, had reasoned the only way to shake the fanatically tenacious Spitfire pilot off his tail was by diving right to the wave tops. Unfortunately, he pulled up a fraction of a second too late and made a crude belly landing on the water. He managed to get out of his cockpit before the Macchi settled to the bottom, but spent several hours in the Mediterranean, swallowing huge gulps of salt water as high waves rolled over him. Just as he was about to give up all hope of survival, an Allied rescue launch came by and took him to Gozo.

On June 27, the Italians took another drubbing as four Spitfires jumped 12 Macchis. "We got three of them," recalled Bob Middlemiss, a 22-year-old Montrealer taking part in his first Malta combat. "We could see the wreckage of all three close together on the water."[21] Middlemiss got one of the enemy planes and damaged another. It was an excellent start to what would be a short but unforgettable stay on the island for him.

There was little combat during the rest of the month; that gave the defenders a false sense of security. Adding to the euphoria was the knowledge that they had shot down 71 enemy planes in June for the loss of only 25 of their own aircraft. In fact, the British High Command felt so sure that the situation was under control that they ordered an entire squadron of Spitfires flown from Malta to the Middle East, where they would be used to help the British Eighth Army battle Rommel. In a single stroke the paper-pushers in London had robbed the island of a dozen front-line fighters. Malta still had about 80 Spitfires left, but it was a serious blow, because the Germans and Italians were pouring reinforcements into Sicily. Two Luftwaffe bomber squadrons and one fighter unit were on their way from the Russian Front, and the Italians were sending another 32 Macchis south. An immediate invasion of Malta may not have been in the cards, but the Axis airmen were planning to launch their biggest blitz yet in July.

CHAPTER 7

THE BLOODIEST MONTH

The Axis aviators on Sicily were in a buoyant mood as July opened. Reinforcements had arrived at the end of June, and they were confident that victory was finally at hand. The Germans were especially euphoric because one of the new units was none other than Fighter Wing No. 77, a 144-plane group that had just left the Russian Front with an astonishing total of 635 victories to its credit. Its leader was the legendary ace Heinz Baer, who many insisted was the best pilot in the Luftwaffe.

A farm boy from eastern Germany, Baer was a strikingly handsome 29-year-old with finely chiselled features. His outgoing nature and keen sense of humour made him enormously popular with his men. He had joined the Luftwaffe in 1937, hoping to get enough flying experience to become a commercial airline pilot with Lufthansa. But when war broke out in September 1939, his dreams of a career in civilian aviation went out the window. He flew in both the Battle of France and the Battle of Britain, destroying one French and 17 British fighters. Later, on the Russian Front, he shot down poorly trained Soviet pilots at a dizzying pace, bagging five in a single day in June 1941 before adding six more in one day two months later. He also proved to be an incredibly tough individual with an exceptionally strong will to live. Once, after being shot down by a Spitfire over the English Channel, Baer swam for two hours through high waves, reaching a buoy just before night fell. He hung on for dear life for several more hours before finally being picked up by a German motor-torpedo boat. A year later, in an even more remarkable display of grit, he survived for two days behind Russian lines after being shot down. He managed to bail out of his fighter but landed heavily, breaking his back in two places. Most men would have given up, turning themselves in to the nearest enemy soldiers. But Baer hid by day and walked towards his own territory by night, covering 30 kilometres in 48 hours before reaching his own lines.

By the time he arrived on Sicily, he had 113 victories to his credit. And he was not the only ace in Fighter Wing 77. At least seven other pilots had 20 or more kills each, including Fritz Geisshardt, who had 83 Russian planes to his credit, and Siegfried Freytag, who had 49 victories behind his name.

On the Italian airfield, the pilots were also brimming with confidence. Mussolini himself had flown to Sicily on June 24 to present medals to 13 aviators who had done well during the winter and spring air battles. Along with him had come reinforcements in the form of one new bomber squadron and three additional fighter units led by the popular and charismatic Aldo Remondino. Among the 32 Macchi pilots under his command were several of the most skilled fliers in the Regia Aeronautica.

"It was clear not only from the number of new planes flying in, but also from the calibre of the air crews, that the High Command was serious about winning, and that was a big boost to everyone's morale," recalled Italian pilot Ronaldo Scaroni. "We knew we had the English badly outnumbered and we didn't see how we could possibly lose. There was a feeling that the whole thing would be over by the end of the summer at the latest. Maybe even sooner. I'm afraid we badly underestimated the determination of the RAF pilots to hold out, no matter what."[1]

That the defenders were not about to roll over and die despite the major new threat facing them on Sicily was amply demonstrated on July 1, when they shot down four Axis planes with the loss of just one Spitfire. In a wild dogfight the next morning, "Shorty" Reid shot down an ME-109 for his fourth victory, but his badly damaged Spitfire flipped over on landing and had to be written off. For once, Reid's small stature paid off. Although his canopy was shattered, he was so short that his head failed to hit the ground as he dangled upside down from his safety harness.

Buzz Ogilvie had an even narrower escape when his radio failed him just as he was closing in on a Messerschmitt. "I had just made my attack on it when six more of them came at me from above," he recalled later. "Someone called out 'Break!' but my radio wasn't working." Ogilvie didn't know he was in trouble until a cannon shell slammed into the fuselage just behind his head.

> My aircraft caught fire and I was thrown into a spin. I wanted to bail out but I couldn't get the canopy open. Eventually I got out of the spin and was sort of sideslipping. I didn't know what my height was because of the smoke. When I was about 1,000 feet up I got the canopy open and had one foot over the side when I decided I was too low to jump. Takali airdrome was right underneath me. I had no power so I used a crank to get the wheels down and made a deadstick landing. I jumped out because I was afraid the aircraft would explode. I grabbed my parachute and was walking across the field when Laddie Lucas motioned to me to go back. The 109 that had shot me down was trying to kill me on the ground. I dove under the Spitfire, which was a stupid thing to do, because that's what he was trying to hit. But it's not easy to hit a target on the ground if your aircraft is being buffeted by wind. Your bullets just spray on you. Anyway, he missed me by 20 feet. I could see his cannon shells exploding into the ground 20 feet from me.

Ogilvie experienced another close call shortly afterwards, and again faulty equipment was to blame. "I was taking off one time when my number two said I'd lost a wheel. The ground crews did as good a job as they could with what they had out there, but sometimes these things happened. The ground controller told me to make a one-wheel landing at Takali. I feared I'd cartwheel all over the place if I did that. Fortunately, my CO said, 'Buzz, make a wheels-up landing. You're going to kill yourself if you try to land with that stub hanging out.' The controller started arguing with him, but the CO said to me, 'Buzz, this is an order, make a wheels-up landing.' I cut my engine just before I hit the ground but I still bent one blade of the propeller and made some dents in the underbelly. I think I made about five or six crash landings [on Malta], and I was shot down once."[2]

The day Ogilvie was shot down there was another ominous development for the Allies. Italian pilot Furio Doglio Niclot opened his Malta account by shooting down a Spitfire. At 34, Doglio Niclot was old for a fighter pilot, but he was an ambitious individual who was determined to make a name for himself. What's more, as one of Europe's top test pilots before the war, he had the talent to do it. "We were certain he could outfly anyone in the RAF," Macchi pilot Ronaldo Scaroni said later.[3]

Combats were frequent and bloody over the next several days. Two Spitfires were lost on July 3, but the defenders took revenge the next day by shooting down three Cant bombers. Led by Englishman Laddie Lucas, the Allied pilots raced through escorting enemy fighters to take out all three Cants in one pass. Bob Middlemiss, who shared one of the victories with Raoul Daddo-Langlois, credits Lucas's leadership for what was a near-perfect bounce. "Initially, when our squadron ran into Cants we didn't seem to have much luck. We were opening fire too far out because they were so big that they looked closer than they really were. This time we squeezed in much closer. That was the trick, to get in close before you opened fire."[4]

The long-suffering Cant crews took it on the chin again two days later, when eight Spitfires rose to challenge three of the big bombers and their escort of 30 Macchis. George Beurling broke through the fighter screen and, attacking head on, lined one of the Cants up in his sights. The two planes were coming together at a combined speed of almost 800 kilometres per hour, but Beurling managed to catch the lead bomber with an accurate burst that killed the pilot at once. Another squirt set an engine on fire. The machine looked to be finished but, in an extraordinary display of courage, an Italian gunner left his gun port and took the pilot's seat. Somehow, he managed to fly back to Sicily, where he crash-landed the crippled ship. Turning on the Macchis, Beurling shot fighter pilot Franceso Montagnani down in flames. Wasting not a moment, he went straight for a second Macchi. The Italian saw him coming at the last second and dove steeply in a frantic bid to escape. But Beurling would not let him go, chasing the Macchi from 6,000 metres all the way down to 1,500 metres. Finally, when the enemy pilot either had to pull up or dive into the sea, Beurling caught him with a killing burst. The Macchi exploded in "a million pieces," Beurling wrote.[5]

The day was not over for the formidable Spitfire pilot. Near sunset, he led four Allied pilots into an attack on two Junkers-88s escorted by 20 Messerschmitts. Two Germans dove on Beurling, intending to

Pilot Bob Middlemiss in the cockpit of his Spitfire airplane. Courtesy of Bob Middlemiss

make short work of him. But he easily outmanoeuvred them. Circling quickly around in his tighter-turning machine, he caught a yellow-nosed ME-109 with a three-second burst. The volley, which came from an amazing 725 metres' range and a nearly impossible angle, hit the German fighter in the fuel tanks, sending pilot Toni Engels to a flaming death. While all of this was going on, the other Spitfires got loose among the Ju-88s, sending two of them plunging into the sea.

In one day the Allies had shot down 15 enemy planes, four of which had gone down before Beurling's guns. Only one Spitfire had been lost, its pilot falling victim to Doglio Niclot.

Fighting on July 7 was not so one-sided, at least partly because Kesselring increased the sizes of the formations he was sending out on each mission. During the dawn attack, for instance, 54 Axis fighters and 12 bombers raided Luqa. Only 17 Spitfires scrambled to meet them, and in the ensuing clash each side lost three planes. Perhaps even more disturbing was the fact that one of the Spitfires had been blasted out of the sky by Doglio Niclot, giving the rising Italian star three victories in a single week. Fortunately, all three Allied pilots downed that morning were able to parachute to safety.

In an afternoon attack two more Spitfires were lost, but again both pilots were saved. Bob Middlemiss was one of the fliers forced to jump from his shattered Spitfire. "The day I was shot down, the squadron only had 10 aircraft for readiness," he told the author 55 years later.

When the raid approached our ground control people sent off two sections of four aircraft, leaving Raoul Daddo-Langlois and myself on the ground. At that time on Malta the saying was, "It was safer in the air than on the ground." We kept after the ground control people to allow us to take off. We were finally scrambled and flew south, climbing to try and gain altitude to be above the bombers. Unfortunately, when we ran into the bomber stream we were only at the same altitude. Daddo-Langlois said, "Shall we have a go?" — to which of course I agreed. Raoul fired at and destroyed a Ju-88, with one of the escorting ME-109s coming down on his tail. I got behind the 109 and shot it down, knowing full well as I did so that its number two would be nearby. He was, and he got me. As I was breaking left and looking over my shoulder I was hit by his cannon shells. I was wounded in the back and down my right arm. The aircraft spun down out of control. I undid my straps and attempted to bail out. Being in a spin, the centrifugal force would not allow me to escape. I sat back down, stopped the spin, and rolled the aircraft over and successfully bailed out.

Middlemiss was out of his burning ship, but his problems were far from over.

When I landed in the water there were more troubles to face. I pulled the dinghy out, remembering to turn the valve on the CO_2 bottle slowly. I did this until it came to a stop and then turned it all the way back — but no CO_2 came out to inflate the dinghy. Attached to the dinghy by cord was a hand pump, which I tried to fit to the valve for inflating the raft, but only having one good arm, the cord kept tangling and I could not attach the pump.

Keeping his head, the badly wounded the Canadian pulled out a hunting knife, cut the cord, and finally attached the pump to the valve. Then, with great effort, he slowly pumped air into the dinghy, climbed aboard, and started paddling towards Malta.

> To make matters worse, the squadron were looking for me on the other side of the island. I was in the water three or four hours before they found me. Luckily, Paul Brennan, an Austalian, and Flight Sergeant de l'Ara, who were out covering some minesweepers, spotted me in the water. They made a pass and recognized the large British Mae West; otherwise they may have fired at the dinghy. Sad to say, we did lose people being shot up in dinghies. Having recognized me, they radioed for an air-sea rescue launch. It soon appeared and had me on board. They wrapped me in blankets and gave me a large shot of navy rum — which nearly made my eyes pop out. Back on shore I was taken to hospital and operated on by Captain Rankin. He later told me that I was lucky that I was leaning forward when I was hit — otherwise the shrapnel would have punctured my lungs.[6]

Middlemiss was not the only RAF casualty that day. In the evening, two more Spitfires were lost, and this time both pilots died. Three more Axis planes were shot down, however, including two bagged by British ace Paddy Schade. Schade had destroyed six enemy planes in five days, making him Malta's leading fighter pilot with a total of 13 victories. Amazingly, his feats were completely ignored by the authorities. He was still only a sergeant and he had not been granted a single decoration. In the days ahead this exceptionally gallant pilot's victory score would be surpassed by George Beurling, and his story would be all but forgotten. The RAF would eventually get around to giving him a Distinguished Flying Medal, but it was precious little return for his feats over Malta.

Two more Axis planes were destroyed that day by Australian Slim Yarra, who thereby gained his 11th and 12th kills over the island. There was a dreadful end to the day's fighting when four Italian airmen died trying to escape from a crippled Cant. The first two bailed out only to be killed by Maltese anti-aircraft gunners as they dangled helplessly under their parachutes. The other two were late getting out an escape hatch, jumping while only a few hundred feet above the ground. There was no time for their parachutes to open, and both plunged to their deaths.

Slowly but surely, the Germans and Italians were winning the war of attrition. They were losing more planes than they were shooting down, but they could afford to. They had gone into the month with 800 aircraft on Sicily compared to just 80 Spitfires on Malta. Needless to say, they could take heavy losses and still win easily, provided that they continued to bag a steady toll of Spitfires.

They did just that on July 8, shooting down four British fighters for the loss of seven of their own machines. The day would have been even worse for the defenders if not for the marksmanship of George Beurling. In the morning raid he got behind an ME-109 and gutted its engine with a two-second burst. The enemy fighter flipped over on its back and dove straight into the Mediterranean just south of Gozo. Turning on a second Messerschmitt, he shot it down too. Unfortunately, no one saw it crash, and he was only credited with a "probable" victory. Still not finished, Beurling went after a Junkers-88, setting its starboard engine on fire before being driven off by five German fighters. A few minutes later he was back, chasing a Messerschmitt off the tail of fellow Canadian Willie-the-Kid Williams.

On July 9 another two Spitfires were lost, including one in which French-Canadian pilot Guy André Lévy-Depas was killed by an alert Ju-88 tail gunner. Fellow Canadian Wally McLeod overhauled the retreating Nazi bombers and shot one down, despite the fact that only one of his cannons was working.

Next day, Beurling was back in the forefront, using new tactics to destroy an ME-109. The ace dove under his victim and then pulled up his nose before raking the German's belly from prop to rudder. The pilot, Hans-Jurgen Frodien, was killed instantly. That same day he shot down an Italian, separating a Macchi from a formation of seven enemies before dispatching it. His account of the fight makes it clear that his opponent, a Sergeant Visentini, was a skilful pilot. "The Eyetie went into a steep dive, pulled out and twisted away, rolled and pulled into a climb," Beurling wrote later. "Finally he went into a loop at the end of his climb and I nabbed him just at its top. A two-second burst blew his cockpit apart. The pilot bailed out in a hell of a hurry."[7] Beurling, who could often be a cold-blooded killer, showed compassion on this occasion, giving the man's position to an air-sea rescue team. As a result, Visentini survived and spent the rest of the war in a prison camp.

While Beurling was taking care of the enemy fighters, other Allied pilots were shooting down no less than four Ju-88s. But Doglio Niclot, once again in the thick of the action, destroyed two Spitfires. He scored yet again the next day, giving him six victories since the month had begun. Clearly, something was going to have to be done about this troublesome enemy pilot.

Both Doglio Niclot and Beurling were airborne on July 12, and both enjoyed spectacular success. The Canadian scored first, shooting down an Italian Reggiane fighter piloted by Francesco Vichi. Sneaking up behind his unsuspecting victim, Beurling sent him down in flames with a one-second burst. Moments after landing back at Takali, however, he was informed that one of his squadron mates was missing. Beurling volunteered to go out looking for the man, who he hoped might be adrift in a life raft. At the same moment, Italian pilots Aldo Quarantotti and Carlo Seganti were lifting off from Sicily, hoping to find some sign of the missing Vichi. Beurling, who had almost superhuman eyesight, spotted the two enemy pilots flying low over the water and moved in swiftly for the kill. In the next six seconds he snuffed out two lives. His first burst hit Seganti's Macchi in the fuel tank, and it exploded in an orange fireball. Seconds later he lined up Quarantotti in his sights. What happened next was nothing short of sickening. "I came right up underneath his tail," Beurling recalled later. "I was going faster than he was; about 50 yards behind. I was tending to overshoot. I weaved off to the right, and he looked out to his left. I weaved to the left and he looked out to his right. So, he still didn't know I was there. About this time I closed up to about 35 yards, and I was on his portside coming in at about a 15 degree angle. Well, 25 to 30 yards in the air looks as if you're right on top of him because there is no background, no perspective there and it looks pretty close. I could see all the details in his face because he turned and looked at me just as I had a bead on him." Beurling squeezed the trigger and watched as a cannon shell slammed into the terror-stricken Italian pilot.

"One of my cannon shells caught him right in the face and blew his head right off. The body slumped and the slipstream caught the neck, the stub of the neck, and the blood streamed down the side of the cockpit. It was a great sight anyway, the red blood down the white fuselage. I must say it gives you a feeling of satisfaction when you actually blow their brains out."[8]

It is hard to understand today how anyone could be so callous. But Beurling was motivated by both fear and hatred. The Italian and German pilots had already killed scores of his friends, and it seemed likely that they would get him before long, too. It is important also to keep in mind that some of what he had to say was nothing more than false bravado. Indeed, his brother, David, later told author Brian Nolan that George had nightmares about this incident for the rest of his life. Sometimes, he was so haunted by the memory of Quarantotti's exploding head that he would "cry all night."[9]

While Beurling was shooting down three enemy planes, Doglio Niclot was knocking a pair of Spitfires out of the sky, giving him nine victories and the title of Italian ace of aces. The Regia Aeronautica's top gun prior to his amazing scoring streak had been Aldo Buvoli, but Buvoli had been shot down by Wally McLeod on June 23. In any case, Captain Doglio Niclot had no time to savour his new status as he flew home. On his way back to Sicily, he came across a damaged Ju-88 that was being harried by a Spitfire. Although he was out of ammunition, the courageous Italian pilot aggressively attacked the British fighter, chasing it off. The German pilot was so thankful that, instead of landing at his own airfield, he followed the Macchi back to its base at Gela. Seconds after landing his bomber, the Luftwaffe pilot ran across the tarmac, grabbed the startled Doglio Niclot in a bear hug and kissed him on both cheeks. The Italian airforce was equally impressed, bestowing the coveted Medaglia d'Oro on its leading ace.

Beurling, who now had a dozen victories to his credit, was recognized too. The British granted him a Distinguished Flying Medal. They also tried to make him an officer, but he turned the commission down, saying he preferred to carry on as a sergeant-pilot. His only interests were flying and fighting. He feared if he became a lieutenant he would have to spend some of his time practising leadership responsibilities that frankly bored him. Besides that, he was really just one of the boys at heart. Because of his limited education and a thinly disguised inferiority complex, he felt far more comfortable in the company of the sergeant-pilots than he did around officers.

Aircraft rigger George Demare, who took care of Beurling's plane, recalled that the ace regularly socialized with the ground crews — something that was completely unheard of in the RAF.

"One evening a few of us were enjoying a quiet pint in the Rovers Arms pub when Sergeant-Pilot Beurling walked in and asked if he could join us. We happily pulled over another chair, and there he spent the evening with us sipping on a soft drink. He shunned alcohol but did not mind if we imbibed. After pubbing he came with us to our barracks, where we spent the balance of the evening listening to records on an ancient gramophone. When eyelids got heavy George asked if we had a spare bed. 'I don't feel like going back to my billet,' he said. He became our overnight guest."[10]

Demare added, "Beurling spent much of his time talking with the ground crew, where he would expound at length about the art of deflection shooting, which, combined with his incredible vision, won him such fame and success in Malta."[11]

The other pilots at Takali spent their spare time relaxing as best they could in Malta's sweltering heat, but not Beurling. He spent countless hours working on the principles of deflection shooting. Essentially, what that amounted to was trying to figure out how far to "lead" an enemy plane so that it would fly right into your burst of fire. You had to calculate the speed of your opponent, how fast your bullets would fly, and your angle of fire, all in a split second, at the same time watching your tail for opponents. It was a tricky business, but Beurling quickly mastered it. He also found a unique way to practise his shooting, despite the ban on gunnery tests. Pilots were not allowed to take their planes up for test firings because there were no extra machine gun bullets or cannon shells to spare. Beurling got around the problem by blazing away at Malta's countless lizards with a pistol. Dressed in a khaki shirt and grease-smudged shorts, he stalked the tiny creatures for hours in the burning sun.

Other pilots thought he was a little crazy, until Italian and German planes began falling before his guns like rain drops. By mid-July his marksmanship had become legendary. Once, he reported firing five cannon shells into the cockpit of an enemy plane. Allied soldiers who inspected the wreckage on the ground found its cockpit had indeed been hit by exactly five rounds. Spitfire pilot D.J. Dewan, who flew with Beurling, told the author that "he was successful for many reasons, but the two most important were his eyesight and his knack for deflection shooting. He used to report sightings of aircraft many seconds before others saw them, and he knew whether he hit them in the front, centre or rear of their airplane, and he usually used minimum ammunition."[12]

Bob Middlemiss still recalls Beurling's eyesight with awe.

"He had without any doubt the best eyesight of any fighter pilot known. When we were not on readiness, we would watch the raids approaching from Sicily from the vantage point of the parapet in Rabat that overlooked our aerodrome of Takali. As the raid approached we would be looking up in the very bright skies of Malta, and Beurling would be counting. He would then say, 'There are 36 JU-88s.' The rest of us were looking in the same direction and saw nothing. Then, after 20 or 30 seconds we would be counting and there would be 36 of them. But by then he would be doing a second count, and he'd tell us, 'There are 48 ME-109s escorting them.' Again, some 20 or 30 seconds later we would see the 109s. And there would be 48 of them."[13]

Aircraft rigger George Demare made it clear that in addition to his ability to shoot, Beurling was a superb pilot who had an instinctive feel for an airplane. Once, while he as still in England, the ace took him up for a spin in an old two-seater and gave him the ride of his life.

My excitement began with a routine takeoff followed by our buzzing of a rugby game in progress. Down over the goal posts we flew, causing the startled players to hug the ground, then up over the other goal posts and away. Next we swooped down over a herd of cattle, then over a potato field so low we had to climb to clear the hedge at the far end. More excitement was provided by flying between two trees with inches to spare. Following those low-level escapades, it was up into the high skies with a spiral climb, then a variety of loops, turns, stalls and spins ... For the grand finale Beurling took us into a power dive — straight down at a horrendous speed. This caused me some concern as I noted the ground fast approaching, and I envisioned myself splattered among the wreckage of our kite. I considered bailing out, but never having learned parachute drill, I decided to wait till George bailed out and then copy his motions. Alas! the ground was so near I abandoned all hope. Then less than 100 feet from the ground Beurling executed a vertical hairpin turn and we were skyward bound. After a few more aerial manoeuvres we came in for a smooth landing.[14]

As good as Beurling was, however, he could not escape the sting of enemy bullets forever. He was wounded on July 14 when three ME-109s and a pair of Italian Reggianes jumped him. He banked away from the Germans, deciding to allow the Italians to have a crack at him instead, figuring they could do less damage. When he got back home he counted 20 machine gun bullets in his plane, including one that had grazed his left heel. The only reason he had not been shot down was that the Reggiane did not come equipped with cannons. Nine days later, he retaliated by shooting the wings off a Reggiane with a deflection shot. He damaged a Junkers-88 in the same mêlée.

Despite Beurling's mounting score, the defenders were in serious trouble. During the first two weeks of July, 39 of the island's 80 Spitfires had been shot down. At that rate, there would not be a fighter plane left on Malta by the end of the month. Desperate to keep the garrison fighting, Winston Churchill ordered the carrier *Eagle* to deliver another shipment of Spitfires. So it was that on July 15 a contingent of 32 Spits flew into Malta, bringing with them nine Englishmen, nine Canadians, seven New Zealanders, three Australians, one Rhodesian and three Americans serving with the Royal Canadian Air Force.

One of the new arrivals, Rod Smith of Regina, was surprised to find that his brother, Jerry, was already on Malta. Within days the pair would be fighting side by side in the same flight.

Axis fliers continued to shoot down Spitfires on an almost daily basis. On July 20 two Canadian pilots were knocked down, and although Jimmy Lambert escaped with only minor wounds, Hugh Russel was killed. Two days later another two RCAF fliers went down in flames, and this time both perished. Jean Paradis, a 25-year-old from Shawinigan Falls, Quebec, was the first to go. "Shorty" Reid saw Paradis's Spitfire hit the water and circled overhead, radioing its position to a rescue launch. While he was performing this act of mercy, the ace was jumped by a lone ME-109. Reid instantly rolled out of harm's way and shot the German down with one burst. It was his sixth victory over Malta, but it was also his last. Moments later, a second Messerschmitt dove out of the sun and killed him.

Beurling was distraught at the news of Paradis's death. The fellow Quebecer had been his only close friend on the island, and the two had spent many carefree hours swimming and talking. When Paradis died, Beurling allowed himself no further friends. If he did not get to know people well, he reasoned, it would be easier to cope with their deaths. He also began referring to the Axis airmen as "those goddamn Screwballs."[15] He did it so much, in fact, that his fellow pilots nicknamed him "Screwball," and the name stuck.

Regardless of what he was called, Beurling was clearly the best fighter pilot on either Malta or Sicily. He proved that conclusively on July 27, putting on a one-man show that RAF veterans still recall with awe. Taking off at dawn with seven other Spitfire pilots, he led them into an attack on seven Ju-88s being escorted by at least 40 Macchis and Messerschmitts. Beurling singled out a flight of four Macchis and closed in on the tail-end-Charlie, an experienced pilot named Faliero Gelli. Gelli, who had two kills to his credit, never saw Beurling coming. Cannon shells suddenly slammed into his radiator and engine, and his plane began shaking apart. He could, he recounted later, actually see chunks of his wings flying off. The next thing he knew he was spinning down out of control with black smoke gushing from a badly skipping motor. He managed to pull out of the death dive over the island of Gozo, but it was obvious his plane was too badly damaged to carry him home. Too low to bail out, Gelli glided in for a crash landing, barely missing a church steeple before setting his machine down in a farmer's field with teeth-jarring force. Gelli, who had been scheduled to go on leave right after the mission, was tossed violently into the instrument panel. When he was pulled from the wrecked aircraft by Maltese civilians, his head had swollen to twice its normal size.

Only seconds after he wounded Gelli, Beurling killed Captain Doglio Niclot. He hosed the Italian's plane from end to end. The Macchi exploded in midair and its pilot, who had claimed his 10th victory just two days earlier, was killed instantly. Beurling was taking dead aim at his third Macchi when he suddenly caught sight of two ME-109s flying underneath him. Diving under them, he pulled up and fired a burst into the nearest Messerschmitt's fuel tank, sending it down in flames. A fourth burst slammed into the other German fighter, tearing chunks of metal off its wings and rudder. The enemy pilot managed to dive out of the line of tracers, and limped home in his badly damaged ship.

Despite this virtuoso performance, Beurling still was not done for the day. Landing only to refuel and reload, he took on two ME-109s. One of them, flown by Lieutenant Karl-Heinz Preu, an ace with five Spitfires to his credit, gave the Canadian one of the toughest fights of his career. They dogfought for several minutes, looping, diving and circling around one another, each looking for an opening. Realizing he had met his match, Preu lost his nerve and tried to dive for home. Beurling was after him in less time than it takes to tell. Clinging to the Messerschmitt's tail, the Canadian caught his man with a one-second burst that sent him tumbling into the sea. The second 109 now approached, but Beurling scored hits on it too, sending it back to Sicily trailing a cloud of black smoke.

That night, New Zealander Noel Pashen wrote in his diary, "We got the drop on them, and in all, 13 were destroyed. Parachutes were dropping in everywhere. Highlight of the day was Screwball Beurling, who shot down three and probably four — he's a wizard."[16]

In fact, Beurling had destroyed four planes and damaged two others. More importantly, he had killed two enemy aces, including the man who was the heart and soul of the Italian airforce. In just over three weeks Doglio Niclot had claimed 10 Spitfires, including six confirmed single-handed victories, three shared kills and one "probable" conquest.

"When he died, some of the fighting spirit of the Regia Aeronautica died with him," observed pilot Ronaldo Scaroni. "There was a feeling that if Doglio Niclot couldn't survive, none of us could. For the first time we began to doubt that Malta could be taken."[17]

Morale among the German fighter pilots was shaken that day as well. For in addition to Preu, high-scoring ace Siegfried Freytag had also been shot down. Fortunately, he managed to bail out and was rescued by a German seaplane. Still, the knowledge that a 49-kill ace could be bested by Malta's defenders was sobering news indeed to some of the less experienced German pilots on Sicily. The Luftwaffe bomber crews were also beginning to waver in their enthusiasm. For while Beurling had been engaged in his almost maniacal killing spree amidst the Axis fighters, other Spitfire pilots had shot down three Junkers-88. Next day, three more Ju-88s were shot down, with the Smith brothers, Rod and Jerry, playing a role in two of the kills.

Still, the Axis fliers kept coming. In a bitter dogfight on July 29 one of them almost nailed George Beurling. Almost, but not quite. German pilot Karl-Heinz Witschke sent a burst of fire right into Beurling's cockpit, blowing his canopy clean off. Miraculously, the ace was not hit and, as the ME-109 roared past him, he latched onto its tail. Witschke twisted to escape, but Beurling hit his plane with a one-second burst that wrecked the engine and set the fuel tank ablaze. The German bailed out, but his parachute was on fire and he plunged to his death.

The victory gave Beurling 16 kills for the month and 18 for the war. That was enough for his superiors. They made him an officer the next day. This time, they did not offer him a commission. They simply *ordered* him to accept the promotion.

Bob Middlemiss was there when it happened. "Beurling and I were to visit Wing Commander Jumbo Gracie for an interview for our commissions," he recalled.

"I arrived at the Wingco office and sat outside the room on a chair, with just a beaded curtain dividing me and the office. I was dressed in my best blue uniform, shoes, buttons all polished and sparkling, but there was no sign of Beurling. Suddenly he arrived off the aerodrome, where he had been working with the airmen [ground crews] on the guns of an aircraft. He was in his khaki shirt and shorts, sweaty, oily and dusty. He asked me if he could borrow my comb. He was not the least bit concerned about the interview. When he went into the office I could hear the conversation between him and the Wing Commander. Beurling told the Wingco he really did not want a commission, that the airmen would not look up to him and would have to salute him and such. Wing Commander Gracie replied that he was the type that the men looked up to and would be proud working for. Of course, he was commissioned. He was also granted a second Distinguished Flying Medal. He did not appear overly impressed, however, and continued to live with the sergeant-pilots.[18]

Beurling did not realize it, but the authorities had been forced to promote him. The attention of the whole world was now riveted on the siege of Malta, and its stubborn defence by a handful of RAF pilots was making headlines in every Allied nation. Beurling, as the top-scoring ace on the island, was front-page news. Reporters were clamouring for information about him. And they were beginning to ask embarrassing questions, such as "Why was the top gun on Malta still only a sergeant?" It would not do to say, "Because he refused to be promoted." So the RAF rectified the situation by hastily promoting Beurling.

On the last day of the month the Axis fliers shot down three Spitfires, but there was little cause for celebration on Sicily. True, the Germans and Italians had destroyed or seriously damaged over 50 Spitfires in July, but they had lost a staggering 137 planes. And because a second batch of 28 British fighters had flown in from the carrier *Eagle* just before the month ended, there were as many Spitfires on Malta at the end of July as there had been at the beginning.

It was not just the number of Allied planes on Malta that disturbed General Kesselring, it was the audacity of the Commonwealth pilots. Kesselring was almost beside himself on July 28 when he received word about what may have been the most humiliating incident Axis fliers suffered throughout the entire siege. It happened when a Malta-based Beaufort bomber flown by South African pilot Teddy Strever was shot down by Italian fighters. Despite the fact that both his engines had been damaged, Strever managed to make a good landing on the water, and all four members of the crew were able to scramble into a liferaft before their plane slipped beneath the waves. They were a long way from Malta, however, and it seemed doubtful that they would be rescued. Fortunately, an Italian seaplane spotted them, landed alongside their dinghy, and took the four airmen prisoner.

The Italians flew them to Greece, where they received their first good meal in months. Next morning, they were packed back on the seaplane and told they would be flown to southern Italy. Once on the Italian mainland, they were to be taken by truck to a prisoner of war camp near Rome. Flying with them was one guard and four unarmed Italian airmen. What happened next is something that would be rejected by most Hollywood script writers as being too improbable. Shortly after the Cant took off, the four Allied fliers jumped the guard, overpowered him and, using his pistol, forced the pilot to turn for Malta.

Needless to say, flying into Malta in an aircraft bearing Italian markings was not the safest thing to do and, before it could land, the seaplane was attacked by four Spitfires. The pilot managed to evade all four, however, and landed on the water not far from the island. British soldiers who came out to capture the crew were astonished to find four Allied airmen sitting on the wings along with their five Italian prisoners. The plane, which had been only slightly damaged by the Spitfires, was towed into Grand Harbour. Strever and his three crewmen, meanwhile, were all decorated for gallantry.

The Italians were so badly shaken by this incident and the other events of July that Mussolini ordered a temporary halt to daylight operations. The Germans also decided to scale back their raids during August, although they would occasionally show up in force. For the time being, at least, the defenders had the Axis airforces under control. That would dramatically reduce the bomb tonnage falling on them, but it would not put food in their mouths. And with only three weeks' supply of food left, Malta was once again facing starvation.

CHAPTER 8

THE SANTA MARIA CONVOY

An almost surreal calm settled over Malta with the coming of August. In fact, there was not a single daylight raid on the first day of the month, which came as a pleasant surprise to everyone on the sun-scorched island. It was just as well that the Axis aviators stayed on the ground, because the heat was so oppressive that pilots on both sides could suffer serious burns just by touching metal parts of their airplanes with their bare skin. Needless to say, that could make scrambling into a Spitfire a dangerous task. Besides that, the Malta Dog had struck with a vengeance, putting several fliers on their backs. One of the sick included George Beurling, who was so ill he had to be helped in and out of bed.

Hunger was also becoming an increasingly serious problem. Beurling, for one, had lost 35 pounds (about 16 kilograms) since arriving in June, and now weighed just 140 pounds (64 kilograms). Now he was throwing up after every meal; before August was over, he was down to a skeletal 115 pounds (54 kilograms). Most of the other fliers were just as gaunt. Pilot Dallas Schmidt recalled later that food was so scarce, bread was doled out by an officer who used a ledger to keep track of the four slices he gave each man per day.

Perhaps because many of the Allied pilots were in no shape to stand up, let alone fight, they began coming out on the wrong end of the few dogfights that were taking place. Between August 2 and 4, for example, four Spitfires were shot down without the defenders claiming a single kill in return. The situation improved four days later when Beurling struggled out of his sickbed to fly his first mission in more than a week. He led four Spitfires into an attack on 20 Messerschmitts, catching one of the enemy planes with a three-second burst that sent it plummeting into the sea. Moments later three ME-109s latched onto his tail, riddling his engine with machine gun and cannon shells. Gliding out of the fight, Beurling decided he was too low to bail out, so he pancaked his crippled Spitfire in a farmer's field. The crash-landing was so severe that he was knocked cold. When he woke up, he found his arm was cut and the nose of his fighter was just yards from a stone wall. Had he waited another second before setting down, his machine would have slammed into the rocks. Unperturbed, Beurling walked to the nearest road and hitch-hiked back to Takali.

Frank Jones also downed a German in the scrap. The two kills seemed to rejuvenate the defenders. On August 10 they claimed three ME-109s in a morning dogfight for the loss of only one Spitfire. One of the Nazi machines was downed by Wally McLeod, who was beginning to fantasize about surpassing Beurling as the top Canadian ace. McLeod closed to within 70 metres of a Messerschmitt before blasting it to pieces. He was so close that chunks of the exploding German plane embedded themselves in his Spitfire. The enemy pilot was hurled free by the blast and floated down with his parachute, landing in the water. McLeod flew low and noticed the German was making no attempt to inflate his rubber raft. Assuming it must be defective, he tossed his own dinghy overboard. The German waved his thanks but made no attempt to climb aboard McLeod's raft, either. McLeod learned the reason when he got back to base. One of his cannon shells had ripped straight through the man's chest, exiting out his back. He died in a rescue launch before reaching shore. Although it was fruitless, McLeod's act of compassion, so rare for him, created something of a sensation in the Allied press. One newspaper reported he had "extended the hand of friendship to a vanquished foe."[1]

Before the day was out, the German would be joined in death by one of Malta's most promising young pilots, Jerry Smith. The Regina native chased a Ju-88 out to sea near dusk, shooting it down for his fourth kill. Sadly, he was not seen again and no one knows for certain what happened to him, although it seems likely that he was killed by return fire from the Junkers. His brother, Rod, was among the pilots who searched in vain for him before all light vanished from the sky.

While these bloody but indecisive skirmishes were being fought over Malta, the British High Command was sending another convoy of supply ships steaming towards the island. This time it would be a truly massive effort, with 13 transport vessels and one oil tanker sailing from Gibraltar. Protecting them would be one of the mightiest armadas ever assembled. In all, four aircraft carriers, two battleships, seven cruisers, 24 destroyers and four corvettes were on escort duty. It was a formidable force that Winston Churchill hoped would be capable of guiding the convoy safely through the gauntlet of Axis planes, ships and submarines that awaited it. If all went well, the freighters would deliver 85,000 tonnes of food, aviation fuel and ammunition to Malta. The tanker, an American ship named *Ohio*, was carrying 12,000 tonnes of desperately needed oil.

The convoy and its escort, totalling 55 ships, set sail on August 10. Unfortunately, an Italian spy in Morocco spotted the fleet as it pulled out, and the Axis forces were soon ready to attack. Some 650 warplanes on Sicily and Sardinia attempted to stop the Allied ships, with the help of 19 submarines, 17 surface ships and scores of fast motor-torpedo boats.

The Axis forces drew first blood when German U-boat commander Helmut Rosenbaum slipped past a flotilla of destroyers and put four torpedoes into the aircraft carrier *Eagle*. The venerable old ship shuddered under the impact of several internal explosions, capsized, and disappeared beneath the waves, all within six minutes of being hit. A young British sailor named Frank Treves never forgot the sight of *Eagle* going to its grave as he looked on from a nearby ship. "I was very young and extremely frightened," he recalled. "The attacks were terrifying; I cannot think of another word. The worst for me were the Stukas; their sirens made a most appalling noise. The sky was absolutely mottled with flak from the ships ... To me the worst sight of all was seeing *Eagle* go down, because you could see both planes and men sliding into the sea; you could actually hear the screams and yells ... It was terror, absolute terror."[2] More than 900 men were saved by British destroyers, but 160 others went down with the carrier.

Next an Italian submarine struck, sinking a cruiser and badly damaging a second British warship before putting a torpedo into the *Ohio*. Fortunately, the tanker was not seriously damaged, and it was able to keep its course for Malta.

With so many Allied warships taking part in the battle, some Axis losses were inevitable. Two Italian submarines were sunk. One was sent to the bottom in particularly dramatic fashion by the destroyer

Three Malta defenders. From left, Smokey O'Neil, Eric Crist and Jack Ryckman. Courtesy of Eric Crist

Ithuriel, which forced it to the surface with depth charges, then rammed it, slicing the enemy vessel in half.

So far, German and Italian subs had been causing most of the damage, but that was about to change. The Axis pilots had been kept at bay for several days by Allied pilots aboard the three surviving aircraft carriers but, as the convoy pushed on into the Mediterranean, the carriers had to turn for home. The seamen were on their own.

Furious attacks by enemy planes and motor-torpedo boats sent nine of the merchantmen to the bottom, along with two more escorting Royal Navy ships. Several Italian cruisers came out to challenge the survivors after that, but turned back after British warships damaged two of them.

As the four remaining merchantmen and the *Ohio* neared Malta, Allied fighter pilots on the island swung into action, providing them with invaluable air cover. On August 12, Canadians Johnny Sherlock and Buzz Ogilvie, flying with a South African pilot named "Zulu" Swales, had a dramatic encounter with a German bomber. "I lost my oxygen and had to fly lower," Ogilvie recalled in a 1997 interview. "I dove down, and lo and behold I bumped right into a Heinkel-III. I made an attack, and

123

one of its engines started to smoke. I told the other guys what I was doing, and Johnny and Swales came down to help out."[3]

Sherlock picks up the story: "It happened about 100 miles east of the island and was a perfect interception. Four of us had taken off, but my number two had gone back with wireless trouble. Buzz Ogilvie and Swales got the first shot at it. I was up higher, came around and took advantage of a cripple. It was already smoking. I fired at it and it went straight in. There were no survivors. I circled the spot, thinking I'd signal a 'May Day' if anyone got out. No one did."[4] When they got back to Malta, Swales and Sherlock insisted Ogilvie be given full credit for shooting down the silver-coloured machine, which went into the record books as their squadron's 100th confirmed victory.

Next day, Rod Smith shot down an Italian bomber just as it was about to drop its payload on what was left of the convoy. At almost the same moment, three Spitfires flown by George Beurling, Frank Jones and V.H. Wynn caught a lone Ju-88 that had apparently become separated from its formation. Jones attacked head on, scoring hits on the wings and nose. Wynn moved in next, reporting his tracers had struck the plane's fuselage. Despite all the damage, German pilot Hans Schmiedgen had somehow been able to keep his ship airborne. But now Beurling swooped down, shooting off the bomber's starboard engine with a burst that sent the Junkers crashing into the sea. All four of its crew perished. The victory, Beurling's 20th of the war and the 18th since his arrival on Malta, would go into the record books as his only "shared" kill. Two more Ju-88s were downed by other pilots in another dogfight, but four of the island's Spitfires were also lost.

That night, three damaged merchantmen limped into Valletta harbour, and the next day, a fourth transport made it to Malta. In all, they brought with them 32,000 tonnes of precious supplies. It was a far cry from the 85,000 tonnes that the islanders had been hoping for, but it would be enough to keep them going until at least the middle of October. If Ohio could somehow get through with its oil shipment, the convoy battle would have to be deemed a major success, despite the terrible losses that had been suffered.

The Luftwaffe and the Regia Aeronautica seemed to realize what was at stake, because they made a determined bid to sink the Ohio before she could reach Malta. One Italian Stuka divebomber pressed home its attack with such vigour that it slammed right into the tanker's deck! Several other enemy planes damaged the *Ohio* with bombs and gunfire, but the ship and its gallant crew kept coming. She was within a few hundred metres of Valletta harbour when she began listing badly, taking on water at a fearsome rate. Those looking on from shore were convinced that the *Ohio* was finished. But now help arrived in the form of two Maltese tugs. Lines were connected to the shattered tanker, and she was successfully towed into Valletta.

Those who watched her limp in from the shore have never forgotten the scene. "*Ohio* had a big hole in the hull," Myriam Mifsud said decades later. "How it got in was by a miracle. That's the only word for it. Everyone believed it was a miracle, because *Ohio* arrived on August 15, which was the Feast of Santa Maria. We called it the Santa Maria convoy after that."[5] Miracle or not, the arrival of the *Ohio* and the other survivors proved to be a huge boost to morale all over the island. "When the convoy came through, people were cheering in the bastions," Mifsud recalled. Civilian George Porter has similar memories. "Some boats came in half-destroyed because they had hit mines," he said. "One was badly damaged by shrapnel — we filled the holes with a whole lot of wooden plugs, believe it or not. The *Ohio* had a plane that crashed on it, but it made it, crawling through."[6]

Strangely, the Axis fliers made no attempt to bomb the surviving ships at dockside. Possibly they had enough after several days of hard fighting. Malta's Spitfires, after all, had shot down 14 enemy planes during the convoy battles, and fire from navy ships and British carrier pilots had accounted for several dozen more.

In any case, Kesselring's decision not to throw everything he had at *Ohio* would prove to be one of the biggest blunders of the siege. The battered tanker's oil was unloaded just before she sank to the bottom of the harbour. She was the 14th Allied ship to go down in what became known as Operation Pedestal. In all, more than 500 Allied sailors and merchant sailors had been lost — but their sacrifice had not been in vain. "Before the Santa Maria convoy came in we had just four days of food left on the island," civilian Milo Vassallo recalls now. "Afterwards, we had enough food and oil to see us through."[7]

Malta received another boost on August 17, when 29 Spitfires flew in from the carrier *Furious*. For the first time in the war, the island had more than 100 fighter planes with which to defend itself. Another first came the next day, when General Kesselring decided not to launch a major strike against the island's airfields following the arrival of RAF reinforcements. On August 19 a heavy rainstorm grounded both sides, but the next day, when the skies cleared, there was still no sign of the enemy.

Kesselring had made another crucial mistake. Now was not the time to ease up. He still had the defenders badly outnumbered and should have taken advantage of that fact by keeping the pressure on, day and night, as he had done in July. Fortunately for the Allies, he was losing his stomach for a bloody war of attrition. More to the point, he was being out-generalled by his British counterpart, Air Vice-Marshal Lloyd.

Emboldened by their growing strength, the defenders went on the offensive for the first time, sending 18 Spitfires to Sicily to seek out the enemy. Amazingly, not a single Axis machine was encountered, and not one shot was fired at them from the ground. Still, as George Beurling wrote later, it was a boost to their morale to fly over the enemy's backyard for a change.

A week later, with the Germans and Italians still refusing to come out and fight, the Spitfires were sent out to raid three Sicilian airfields. Led by Englishman Walter Churchill, a decorated ace with eight victories to his credit, the attackers caught the enemy completely by surprise, destroying 10 Axis planes. Tragically, however, Group Captain Churchill, a 35-year-old who was in poor health, was shot down and killed by anti-aircraft fire. One other Spitfire was also lost, but the pilot survived to become a prisoner of war.

Because of the slackening Axis air activity over Malta, the island's aircrews were finally able to step up their attacks against Italian supply ships headed for Africa. The day after the raid on the Sicilian airfields, RAF bombers sank two enemy vessels, and a Malta-based submarine sent a third to the bottom. All three had been loaded with fuel and tank shells that Rommel had been counting on for a new offensive in Egypt. Without them, he had to limit his Afrika Korps to a few probes against British and Australian positions. A few days later, Malta's bombers struck again, sinking both a merchant ship and the Italian motor-torpedo boat that was escorting it.

One of the leading bomber pilots on Malta was Dallas Schmidt, who won the Distinguished Flying Cross for scoring a direct bomb hit on a transport ship and for shooting up an enemy destroyer with machine gun and cannon fire. When the Axis tried to get supplies to Rommel aboard transport planes, Schmidt again rose to the occasion. In one episode, Schmidt and South African pilot John Clements shot down a German flying boat. Moments later, the two joined with several other Allied pilots in an attack on a formation of 46 lumbering Axis transport planes. With no enemy fighter escort in sight, the RAF fliers were able to shoot down six planes for the loss of only one of their own machines. Schmidt led the way, destroying two Ju-52 transports before his own twin-engine Beaufighter was damaged by return fire from a German gunner.

A few weeks later the aggressive pilot was back in action, shooting down another transport plane. Not long after that, he became an ace by bagging an Italian plane. Before the year was out he would destroy three more of the big supply planes.

His closest brush with death would come not from Axis aircraft, but rather from anti-aircraft fire directed his way by a German warship. With his controls shot out, he tried to get home by alternating engine speeds and using his ailerons. According to an official report of the incident, "by means of jerks and lurches he got the aircraft back to Malta."[8] Once over his own airfield, however, he discovered the plane was too badly damaged to land. Faced with no other option, both he and his navigator bailed out, and were back in the squadron mess before nightfall.

Schmidt, of course, was by no means the only successful Beaufighter pilot on Malta. Another, Harry Donkersley, won two DFCs for sinking or running aground several enemy ships. The citation to his second medal read: "In sorties against enemy shipping this officer has achieved much success. One night he captained an aircraft detailed to drop flares over Italian naval units and accomplished his task successfully. Several nights later he attacked and sank a small merchant vessel. On another night he participated in an action against an important enemy convoy in the Mediterranean. As a result, other air and surface forces were enabled to strike successfully. Two merchant vessels were sunk and two badly damaged."[9]

Another Beaufighter pilot, American Warren Sutton, spotted an Italian convoy in the moonlight and radioed its position to Allied warships. As a result, according to his DFC citation, "the convoy was almost totally destroyed."[10]

With General Kesselring refusing to send large formations over Malta during daylight hours, most of the aerial combat seen over the island during the month of August took place at night. Small numbers of Italian and German aircraft made periodic strikes throughout the month, as indeed they had since the siege had begun. But just like the Luftwaffe and Regia Aeronautica day fliers, they found the defences tough to crack. It would take a separate book to adequately cover the exploits of the Allied night fighter pilots on Malta.

The easiest way to tell the story of Malta's nocturnal war might be by studying the career of the island's leading night fighter ace — Carl "Moose" Fumerton. Born in Fort Coulonge, Quebec, in 1913, Fumerton was a tall, muscular man with a background that included mining, hunting and work as a lumberjack. As a boy he had excelled in hockey and football. He was also adventurous, having spent much of the Great Depression prospecting for a mining company in remote regions of the Northwest Territories. Along the way he had also found the time to study mapping, surveying and geology, and to qualify for a private pilot's licence. When war came in 1939 he was quickly accepted by the RCAF. His wings were pinned on his chest in the spring of 1940 by Air Marshal Billy Bishop, the legendary First World War ace. "It was a thrill," Fumerton said in a 1997 interview. "He was quite friendly." Eight of the 29 young men who received their wings from Bishop that day were destined to be killed in action.

Once he got to England, Fumerton found himself assigned to night-fighting duties. His plane, the twin-engine Beaufighter, was not immediately to his liking. For one thing, it took a firm hand to keep it straight and level during both takeoffs and landings. For another, he discovered it could not retain altitude if one of its engines quit. Other members of his squadron had the same misgivings about the big machines until a lady flier delivered one of them to the airfield. She was almost dainty, standing about five foot one and weighing not much more than 100 pounds (45 kilograms). As she climbed down out of the cockpit she swung a parachute pack over her shoulder that was almost as big as she was. "If it had been a staged performance, it couldn't have worked better," Fumerton recalled. "It provided quite a psychological boost. After that, everyone got down to business flying the Beaufighter."[11] In due course the pilots began to appreciate the plane's awesome firepower. Early models of the Beau may have been difficult to fly, but if you did manage to work yourself into position behind an enemy plane, you could bring an incredible six machine guns and four cannons to bear on the target. That gave the plane more punch than any other fighter produced by either side throughout the war.

Posted to a squadron in Egypt, Fumerton saw his first action on March 3, 1942, when he caught a Heinkel bomber in the moonlight over the Suez Canal. He went for it like a cat pouncing on a mouse, only to run headlong into a stream of fire from the bomber's alert rear-gunner. Bullets slammed right into the cockpit, shooting away most of Fumerton's gunsight. Shattered plexiglass cut his face, and a shell nicked his right leg. Another salvo knocked out one of his engines. Keeping cool, Fumerton returned the fire, hitting the Heinkel in both motors. Within seconds both planes were going down in flames. Fumerton managed to pull up in time to execute a masterful emergency landing on the desert floor, but the German machine plunged straight into the nearby Mediterranean Sea.

A few days later, Fumerton learned that the crew of the Heinkel had been taken prisoner and that, amazingly, the rear-gunner was a Jew who had successfully hidden from the Nazis by enlisting in the Luftwaffe!

Fumerton spent three days in hospital, but was back in action a month later, shooting down two HE-IIIs in one night. On June 22 he flew to Malta, along with his radar operator, fellow Canadian Pat Bing, to help the defenders deal with an ever-increasing number of night raids. Like all newcomers to the island, the pair did not have to wait long before being thrown into the fray. It happened on the night of June 24, when three Italian Stukas set out from Sicily shortly after nightfall. Weather conditions were deteriorating rapidly, and the leader wisely called off from the mission, signalling his men to return to base. Faulty equipment caused his message to be garbled — the other two divebombers continued on their way. One of them ran headlong into Fumerton and Bing just north of Malta. One quick burst sent the Ju-87 down in flames. The two returned to Luqa airfield to reload and refuel, and were quickly off again in search of more victims. Just before dawn they found what they were looking for. Bing spotted a Cant bomber on radar and directed Fumerton to the spot. The Quebec pilot did the rest, blowing the tri-motor aircraft in half with a prolonged burst.

Five nights later, on June 29, the duo struck again, shooting down a pair of Ju-88s that were attempting to bomb Hal Far airfield. Fumerton caught the rear-gunner of the first bomber napping and was able to finish off the Junkers without difficulty. The second opponent proved more troublesome, with the gunner managing to damage the Beaufighter before Fumerton's return fire killed him. Moments later, the enemy machine fell into the sea, where its wreckage was observed to burn for several minutes. Fumerton added three more Ju-88s to his growing score in July, destroyed a Cant on August 14, and added yet another Junkers on August 28, giving him nine kills over Malta.

Unlike some leading aces, who seem to have been motivated by blood lust, Fumerton took no pleasure in killing. "You think of the people [in the enemy plane]. You know what's being done to them. You really feel sorry for them. At least I did. But you had to do it. Think what Europe would be like today if Hitler had won."[12]

At first, the German and Italian planes came over in bright moonlight, which made it easier for them to bomb their targets. But after Fumerton and Bing and their mates started clawing them down on a regular basis, they began flying strictly on moonless nights. Often, the defenders were guided to their target by ground controllers. But just as often they found their prey by themselves. "There was an Italian fellow on Mount Etna who was jamming all the radar, but he gave up after a month or so," Fumerton recalled. "He probably didn't realize how well he was doing. If we couldn't find them on radar we'd fly north along their flight lines. We picked a lot of them up on our own." Once the enemy was spotted, Fumerton was a tiger in the cockpit. Asked whether he caught most of his victims over Malta or Sicily, he told the author, "Wherever they were we were after them. You tried to get in fast, break fast and do your shooting."[13]

Along the way, Fumerton and Bing had their narrow escapes. Their most harrowing adventure came on the night of August 10, when they took off to intercept an enemy flight headed for Malta that had been detected on radar. Fumerton was closing in on a bomber when all hell broke loose. "I don't know what happened," he says now. "I was scanning the air ahead of me and above. Pat had his head in the box [radar sets]. In those situations your total concentration is in picking it [the enemy plane] up. Suddenly there was a loud bang and one engine stopped. Twenty seconds later there was another bang and the other engine stopped."[14] They did not know if they had encountered a mechanical problem or a sharp-shooting German rear-gunner. But they knew they were in big trouble. Fumerton had only two options — bail out or land on choppy seas in the middle of the night.

Neither was a very happy prospect, but Fumerton radioed their position so rescuers would at least have some idea of where to start looking for them. Then, turning to Bing, he announced he was going to try to set the doomed machine down on the water. As the Beaufighter neared the waves, warmer air hit the windshield, causing it to mist over. Fumerton was effectively blinded, but there was no turning back now. He caught a glimpse of huge whitecaps coming up to greet them just before impact. Shouting to Bing to open the hatch, he pulled back on the joystick and executed an amazingly gentle landing. The two men scrambled out onto one of the wings with only moments to spare. Then, Bing disappeared back into the cockpit to retrieve a good luck charm! He got out just before the Beaufighter slipped beneath the waves. As it went down, Fumerton could see the green lights of the control column still shining in the dark.

By now the airmen were alone on the dark, wave-tossed Mediterranean. To make matters worse, Bing's rubber raft would not inflate and the men, who both stood over six feet tall, had to share Fumerton's five-foot-long dinghy, which was designed for one person. "I was sitting upright as best I could and Pat was stretched between my legs with his legs drifting several feet behind. 'Pat,' I said, 'I hope there are no sharks here!' His reply, a dour 'I hope so too!'"[15] They managed to stay afloat long enough for a rescue launch to spot Bing's flashlight and take them to safety.

Another night, they mistook a Ju-88 for a Beaufighter. "It was usually our custom when two of us were patrolling to do practice runs on one another," Fumerton said. "This particular night two of us were up — I was given a vector, we picked up the blip [on radar]. I was delighted. I closed in, pulled up and tucked myself inside the wing of the other Beau and prepared to wave at the other pilot. In one split second I realized it was a Ju-88 and the horrified face I was looking at was German. Fortunately the reaction of the Ju-88 pilot in doing a wing-over was so fast that the rear gunner, who couldn't have been more than 25 feet away and in perfect position, didn't get a chance to blast me."[16]

Like Malta's day fighter pilots, the night fliers also encountered dangers on the ground. "There were a lot of bombings, and sometimes the bombs sounded awfully close. I remember once Bud Connell [a Spitfire pilot] was in a slit trench when a bomb landed within three feet of him. He could put his hand out of the trench and touch the crater. It shook him up."[17]

The night fliers faced other dangers as well, including trying to find their way home in the dark. If they got lost they would eventually run out of fuel and have to land on the sea. But Fumerton had a sixth sense that always brought him back safely. "I never did have any trouble getting back, probably because of the type of work I did before the war. I did a lot of traversing through the bush. I was a lumberjack and I did a lot of prospecting. I'd walk 20 miles one way, move over a few miles, then move back again. You just acquired that sense of where you were."[18]

Night raids were remembered by many survivors of the siege as the worst experience of all. Not being able to see the enemy made people feel especially helpless. And of course being denied a good night's sleep made it difficult for both civilians and military personnel to function efficiently the next morning.

The raiders usually started coming over between 10 p.m. and 11 p.m. Some dropped flares that burst about 1,500 metres above the ground, then floated slowly to earth, washing several square kilometres of the island in a glaring yellow glow. Sometimes a single Junkers-88 would keep the whole population awake for hours. It would circle round and round just offshore, occasionally darting in to drop bombs or flares. Often, the all-clear did not sound until morning.

Some of the Axis planes dropped delayed-action bombs that went off at the break of day or at intervals throughout the morning and afternoon. The knowledge that unexploded weapons might go off at any moment kept people on edge for hours. Pilots often had to wait for bomb disposal units to dismantle a deadly device embedded in the ground beside a Spitfire.

For the Axis crews as well, night bombing was a frightening experience. German pilot Helmut Zlitz, who flew 110 raids over England, including 64 daylight operations against London, remembers his nocturnal missions over Malta as the toughest assignments he ever faced. "I will never forget it. There was heavy anti-aircraft fire and many, many searchlights. Sometimes it was so light [from the searchlights] that we realized we could see every ship in the harbour. Searchlights got hold of us once, but we slipped away because our airplane was painted completely black." Zlitz, who had been a 26-year-old farmer from East Prussia when the war began, said the hardest thing about a night flight to Malta was the last hour before takeoff. "Before we started to fly we were restless. You think about what will happen. But as soon as the green light came [ordering the crews to take off] everything was forgotten. You didn't think about getting hit. You were too busy to think about it."

Zlitz had great respect for the Allied night fighter pilots. "They were human beings like me, doing their job. We had to fight each other. Maybe if we had met before the war we would have been friends. The politicians made the war, then sat at home. We had to fight it."[19]

Italian Cant crewman Tony Ferri found flying over Malta in the dark much more frightening than facing waves of Spitfires in the daylight.

> Once we were hit by flak and our pilot was badly wounded. He almost made it back to Sicily before he died, right in his seat. The plane continued on a level course, but there was no way we could land without him. Two of us bailed out, but the rear gunner wouldn't leave the plane. He had once told me he was terrified of the thought of bailing out, that he would never do it, no matter what. I was yelling at him at the top of my lungs to come with us but he stared back blankly. He seemed to be in a trance. Anyway, we had no time to argue with him. We jumped. As I floated down under my parachute I could hear the bomber's engines as it continued to head northwest [towards

the Tyrrhenian Sea]. In my mind's eye I could see the gunner, up there by himself, looking out at the stars as the plane droned on into the night, knowing it had to run out of fuel sooner or later. It's an image I can't get out of my mind to this day.[20]

The Cant was never seen again.

Ferri's dreams would also be haunted for years by another equally terrible incident.

After one raid two or three planes came back with dead men on board. The planes were shot to pieces. You couldn't figure out how anyone could have gotten out of them alive. I helped carry them out. We placed the bodies in a hangar, four of them, and covered them with blankets. They were so young. Their eyes were open, I remember that. I had never seen a dead person before, except my grandfather, and that was different. People who have died violently don't look anything like they show you on TV. They ["victims" of TV violence] look like they've gone to sleep ... It's nothing like that. Sometimes I still see those poor kids in my dreams, lined up on that hangar floor. I wake up in a cold sweat every time.[21]

CHAPTER 9

MALTA'S UNSUNG HEROES

Boredom began creeping into the lives of the defenders as September 1942 opened. For the first time in months there was virtually nothing for the fighter pilots to do. They sat in their cockpits for hours at a time, ready to take off at a moment's notice. But on the first day of the month not one alert was sounded. Frustrated with this inactivity, the Allied fliers flew to Sicily the next day, buzzing several enemy airfields. Still the Luftwaffe and the Regia Aeronautica stayed on the ground, content to let the RAF waste precious aviation fuel.

During the few dogfights that did take place at this time, the Axis forces usually had the upper hand. German pilots shot down a Spitfire over Malta on September 8 without suffering any losses of their own and, the next day, American ace Claude Weaver was lost. The Oklahoma City pilot, who had joined the RCAF before Pearl Harbor, had just dived on a Macchi when two more Italian fighters jumped him, forcing Weaver to crash-land on a Sicilian beach, where he was promptly captured. His loss was keenly felt, because in just a few months on Malta he had shot down 10 enemy planes.

Lord Gort took advantage of the slackened enemy activity to formally present the George Cross to the Maltese people. Some 5,000 civilians crowded into Valletta's Palace Square for the ceremony, which was held on September 13. As Gort presented the medal to a local judge, three Spitfires circled overhead, providing air cover.

It was a happy occasion, although British soldier William Keen clearly remembers hearing grumbling from the crowd. "People were crowded around but they weren't very concerned about the George Cross. They were more concerned about getting some food in their bellies. I heard remarks like, 'It's food we want, not George Crosses.'"[1] But schoolgirl Myriam Mifsud thinks Keen was simply overhearing

British soldier William Keen, on Malta. Courtesy of William Keen

the complaints of a few grousers who were in no way representative of the majority of their countrymen. Asked if she felt ordinary Maltese were proud of the honour, she replied, "Oh God, yes!"[2]

Finally, on September 15, the Axis planes started showing up in significant numbers. Two Spitfires were shot down and a third was badly damaged. In return, the defenders lightly damaged a single Italian fighter. The next day the Germans almost bagged George Beurling. The ace was flying with British pilot Eric Hetherington when they encountered a formation of eight ME-109s. Outnumbered four to one, the two Allied pilots fought for their lives for more than an hour before the Germans finally turned for home. When he got back to Takali, Beurling counted several bullet holes in his tail and wings.

Perhaps the most dramatic air battle of the month broke out September 25 when 10 Spitfires tangled with a dozen Messerschmitts. Diving out of the sun, Beurling shot one of the Germans down in flames with a two-second burst fired from 275 metres' range. Swerving to line up a second victim, he damaged it with a salvo triggered from 325 metres out. Seconds later he saved British pilot Ernie Budd's life by blasting an ME-109 off his tail. The German bailed out but, before he could land in the sea off Malta, he was machine gunned in his parachute by another Messerschmitt pilot who mistook him for a helpless Allied pilot. Beurling was so sickened by the sight he almost vomited into his oxygen mask.

With his two victories, Beurling had now destroyed 20 enemy planes since arriving on Malta. But the man who hoped to eventually overtake him as top Canadian ace scored again the next day. Leading three Spitfires into an assault on 20 ME-109s, Wally McLeod shot down one Nazi plane and drove off the rest. This accomplishment gave him five victories, officially making him an ace, and he was awarded a much-deserved Distinguished Flying Cross. His score likely would have been much higher except for the fact that McLeod was harder hit by illnesses than most of the other pilots on the island. On a couple of occasions he was so weak from hunger and the Malta Dog that ground crews found him unconscious in the sweltering heat of his cockpit just before takeoff.

While the Spitfire pilots were engaging in these sporadic dogfights, Malta's bomber crews were continuing to take a heavy toll of Italian ships. Eleven transports were sent to the bottom that September, robbing Rommel of tens of thousands of tonnes of supplies. The situation was so serious that during the first two weeks of the month, he got only one-quarter of the gasoline and tank shells he needed to maintain his offensive. As a result, the Afrika Korps found itself incapable of mounting any kind of major attack at this time.

One of the key reasons for all the trouble the Desert Fox was in was that Malta's bombers and submarines often knew exactly where to find the Axis convoys. And that was due in no small measure to the peerless work of an eccentric young British reconnaissance pilot named Adrian "Warby" Warburton.

The son of a British naval officer, Warburton had been christened aboard a Royal Navy submarine stationed at Malta during the last year of the First World War. After graduating from school in the United Kingdom, Adrian took a job in a bank, where he soon found himself bored to tears. Eager for adventure, he joined the Royal Air Force in January 1939, just eight months before the war began. He dreamed of being a fighter pilot, but his instructors were not impressed with his flying abilities and decided instead to assign him to a reconnaissance squadron. Posted to Malta in 1940, he found himself flying a lumbering old Maryland twin-engine bomber.

Swordfish torpedo-bomber. Photo by the author

Warburton's debut was nothing to write home about. On his first flight he hit the airfield's perimeter fence with his tail wheel and almost crashed. He persisted, however, and soon became a topnotch pilot. Flying up and down the Italian coastline almost daily, he started coming home with excellent pictures of enemy airfields and harbours. It was important work, but it did not appeal to the 22-year-old, who was yearning for more action. He wanted a transfer to a fighter squadron. When he could not get one, he decided to use his Maryland as a fighter. After taking his photos on October 30, 1940, he attacked an Italian Cant and shot it down. Circling low, he took a picture of the crashed enemy machine just to make sure his victory would be confirmed. From then on there was no stopping him. He was constantly attacking swift Italian fighters in his Maryland and, before long, he was an ace with 10 kills to his credit.

At the same time, he was gaining a reputation as the best reconnaissance pilot in the RAF. Italian naval installations were heavily defended by both fighters and flak, but that did not stop Warburton. He consistently came home in a badly damaged aircraft with spectacular pictures. Once, he flew so low that his photos actually showed the laundry of Italian sailors hanging out to dry on the deck of a battleship!

The British put the work of this intrepid spy in the sky to good use. After he came back from Taranto harbour one day in November 1940 with pictures that showed exactly where all of Italy's biggest warships were moored, torpedo-bombers were sent out to attack the place. They struck with devastating effect, sinking three battleships and seriously damaging two cruisers. The powerful Italian fleet never fully recovered from the setback, spending much of the rest of the war in port.

Emboldened by his success, Warburton began taking frightful risks. On December 15, 1940, he came right down over the deck of an Italian submarine, flying through a hail of anti-aircraft fire to damage it with machine gun and cannon shells. On Christmas Eve he added to his growing reputation by shooting an Italian bomber down in flames over Naples. Two days later, he engaged no fewer than nine enemy fighters at once, before escaping with new pictures of Taranto harbour. On another occasion, Warburton was nearly killed when an Italian fighter pilot poured a burst right into the nose of his Maryland. One shell ricocheted off the instrument panel and struck him in the chest. Fortunately, its force was almost spent by the time it hit him, and he was able to fly home with nothing more than a bad bruise over his heart.

The men who flew with him insist that Warburton was completely fearless. "The most remarkable of the many personalities in Malta was Adrian Warburton," Spitfire pilot Duncan Smith recalled. "Warby was moulded in the buccaneer style, and his exploits captured the imagination. Immensely brave, he delighted in taking fearful risks, and would go out of his way to embarrass the enemy by the brazen impudence of his photographic reconnaissance missions. Apart from his normal work, which ranged over the whole Mediterranean, he had a fine record as a fighter pilot. On the streets and in the bars he was immediately recognized and would be greeted affectionately by civilians and servicemen alike."[3]

Duncan Smith recalled escort missions he flew with Warburton as among the most harrowing experiences of his combat career. "Once Warby decided to take pictures of Syracuse, and without wavering I found myself following him into the harbour at zero feet to be met by the strongest ack-ack fire. We flew up, down and out with everything shooting at us, and the only reason we escaped was because the enemy could not depress their medium guns sufficiently — we were so low."[4]

Wellington bomber crewman Wilfred Baynton. Courtesy of Wilfred Baynton

On another occasion Duncan Smith was covering Warburton's Maryland in his Spitfire when four ME-109s suddenly appeared. "I told him to turn so that we could make good our escape out to sea," he wrote later. "On the R/T [radio] he said: 'Sorry, old boy, got to finish this run — you see them off — you've got the guns.' I had a hell of a time of it before Warby called to say he was headed out to sea and why was I not following to protect him ... The experience only made Warburton laugh his head off when we landed."[5]

On the ground Warburton was much like George Beurling — an unorthodox loner who lived by his own rules. Wilfred Baynton, a 19-year-old wireless operator/air gunner who served in the same squadron, remembers Warburton as "a rather slight, blond fellow who wore his battle dress pretty casually."[6] In fact, he was often seen in the mess or on the airfield wearing slippers, pyjamas and a grease-smudged cap.

Alex Stittle, a young Canadian flier, remembers Warburton as "a great guy. He was a polished Englishman with a very polished accent, but he liked Canadians. He was a regular guy. He would wrestle with guys on the bus on the way down [to the tarmac]. The authorities didn't like him because he wore really baggy pants. But what could they do? He was good and he loved the place. He couldn't understand why anybody wanted to leave Malta. He'd say, 'Where can you get more action than this?' And his photos were something else. But if nobody chased him it was a dull day for him. For most of us there was too much action, but he really loved it."[7]

Baynton found him to be a remote figure. "I only saw fleeting glimpses of him" in the mess.[8] The main reason for that was that Warburton lived off the base with an English nightclub dancer named Christine Ratcliffe. Ratcliffe, a strikingly beautiful blonde, was a character in her own right. And like Warburton, she was one of the heroes of the siege. She had been performing for British troops on the island in June 1940, when Italy declared war on England, leaving her and the rest of her troupe — a colourful collection of young women nicknamed the "Whizz Bangs" — marooned. For the next three years she worked by day in the RAF's underground operations room, then spent her evenings entertaining soldiers, sailors and fliers with shows all over the island.

She soon gained a reputation as a woman who would not run for cover, even when bombs were raining down just outside the bar in which she was performing. Once, when a bomb exploded nearby, sending the customers diving under their tables, Ratcliffe kept on dancing. Asked later why she had not sought shelter, she said matter-of-factly, "If you're for it, you're for it. There's nothing you can do, if your time is up now, is there?"[9] The authorities were so impressed with the work she did to keep up the morale of Allied troops that they granted her the Medal of the British Empire in 1943. Unfortunately, the story of Adrian Warburton and Christine Ratcliffe does not have a happy ending. Both survived the siege, but Warby was killed in action later in the war and his lover never recovered from the loss.

Another hero of the siege was Josephine Fursman, a 34-year-old Maltese housewife who gained a reputation as something of an angel of mercy among the young fighter pilots. Fursman, who lived in a small village near Takali airfield, was almost like a mother to some of the teenaged fliers. "I'd watch them getting on the bus to join their squadron," she recalled in a 1997 interview. "They were so young and vulnerable. Life could be so short. I tried to look after them. You worried from the moment they left until they came back. Sometimes they didn't."

One of the pilots she took a special interest in was Canadian Jerry Billing, who was twice shot down. Both times he was plucked from the sea, and each time Fursman washed his clothes for him. "You had to get that salt water out or it would be the end of the tunic," she said. They became so close that each time he took off to intercept a raid she handed him a flower. Touched by the gesture, Billing began giving her a flower in return. "It was best, fond wishes," she said.[10] Fortunately, Billing survived the war. The two friends held an emotional reunion when Fursman visited Canada 54 years later.

Although Warburton and Ratcliffe received acclaim for their heroism, most reconnaissance pilots, cabaret dancers and ordinary civilians went about their business almost completely unnoticed. It was the same for most of the British sailors who operated the Royal Navy's handful of submarines on Malta. In fact, they played a magnificent role, sinking scores of Axis ships while garnering only a fraction of the attention given to the more 'glamorous' fighter pilots. One sub in particular — HMS Upholder — sent 21 enemy vessels to the bottom. Its commander, the dashing, bearded Malcolm Wanklyn, had once ordered his crew to board an enemy ship after he ran out of torpedoes. They did, allowing the Italian sailors to escape in lifeboats before setting the vessel on fire. On another occasion he won the Victoria Cross, the Commonwealth's highest gallantry award, by slipping through a swarm of enemy destroyers to sink an Italian troop ship loaded with soldiers headed for North Africa.

These successes were not won without paying a high price. Eleven Maltese-based subs were lost, including Upholder, which went down with the loss of all hands. Captain Alistar Mars, who commanded HMS Unbroken, has said that half of all submariners on Malta perished. By way of comparison, only one in every 10 sailors who served on surface ships died. Submarines faced enemy destroyers and motor-torpedo boats, as well as air raids and mines. Just getting in and out of port was a dangerous task, because Axis planes had dropped 30,000 mines in the waters around Malta. They were a menace throughout the siege, because all of the island's minesweepers were quickly sunk by Axis bombers.

Captain Mars thought air raids on the submarine base were the hardest ordeals to bear. They were so frequent, he said, that the subs had to be submerged all day, only coming to the surface at night. "If harbour rest periods are continuously interrupted by air raids, in which the safety of personnel and the submarine are always at stake, where there is little recreation or social relaxation and when home mails are frequently interrupted, one can readily visualize the strain placed on submarine crews operating out of Malta," he wrote later. "In addition, rations were usually poor, basically inadequate and lacked the vitamin and other ingredients essential to the re-establishment of good health after a long patrol. All these factors contributed to physical and mental disabilities which could well prove dangerous."[11]

As hard as the submariners had it on Malta, they had at least one consolation. Like the fighter pilots, they had the opportunity for glory. If they did well they could expect to win decorations and promotions. The troops on the island who were probably the least appreciated were the foot soldiers. Their job was to fight off an invasion that, month after month, failed to materialize. After a time, many Maltese came to view them as freeloaders who were taking up precious food. In reality, nothing could be further from the truth. The infantrymen were involved in everything from unloading ships and repairing airfields to rounding up Axis airmen who had bailed out over the island. Often it was extremely dangerous work and, before the siege lifted, nearly 500 soldiers were killed in air attacks.

For some, just getting to Malta was a harrowing experience. In fact, all three British soldiers interviewed by the author for this book were on board ships that were attacked on the way to the island.

"I had to travel by troop ship, and the Mediterranean was very dicey in those days," Englishman William Keen recalled. "We were torpedoed, and I spent eight hours in the water, clinging to a floating door. I watched the ship turn over completely and saw the bottom of it as it went down. It took about 800 men with it. I was picked up by a British destroyer. I kept on saying to them, 'I've got to get to Malta.' They said, 'You can't go there now.' I had rib injuries. We went back to Cairo and I was flown to Malta."[12]

John McIntyre, a Scotsman who had joined the British Army as a 17-year-old, had a similar experience. He was bound for Malta aboard the cruiser HMS *Manchester* when she was hit by a torpedo. "As we approached Pantileria the captain announced that a large formation of aircraft were 50 miles east and headed our way," he wrote in a letter to the author.

Six of us, who had wiggled out of any duties, had been playing cards on the mess deck below the foward

British soldiers on Malta. John McIntyre, back row, left. Courtesy of John McIntyre

six-inch guns which opened up. We came to life and dove flat on the deck with our heads inboard, as per regulations. Another explosion and the ship heeled over, causing the lockers above our heads to open up and bury us in seamen's gear. A head appeared above the debris and asked for six volunteers to take a cable down to the wheelhouse, which could have been on the moon as far as we landlubbers were concerned, but grabbing the cable we climbed down a hatchway to the steering room. We were knee deep in oil but managed to hand over the cable and scramble up the hatch again. On arriving back on deck we were again accosted by a P.O. [superior officer] asking for volunteers to steer the ship. So down the hole we went again to spend the next half hour holding the rudder in place. We lost something like 200 men. It wasn't a fun time. We went to Gibraltar and we figured we were going home from there. Instead, they marched us along a pier at 2 a.m. and put us on board another cruiser going to Malta.

McIntyre's second attempt to get to the island was almost as eventful as the first. On their first night out he heard the captain cry out, "Stand by to ram!" Moments later, he heard "some ugly crunching sounds as a U-boat was cut in half. Next day, under a beautiful sun and sky, I fell asleep under the shadow of the forward guns, wearing only a pair of shorts." When McIntyre awoke a little later, he had a severe sunburn. "The only white skin I had left was where my death tags were sunk into my flesh. I went to the medical room, was ordered to see the C.O., who ordered me to stand trial." He was accused of administering a self-inflicted wound and forced to do extra duties for a week once he got on shore.

At first, McIntyre found his new home rather pleasant. "Life on Malta for the first few months was beautiful. We were supposed to lie down in the afternoon, but by sneaking out of camp we could run the two miles to the south side of the island and spend an hour diving off the cliffs, until one day some plane wreckage floated in and among the debris was a man's scalp. That was our last swim at that side of the island."13

Harry Kennedy, who joined Britain's Territorial Army in 1939, was bound for Malta in January 1941 aboard a British warship that came under relentless air attack. "When the convoy neared Sardinia they were at you. I was on a fast, light cruiser and she weaved in and out of the convoy, defending it as best she could. We were gunners, so the Royal Navy said, 'You can't just sit downstairs and do nothing.' We fed ammunition to the guns and removed the empty shells. We were happy to be doing something." His ship got through unscathed, but an aircraft carrier in the convoy, the HMS *Illustrious*, was badly mauled. "We pulled into Grand Harbour just behind *Illustrious* and saw her decks just running with blood. She was quite a mess. They were taking bodies off in donkey carts. That was the last convoy to get through for a long time."14

Kennedy got to the island early in the siege, when the Italians were providing the only opposition. They flew in at great height, dropped their bombs, and quickly left. The only aerial defence was provided by three Sea Gladiator biplanes that the locals had dubbed Faith, Hope and Charity. The outnumbered British pilots shot down several enemy bombers over the next few weeks, and the raids slackened. Then both sides upped the ante at almost the same time. The

Malta's 51st light anti-aircraft battery, commanded by Lieut. J.H. Mifsud.
Courtesy of Peter Mifsud

English flew Hurricanes in from the aircraft carrier *Eagle*, the Luftwaffe joined the Regia Aeronautica on Sicily, and the fighting suddenly became deadly serious.

Kennedy, who saw action as an anti-aircraft gunner, soon noticed a more frenzied pace. "The Italian planes had been dropping bombs from 35,000 feet but the Germans came right down at us. They had no fear. They wanted to bomb the island to bits. I saw Stukas dive so steeply that they never pulled out in time. They were gutsy fighters. I was always impressed with the German airforce, I'll tell you that."[15]

There were so many air raids that the gunners soon began running short of ammunition. "We were limited to firing our guns on odd and even days," Kennedy recalled.

> Our barrels were beginning to warp in some cases.
> I remember once there was a Lewis gun that was on
> stand down [meaning it was not supposed to be fired
> that day]. I was in a building with another soldier
> when there was a hell of a bombing going on. We just
> couldn't stand being in a building during a heavy raid,
> so we went out on the parade grounds and there was

146

that Lewis gun, with sandbags all around it. A Stuka
came down and we got the gun going. We were firing
and he was firing back, then we were hit by a bomb
that fell quite close to the sandbag. We got the Stuka,
it went down over the buildings and never came back
up again, but we were knocked out. The two of us
were in hospital when an officer came in and said,
"You fired that gun on the wrong date. I can do one of
three things. I can charge you, I can forget the whole
thing, or I can recommend you for medals." We said,
"Forget the whole thing."[16]

Kennedy and his pal were by no means the only anti-aircraft gunners to risk trouble for ignoring the rules. At Grand Harbour, where
there were batteries directly opposite one another, the gunners were
under strict orders not to fire at low-flying enemy planes. If a gunner
missed his target the shells could easily hit Allied troops on the other
side of the harbour. Before long, German pilots realized that the safest
way to make good their escape after pulling out of a steep divebomb-
ing attack was to hug the waves. They flew so low, Maltese gunner Joe
Mifsud recalled later, that the faces of the pilots were clearly visible.
Once, a German airman arrogantly gave the "international 'up yours'
signal" to a gunner across the harbour from Misfud's position. The
gunner was so enraged that he lowered his weapon and blew the plane
out of the air. The authorities were unimpressed and promptly court-
martialled him for breaking the rules.

Despite such travails, anti-aircraft gunners managed to shoot down
130 Axis planes during 1942.

Most soldiers, however, never got the satisfaction of being able to
shoot back at the enemy. McIntyre recalled spending a lot of time
unloading ships or working at Luqa airfield. The runway was pocked
with bomb craters after every raid, and it was the army's job to get it
operational as quickly as possible. "We got it down to a routine. We
went out there right away. One thing about Malta — there's lots of
rocks. We got them and filled the craters in in a hurry." McIntyre was
also responsible for loading the guns of fighters and for tying torpedoes
under the old Swordfish biplanes. "We tied the torpedoes to them
with a rope; it was really primitive."[17]

Kennedy also recalled spending time unloading ships on the rare occasion when a vessel could get through. "I remember when the *Ohio* and two merchant ships came in. That very day the Maltese dockers went on strike and the poor old infantry had to unload the ships."[18]

While the fighter pilots were often treated like royalty by the civilians, some British soldiers felt they were disliked by the Maltese. "You may not want to hear this, but we hated them," one soldier said. "The general opinion of the British soldier is if we are invaded, the first people we are going to shoot will be the Maltese. They treated us pretty badly. We figured they would have preferred the Italians to us."[19] Another added: "The Maltese weren't very fond of the Germans and Italians but they weren't very fond of us either. We were eating a lot of their food."[20]

Whether they were appreciated by the civilians or not, the soldiers shared the same travails as the Maltese. For Harry Kennedy, the hardest thing to take was "the food, or the lack of it. I got two slices of bread once a week. Some weeks we got a chocolate bar to build us up a bit, but it was mainly corn beef and crackers or dehydrated potatoes or cabbage. We found it better to smoke it [the cabbage] than to eat it. We rolled it up. There weren't many cigarettes around." Before long, he came down with the Malta Dog. "We all had dysentery continuously. I was taken into the hospital and the whole ward was filled up with dozens of guys with dysentery. It was normal. A couple of times I did all-night sentry duty sitting on the can. The relief came and I said, 'Don't bother, I'll be here all night.'" Before long, Kennedy began losing weight at an alarming rate. "The officers would take everyone's weight once a month on a scale. I got down to 102 pounds. Most of the guys were pretty thin. When I joined the army I was about 140 pounds but the weight loss was gradual, so you didn't notice it. It's like being a prisoner of war, I suppose. Some of the guys said, 'Why should Hitler invade? We're all prisoners on Malta already.'"[21] McIntyre found the situation much the same. "Food got to the point where we were receiving one quarter of the rations you got [in the United Kingdom]. There were a lot of skinny people on Malta."[22]

Lack of sleep was another problem. "I was so used to getting broken sleep because of air raids that when I left Malta I couldn't get used to sleeping for the whole night," Kennedy recalled. "I used to get guys to wake me up every few hours."[23]

Social life was virtually non-existent for the infantry. Kennedy recalled the soldiers had to take their rifles with them wherever they went because of the fear of invasion. "You would get 48 hours off, but the island is so small there's nowhere to go. You went to only one place and that was Valletta. You might find some girls, I suppose, and if you had any cash you could get a beer and a meal. But most British soldiers had no money."[24] Keen also recalled there was little to do during off hours. "We didn't have cinema or anything at all."[25]

Conditions were so deplorable that when the army asked for volunteers to join a British commando force that was routinely taking part in extraordinarily dangerous missions behind enemy lines, scores of soldiers put their hands up. "Everybody and his uncle volunteered just to get off of Malta," Kennedy said.[26]

Most survivors believe that the ordeal aged them prematurely. "We were almost all young kids when we arrived," Kennedy noted. "We really didn't understand what we were getting into. But once you were there you started to grow old really quickly." Still, he believes the morale of the troops held up remarkably well. In fact, a fatalistic mood set in that helped many of them cope with the privations. Kennedy recalled, "The attitude was, 'We're not getting out of this damn place.' We were so close to Sicily. The nearest British flag was 900 miles away. We thought there was no way of getting out without getting killed or becoming a prisoner. But there was no damn way that we were going to go down without causing havoc for someone."[27]

Amazingly, as September came to a close, the will of the defenders to resist against all odds was stiffening. It was just as well, too, because in October the Germans and Italians were planning to launch a final, massive assault on the island. This time, they were determined to win the battle or give up the siege.

CHAPTER 10

THE OCTOBER BLITZ

When Adrian Warburton returned from a reconnaissance mission over Sicily on October 9, 1942, the usually unflappable pilot was visibly shaken. Ground crews who asked what was wrong were in for a start. " The whole bloody Luftwaffe is assembling over there," he said, pointing northward.[1] Warburton's film backed up his statement. His pictures showed that airfields all over Sicily were lined wingtip to wingtip with Messerschmitts, Junkers, Macchis and Cants. Intelligence officers counted no less than 570 German and Italian planes — and those were just the ones that were visible in Warburton's photographs. Doubtlessly there were scores of others inside hangars or hidden under the branches of nearby trees. There was no longer any doubt about it — Malta was about to undergo another shattering ordeal by fire.

The next day, the defenders anxiously scanned radar screens, expecting to pick up waves of bombers. Nothing appeared. The only excitement took place when a pair of Messerschmitts sneaked in at rooftop level, looking for something to strafe. They came in so low that they were not spotted by radar operators, and no Spitfires were scrambled to greet them. It looked as if they would be able to make a lightning strike and then head for home. Unfortunately for them, however, George Beurling was up that morning testing a new Spitfire. His eyes caught a glint of sunlight off one of the Messerschmitt's wingtips, and he was after the pair of them at once. The first kill was witnessed by Maltese schoolboy George Scerri. "Beurling zigzagged down so low I thought he was going to crash. He nearly touched the ground then zoomed up under the German plane and fired into its belly, cutting it almost in half. I can't forget that. Whenever he made a kill he'd always come down low and waggle his wings to tell us."[2]

On this occasion the victory waggle had to wait a few minutes, because Beurling was in pursuit of the second Messerschmitt, which was racing back to Sicily. He caught up to the panic-stricken German a few kilometres out to sea, scoring a direct hit on the poor fellow's fuel tanks. The 109, like so many of Beurling's earlier victims, went down in flames with a dead pilot at the controls.

For the defenders there would be little time to celebrate Beurling's two victories. The next day the Luftwaffe and Regia Aeronautica opened the October Blitz.

The first Spitfire pilots off the ground that October 11 had little real idea what was coming. "As we climbed above the haze over Malta, the upper sky became more beautiful than any I had ever seen in the Mediterranean," pilot Rod Smith wrote later. "It was bright blue and crystal clear, with a magnificent bank of cumulus cloud far off to the north-east." Moments later, that idyllic scene was shattered by a sight that Smith still recalled with astonishing clarity 55 years later. "We suddenly caught sight of the oncoming raid, ahead of us and slightly to our right. It was the most awesome sight of our lives, in large part because the background cumulus presented the whole array to a single glance."[3] He counted nine Ju-88s being escorted by at least 60 fighters. The German aircraft appeared to be stacked on top of one another, almost as if they were perched on separate levels of a giant staircase. There were so many planes they stretched from 6,000 metres all the way up to 9,750 metres, with the machines at the higher altitudes giving off long, white vapour trails.

Smith went for the bombers, hoping he could pick one of them off before the Messerschmitts could intervene. Closing in on his target, he took dead aim at the port engine, setting it on fire with a burst from 230 metres' range. The gunners of several Ju-88s were shooting back at him for all they were worth, but Smith ignored them, figuring their low-calibre machine guns were not much of a threat. He broke off the attack only when tracers from a group of cannon-armed ME-109s flashed past his Spitfire, letting him know the escorts were on his tail. He dove sharply to the right, turning as he went, hoping he could shake off his pursuers. Then, suddenly, he had a change of heart. Climbing back up, he went for the crippled Ju-88 again. The move caught the Messerschmitts by surprise, giving Smith perhaps three seconds in which to finish off his wounded prey. This time he aimed

German Junkers-88 burning on Malta. Courtesy of Eric Crist

for the starboard engine, setting it ablaze with a quick burst. Seconds later, the Messerschmitts were after him again. As he dived away, he caught a brief glimpse of the bomber as it blew in half. He had taken an extraordinary risk, but Rod Smith had just scored the first kill of the October Blitz.

More victories followed before the day was out. During an evening raid, Kesselring foolishly sent out 30 bombers without any escort, figuring they could escape detection in the fading light. Instead, they ran headlong into a swarm of Spitfires led by ace Wally McLeod. McLeod shot two of them down, and other Allied pilots destroyed three more. A sixth Ju-88 was so badly damaged that it crashed on landing in Sicily. The stunned pilot was pulled from the wreck, but all three of his crewmen were dead. When darkness fell, the fifth raid of the day was greeted by RAF night fighters who shot down two more Axis bombers. Without question, the first day of the new offensive had been an overwhelming success for the defenders.

Day two was one of non-stop fighting as the Germans and Italians launched five daylight raids. So many planes were knocked out of the sky that as British Spitfire pilot Mike Stephens floated to earth beneath his parachute he saw four aircraft going down in flames at the same time. In all, 27 enemy planes were destroyed for the loss of only seven Spitfires. Wally McLeod got one of the Germans, giving him three kills in 48 hours.

Luftwaffe ace Heinz Baer shot down two Spitfires on October 13, but his performance was overshadowed by George Beurling. The Canadian got loose among eight Ju-88s that morning, knocking pieces off one of them before an ME-109 came to the rescue. Turning quickly to meet this new threat, Beurling shot the Messerschmitt down with a two-second salvo. Another 109 went for him, and he shot it down with a four-second burst. Fortunately, the German pilot was able to bail out before his machine slammed into the Mediterranean. Glancing quickly around, Beurling witnessed a sight that filled him with rage. The Ju-88s were dropping their bombs on a village near Luqa airfield. Two civilians were killed, but Beurling exacted almost instant retribution, chasing the enemy formation 13 kilometres out to sea before overhauling a Junkers flown by Anton Wilfer. Two bursts from 275 metres' range sent the bomber down in flames, killing Wilfer and his crew. In 10 minutes Beurling had destroyed three planes and damaged a fourth.

Newspapers in the Allied nations were filled with stories about Beurling's exploits. One of them reported: "Malta's defenders shot down 17 Axis planes yesterday when Pilot Officer George Beurling of Verdun, Quebec, one of the Empire's ace fighters, got three in a single battle to boost his total to 26 since he got into action. The RAF Middle East news service described Beurling's triple success yesterday as 'a performance which is becoming quite a habit with him.' It added that 'his sense of positioning is instinctive, and he must be one of the best marksmen in the RAF.'"[4]

The next day, George Beurling flew his last combat mission over Malta. Leading three Spitfires, he took on eight Ju-88s and 50 fighters. Recognizing that the bombers were the main threat to the island, he herded one out of formation and sent it down in flames. But a dying rear-gunner scored 30 hits on the Canadian's plane before the Ju-88 slammed into the Mediterranean. One of the bullets nicked Beurling's finger, and another struck him in the forearm. At that moment, two ME-109s dove on his tail, intent on finishing him off. Ignoring them, with the blood flowing from two wounds, Beurling pressed home an attack on an ME-109 in front of him, destroying it with a burst from 410 metres' range. Only then did he turn on the adversaries behind

HELL ISLAND

him. It was almost too late. One of them peppered his tail and wings with cannon shells. The other German shattered the canopy of his cockpit with a well-placed burst. Beurling plunged at 975 kilometres per hour, managing to lose the two Germans on his tail.

At this point he should have hightailed it for home to have his wounds treated and his machine repaired. But Beurling could not resist taking another crack at an ME-109 he saw sailing along below him. Within seconds the Nazi fighter was in the sea. But Beurling's move caught the attention of more enemy pilots. Several ME-109s dropped on him with guns flashing. A cannon shell sliced off the bottom of his right foot, and another grazed his left elbow. The controls were shot from his hands. The Spitfire engine suddenly burst into flames. Beurling, wounded four times and with flames licking at his face, slid back his damaged canopy and attempted to bail out. But he was pinned back into his seat by a rush of air as the burning fighter plane spun down out of control. Strangely, he found himself completely calm. He had sent dozens of men to a similar fate and now, he thought, it was finally happening to him. "This is it. This is what it's like when you know you're going to die," he thought to himself.[5] Then the will to live took over, and Beurling pulled himself out of his stupor. Climbing out of the cockpit, he stood on the starboard wing, trying to work up the courage to jump. The sea was only 300 metres below. Another second or two and it would be too late. At the last moment he closed his eyes and dove over the side. With only 150 metres to go, his parachute opened with a painful jerk. Beurling just had time to kick off his heavy boots before he hit the water. Despite his wounds, he managed to inflate his rubber raft and climb aboard. When a rescue launch reached him, the floor of the dinghy was covered in blood.

L.G. Head, one of the men who pulled him out of the sea, never forgot the scene. "When we picked him out of the water, he was most concerned for a few moments because he was unable to locate a small Bible that he had been given by his mother. He told us that he would not fly without his Bible, and was most relieved when we found it and handed it to him. Before we got ashore, he was most adamant that he was going to fly and fight within a few hours, but it was most obvious to us that the wound in his heel in particular would put him out for some time."[6]

154

Beurling was indeed seriously injured. But you would never know it by reading the jubilant press accounts of this action. One Toronto newspaper gleefully reported:

> Axis air losses over Malta increased to 94 since Sunday with the destruction of 13 more enemy aircraft over the rocky island fortress as the Germans and Italians strove mightily to reinforce and supply their stalled army in Egypt. Nine Axis planes went down in the morning's fighting, three of them before the guns of Pilot Officer George Beurling of Verdun, Quebec, the Canadian ace who knocked down Malta's 1,000th victim three days ago. Beurling now has accounted for 29 of the enemy. Beurling destroyed two Messerschmitt 109s and a Junkers-88 before being forced to bail out of his bullet-riddled fighter, the Air ministry News Service said. He is wet as he fell into the sea, it added, but he was picked up soon after and is little the worse for wear.[7]

In truth, Beurling was an emotional and physical wreck. Besides his wounds, he was clearly suffering from battle fatigue, exhaustion and malnutrition. He had destroyed six enemy planes in two days and eight since the month began, but he was no longer in any condition to fly combat missions. Instead, he was consigned to a hospital bed, where he would remain for the rest of his stay on the island. Malta's defenders had lost their brightest star.

Within 24 hours two other Allied aces, both Canadians, would be shot down. John McElroy, who would finish the siege with 10 victories, had an especially narrow escape when his Spitfire was hit and started going down when the engine ignited. He decided to bail out, but found the canopy hopelessly jammed. Smoke filled the cockpit, and it looked as if he might burn to death. Somehow, he managed to glide in for a forced landing; ground crews put out the fire, saving his life. Rod Smith, who would chalk up six kills over Malta, had an equally horrifying experience as he closed in on an ME-109. He was firing away at his intended victim when, for some unknown reason, he glanced at his left wing and noticed it contained a bullet hole. Assuming he had been hit earlier in the dogfight, he continued to fire at the German fighter ahead of him. Something made him look at his wing again, however, and he saw a second bullet hole, this one less than a metre from the first. Smith did not glance over his shoulder to see if there was an enemy plane behind him. Had he taken the time to do so, he would surely have been killed. Instead, he turned wildly to the left, climbing as he went. The lightning move caused several cannon shells to miss him, but several others slammed into his engine, setting it on fire. Looking back, he could clearly see a yellow-nosed German fighter directly behind him. It was so close he could see smoke coming from its guns. So close, in fact, that it just missed colliding with his plane as it passed under him.

The doomed Spitfire managed to hold together long enough for him to climb to 1,200 metres, at which point he bailed out. Fortunately, he was picked up a little later by a rescue launch. "I could never ask for greater luck than I had on that October morning when two bullets, timed and spaced by chance, gently warned me not to linger," he said later.[8]

With Beurling permanently out of action and Smith and McElroy recovering from the temporary shock of being shot down, others rose to the occasion. Wally McLeod was perhaps the most prominent, scoring his 12th victory on October 16 when he killed German ace Heinz Golinski. Moments before McLeod blasted his ME-109 out of the sky, Golinksi had shot down a Spitfire for his 47th victory. A full 46 of those kills had been claimed on the Russian Front. Days later, McLeod scored again, blasting an Italian Macchi to pieces to give him 13 victories.

It would be a mistake to think the fighting was totally one-sided, despite the exuberant claims of the newspapers. Nine Spitfires were shot down or crash-landed the day McLeod killed Golinski. Such losses were hard to bear, even given the fact that Malta now had more fighters than ever before.

Still, there is no denying the fact that the Luftwaffe and the Regia Aeronautica were taking a terrible drubbing. Bomber pilot Werner Baumbach captured the despair of the German fliers when he wrote in his diary:

> Dante's hell is a reality here. Roth's crew gone. Lieutenant Grigoleit shot down, little Quisdorf missing, Stoffregen down and mortally wounded, Metzenthin's and Lt. Harmel's Ju-88 shot down in

flames. Yesterday evening I had the jumbled-up crews
lined up before me once again. Briefing, target same
as yesterday. With everything we have. Same as yesterday. And early next morning, when we assemble
after the sortie, two, three or four crews will be missing once more. Have not returned from the sortie!
Who will be next? What cruel fate has already decided on the next batch? All of us have got together our
few belongings and tied them up as "casualty pack" by
the time the truck arrives to take us off to the airfield.
I often lie in my bed in a sort of paralysis, dripping
sweat and yet feeling frozen to the bone while gazing
at the blood-red oranges hanging in the leafy trees. It
is a worry, heart-rending worry, which shakes me to
the core and is growing to a horrible, nerve-racking
fever. Since we have been here I have stopped talking
to the men. I could not find anything to say which
would lessen the feeling of hopelessness.[9]

Italian pilot Ronaldo Scaroni said later:

We no longer thought in terms of winning the battle; at least I didn't. My only thoughts were about survival. Pilots were being shot down after seven or eight
trips to Malta. That was the life expectancy. I remember our squadron commander berating us, saying, "If
we don't win this thing we could lose the whole war."
To which I thought, "What does it matter to a dead
man who wins the war?" I no longer had any zest for
the whole dirty business. I just wanted to go home
and be with my girlfriend. I'm sure most of the others
felt the same way. Some of our bomber crews were jettisoning their loads way short of the target so they
could get the hell out of the danger zone as quickly as
possible. I know that for a fact, because I saw it
myself.[10]

Ordinary airmen were not the only ones feeling the heat. Adolf
Galland, the commander of all German fighter forces, was called on the
carpet by Luftwaffe chief Hermann Goering to explain why the blitz
was not achieving the desired results. "The Malta raids resembled more

and more the heartbreaking task of Sisyphus ... our losses increased from raid to raid," he wrote in his autobiography. "Nothing is more demoralizing for a soldier than to see no results from his actions, however great his effort. We had already experienced this over England. Actually, the Malta Blitz was a repeat performance on a smaller scale, with similar disappointments, similar losses, similar failure."[11]

Goering angrily blamed the fighter pilots, declaring they had not done enough to protect the bombers. Galland refused to accept any criticism, insisting his men had done their best. The only reason they were losing, he declared, was because "the English fought gallantly with their backs to the wall."[12]

Sadly, the carnage continued, because neither Goering nor General Kesselring was willing to throw in the towel. On October 17 they sent out another huge force of fighters and bombers. Once again there were brutal clashes. Ace pilot Heinz Baer shot down a Spitfire, but two of Germany's most experienced bomber pilots were killed. One of them, Heinrich Paepcke, died when his Ju-88 collided head on with a Spitfire flown by American Rip Jones. Jones and all four Germans were killed instantly. New Zealander Nigel Park shot down six enemy planes in two days, then died himself on October 25.

Both sides were reeling. The Axis airforces had lost 132 planes during October and, as November began, their fliers were on the verge of revolt. Pilot Werner Baumbach went so far as to write a scathingly bitter letter to the High Command, calling for a halt to the offensive. "In my opinion, daylight attacks on Malta in present circumstances cannot be carried out without extremely heavy losses, and it is even doubtful whether the aircraft actually reach the target," he wrote. "I am told at any rate the 'attempt' must be made, and that we must 'improvise' more. It is with such dangerous catchwords that we are directed from the safe distance of the office stool."[13] A young German fighter pilot shot down over Malta summed up the situation even more succinctly. As Hans Splitz was being led away from his burning Messerschmitt by British soldiers, he looked skyward, caught a glimpse of a torrent of anti-aircraft shells exploding overhead, muttered sadly, "This is hell island."[14]

By now the attention of the whole world was fixed on the siege, and the Allies were beginning to sense that victory was at hand. Late

in October, *Time* magazine reported: "This week Malta still stood, battered and bloody, with guns and planes ready for the next Axis raid.
No spot in the wide world has taken such sustained and savage bombing. To defend it, the British have paid dearly. But they still cling. If
the world wonders, the British have a twofold answer. Malta is worth
the price for strategic reasons. Sixty miles from Sicily, the island is a
constant menace to Axis supply routes in the Mediterranean."[15]

The enemy may have been close to the breaking point, but there
were still tragic losses to be endured on Malta. Teenager George Porter
lost his father and aunt during one of the last air raids. "It was right at
the end of the siege," he recalled in a 1997 interview. "I remember my
father telling me, 'It will soon be over.'"[16] Another heart-wrenching
loss occurred just before the end of October, when a transport plane
took off from Malta under the cover of darkness, loaded with British
civilians, wounded troops and tour-expired fighter pilots. As the plane
came in to land at Gibraltar in the midst of a blinding rainstorm, it
overshot the runway and plunged into the sea, breaking in half. Five
pilots, including aces John "Willie-the-Kid" Williams and Eddie
Glazebrook, perished, along with 10 civilians. George Beurling, whose
wounded heel was covered in heavy plaster, miraculously survived. He
had had a premonition of the crash and took up position near a rear
door as the plane came in to land. Incredibly, he was able to climb out
of the wreckage and swim to safety.

Finally, on November 7, General Kesselring admitted defeat. Daylight
raids were dramatically scaled back and several hundred warplanes on
Sicily were ordered back to the Russian Front. Just a week later, a convoy of four supply ships escorted by 21 destroyers and cruisers sailed
virtually unopposed from Alexandria to Grand Harbour, bringing with
them 35,000 tonnes of food and ammunition. Not long after that, four
more merchantmen made it in unmolested, delivering a staggering
55,000 tonnes of supplies. At the same time, two more batches of
Spitfires flew to Malta from carriers near Gibraltar, replacing virtually
all of the fighters that had been lost during the October Blitz. There
was no longer any doubt about it — the siege was all but over. And
Malta was getting ready to strike back.

For the fighter pilots, everything had changed. There was still the
occasional nuisance raid but, by and large, the Axis fliers were

Spitfire pilot Bob Taggart. Courtesy of Bob Taggart

nowhere to be seen. With fuel and ammunition no longer in short supply, the RAF decided to take the offensive. One of those taking part in the sweeps over Sicily at this time was Spitfire pilot Bob Taggart. "We sometimes carried two 250-pound bombs to attack factories at low level and airfields by dive-bombing," he recalled. "We also attacked railway locomotives and switch boxes with cannon and machine gun fire. I remember once when we bombed a factory, coming in right at deck level. We lobbed bombs right at it and then went over the top and away. That was pretty good. When we attacked locomotives we did it in pairs. We'd come in on the deck, below radar height, looking down the railway lines. The best way to get a locomotive was from head on. Our armour-piercing cannons made them steam up pretty good. That would wreck the locomotive ... they'd always stop in their tracks. Then we'd strafe the cars."[17]

Taggart says anti-aircraft fire was light, making it easy for the pilots to roam over Sicily at treetop level, almost at will. In fact, he once flew so low during a strafing run on a barn filled with ammunition that when the structure exploded, his Spitfire was coated in moss.

As gratifying as it was to shoot up enemy ground targets, what most of the Allied fighter pilots longed for were dogfights. But with so few Axis planes left on Sicily, the enemy pilots usually stayed on the ground during daylight hours. All that changed for Taggart one spring

Bob Taggart, right, with his wife and father, home on leave after a tour of duty as a Spitfire pilot on Malta. Courtesy of Bob Taggart

day in 1943 when he took off with three other Spitfires to try to draw the Luftwaffe out. "We'd been going over in squadron strength and nobody would come up and play, so our CO wanted to take four of us up," he said. "We were refused permission so the CO asked permission to do a practice flight with four planes." Once airborne, the Spitfire leader decided to do his "practice" flying off the coast of Sicily. In the next few minutes, the brash Allied pilots found out why their superiors were not allowing four-plane sweeps over enemy territory. "Six ME-109s came down at us out of the north, and another six were behind us. The CO turned gently into the ones behind us. My number two broke, so I had to go with him to protect him. The ones to the north got us. The CO said, 'Look out!' but before he could finish his transmission I felt a bang that knocked the oil cooler off the aircraft. I saw an ME-109 go past me, so I took a shot at it." Unfortunately, the recoil from Taggart's two cannons and four machine guns put his crippled Spitfire into a stall. Seconds later, he was spinning down out of control. Keeping cool, he pulled out of the spin and bailed out. An Allied rescue launch picked him up, but when he got back to Malta he discovered he had not been the only one hit. "The CO's plane was so badly shot up it had to be written off. His number two was shot down and bailed out ... My number two was never seen again. He was killed."[18] In other words, all four Spitfires had been lost. Clearly, flying from Malta was still anything but a piece of cake, even if the Allies did have the upper hand for a change.

Living conditions had not changed much, either. Although convoys were finally getting through on a regular basis, food was still carefully rationed because of fears that the situation might change at any moment. There had been lulls in the raids before, and there was no guarantee that action would not pick up again. "We were eating hard tack biscuits that had been canned in 1917," Taggart noted. "We had to shake them to get the weasels [maggots] off. They tasted like dried powder." During off hours, the pilots found there was still little to do. "We played a lot of bridge and listened to a lot of old 78 records," he said. They also enjoyed playing practical jokes on the priests who frequently walked past their apartment complex. "All the priests would go by in their big hats in groups. Some guys would take French safes, fill them with water and divebomb the priests. I'm not particularly proud of it now, but we thought it was humorous at the time. It was just kids' stuff."[19]

As important as the fighter sweeps over Sicily may have been, it was Malta's bomber crews who now took centre stage. Several squadrons of Wellingtons flew into Malta during November and December, dramatically bolstering its offensive capabilities. One of the newcomers was a modest young English sergeant-pilot with a jolly-looking face named Reg Thackeray, who would fly an astonishing 40 missions during his 57-day stay on Malta.

> I and my crew flew in to Luqa from a desert landing ground to the west of El Alamein on 26th November 1942. Our six-and-a-half hour flight took place overnight so that our landing was just before dawn. Eleven aircraft flew — we had overload fuel tanks in the bomb bays and each aircraft carried four groundcrew with kit and tools and some spares. I can't believe anybody bothered to calculate the weight, but the old "Wimpy" [Wellington] copes well with that sort of treatment and no aircraft were lost on the

flight. We only had a small amount of kit with us and lived very, very simply. On first arrival at dawn on 28th November we had been instructed to find an area of stone floor in the "Poor House," an old leper colony just outside the boundary of RAF Luqa. Here we put our kit and laid out our blankets. Of course, we had come straight from the desert where we were sleeping in tents on the sand and so were used to "hard-lying" but, at least, we could scoop out sand to the shape of our hips to make sleeping more comfortable and we could not do that with a stone floor.

Thackeray and his crew were immediately tossed into the breach, often flying two operations a night against targets in both North Africa and on Sicily.

We were thrown straight into the deep end. The very next night [after their arrival on the island] we had a trip to Bizerta, one of Rommel's supply ports — then we were switched to Trapani, a port on the west coast of Sicily — we made two visits here on the same night — the first trip took three hours and 50 minutes and the second trip was 10 minutes shorter! Three nights later we made two trips to bomb Luftwaffe airfields in the southeast corner of Sicily. The first trip took four hours and the second, from chocks away to chocks on, was exactly 90 minutes. This indicates how close Sicily and Malta are. Then we switched back to Bizerta and La Goulette, the seaport for Tunis. By the end of December we had also visited Palermo, the capital of Sicily, and Comiso airfield together with five more trips to Tunis and La Goulette. We even operated on Christmas Day but had to bring our bombs back because targets were obscured by cloud. Our last trip of 1942 was to Sfasx, and we returned to attack Palermo docks on New Year's Day 1943. A couple of trips to Sousse and three trips to Tripoli completed our stay on the island. The Eighth Army occupied Tripoli on 23rd January and we were back in

Egypt that same day! We were classified as a Mobile Heavy Bomber Squadron, and we were certainly moved around at a few hours notice.

The bomber crews were continually on call for operations and had to be prepared to fly at any moment.

Generally speaking there were two crews for each aircraft, so each crew went out every other night and the aircraft went out every night. The sequence was broken, of course, by unserviceability of the aircraft or the crew and by the weather. On average, losses were of the order of two and a half per cent, which made a full tour of 40 trips a statistical possibility. Statistics, of course, can prove anything, and there were crews lost on their first trip and some gong happy captains clocked up over 100 missions. I was a "lucky" skipper — never lost an aircraft — was never shot up by night fighters — had only superficial damage from flak over the target — and only lost power on an engine in a couple of cases. I did have to land back on Luqa main runway one night, immediately after take-off, with ineffective controls, and this must be classified as a "shaky do" in RAF slang.

Another close call came on one of his last missions.

I never had a complete engine failure on any of my 40 operations but came close to it on our last trip to Tripoli from Malta. The distance involved was only 200 miles but it was, of course, across open sea. We lost power on one engine going south and could see oil leaking from the top of the engine, but we were young, keen and foolish and getting near the end of our operational tour of 200 hours or 40 missions — in fact this was my 36th mission. So with the agreement of the crew we pressed on and reached enough height to complete our task, which was to disrupt Rommel's transport retreating through Tripoli towards the Tunisian ports and withdrawal to fight again in Sicily and Italy. On the way back the oil loss got worse but the aircraft was lighter so we were able to maintain height with the engine throttled back. This early Mark [type of Wellington] did not have fully feathering propellers so an engine failure usually resulted in a ditching. This we avoided and did a single engine landing as a precaution at Luqa after firing a red Very light [signal flare]. Next day the engine had to be changed for the top cylinder had lifted off the crankcase — the Gremlins were on our side that night for we could so easily have had an engine fire!

Besides the enemy and equipment malfunctions, the bomber pilots had to cope with other dangers. Momentarily abandoning the controls so the co-pilot could take charge of the plane was a hair-raising experience.

Owing to the effect of the sand in the air all radial engines had very high oil consumption and a co-pilot was carried to pump oil from a tank in the fuselage to keep the bearings cool," Thackeray explained. "Again because of the sand, the automatic pilot would not work and the flights could take nine hours! So the captain took off and landed and flew in the target area and shared the long haul to and from the target with the co-pilot. There were no dual controls so there was always a bit of a panic swapping seats.

Weather could also be hazardous.

Meteorological forecasts were poor. The only place west of Malta in Allied hands was Gibraltar and this was 1,000 miles away so things often changed dramatically by the time the weather reached us. Many nights we went out west to Tunis or north to Palermo or Trapani to find towering thunderheads and electric storms.

On the plus side, Thackeray had plenty of faith in his airplane.

I think most pilots will swear by the aircraft they flew regularly and all Wellington pilots certainly do. I know it is said that the geodetic construction with fabric covering was old fashioned but it was immensely strong and the fact that the wings could flex prevented failures in extreme manoeuvres. I have pulled the fabric off in a dive to get out of flak but I never worried about pulling a wing off.

As good as the Wellington was, however, it could not do anything to protect you when you were back on the ground.

I only experienced one major air raid on Luqa airfield. It was on 18th December 1942 — we had returned from a short trip to bomb Comiso in Sicily and 10 aircraft were lined up alongside the main runway at about 10:30 p.m. The aircraft had been refuelled and re-armed for a second sortie to Comiso and the aircrews were standing around eating sandwiches when the sirens went — almost before we could move the runway came under Ju-88 dive-bombing attack. Whilst no-one was killed on the airfield, seven aircraft were destroyed and the remaining three were damaged. Our second sortie was, of course, cancelled and we were never again to attempt two sorties in one night.

Like so many others who were there, Thackeray still vividly recalls the meagre diet that the lower ranks were expected to survive on.

Food rations were pretty grim. Part of the squadron flew to Malta at the beginning of November, and we followed three weeks later. In that short period the change in our friends' appearance was most noticeable — a heavy operational load, poor food, poor living conditions, etc., had all combined to produce a haggard appearance. We took our meals in the Transit Mess [for aircrews passing through from Gibraltar to Cairo and vice versa]. "We" refers to the NCOs — our officers were accommodated in the Hotel Imperial in Sliema and ate in the Officers' Mess on Luqa. We were fortunate, occasionally, to get meals there after a trip, and these I might say were good and "normal." The sergeants lived on soya sausages, corned beef and boiled artichokes. As a special treat we had half a tin of American stewed steak for lunch on Christmas Day with a promise of the other half on New Year's Day. This promise was kept! We were allocated two bottles

Wellington bomber crew at Luqa airfield in Malta. From left: Reg Thackeray, Eric Kerbey, Arthur Harvey, and Bert Ward. Courtesy of Reg Thackeray

> of weak "local" beer from a German-owned brewery outside Valletta. It was said the Luftwaffe used the brewery as an aiming point and as a consequence it was never hit! The officers had a regular run back to Egypt in aircraft going for major overhaul and returned with fresh aircraft loaded with whiskey, fruit and fresh meat. There was no resentment — for a time I had an officer navigator [on his crew] and used to get into his hotel through the back door![20]

Wellington pilot Peter Hoad recalls one officer going to extraordinary lengths to make sure a shipment of booze got through to the island safely. Hoad was getting ready to take off from Gibraltar when an officer asked him to bring along several crates of alcohol for the mess at Luqa. "He brought in a whole bunch of booze and parked it beside the aircraft with an armed guard present until we got off with our valuable cargo." As they approached Malta, they saw that an air raid was underway. "The squadron leader said to me, 'Do you want me to land it?' I said, 'Sure.' He put it down almost like he was kissing the ground. You hardly felt the wheels touch down. I said, 'Good landing,' and he replied, 'I couldn't have you breaking some of those bottles of booze in the back of the aircraft!'"[21]

Thackeray also said there was plenty of beer, both Canadian Black Horse and American Schlitz, to drink. That there should have been so much alcohol available when everything else was in short supply is surprising. As Thackeray noted, "All the time I was there food rationing was extremely strict. Supplies of aviation spirit, bombs and ammunition were brought in by submarine, and we were under strict instructions to waste nothing. We bombed visually and if the navigator, who was also the bomb aimer, could not see the target for cloud, we would wait for clearance or proceed to an alternate target. If this was 'out of sight' then we brought our bombs back to base. There was no question of jettisoning our load unless it would have created problems on landing. We brought our bombs back on two occasions in December 1942 because of ten-tenths cloud cover on main and subsidiary targets."[22] Possibly the authorities made liquor and beer a higher priority than food, fuel, bombs and bullets because they felt alcohol was essential for the maintenance of morale.

In any event, Thackeray recalled, by this stage of the war there seems to have been a little more entertainment available on Malta than had been the case just a few months earlier.

Surprisingly, there were places in Valletta where a meal could be obtained — usually sardines on toast — and these were in the brothels down Strait Street (otherwise known as "The Gut"). I was 21 at the time but was quite satisfied just to have the food. Some cinemas were open, but there was an outbreak of meningitis towards the end of our stay and the cinemas were put "Out of Bounds/Off Limits" to servicemen. There were many clubs operated by the services which ran dances and entertainments at the weekends —and the one I liked best was called the ERAs Club in Floriana, just outside the walls of Valletta. This was a "Navy" club but we were made most welcome as aircrew. In fact, since we were not part of the defensive forces and could be seen to be dishing out some sort of retribution to the Axis forces, we were all very popular. There were female partners at these

dances other than nurses from the hospitals but all
the Maltese girls were most closely chaperoned and
one couldn't follow the old pre-war English habit of
walking the girl home for a kiss on the doorstep![23]

Wilfred Baynton, a wireless operator/air gunner serving with a
Malta-based Wellington squadron, found he had precious little time
to do anything except fly and sleep. "We didn't have many off hours,"
he recalled. "We were on duty seven days a week. Our big excitement
was to rent a boat to ride to Valletta and wander around the streets.
On a typical day you got up about noon, did an air test and had a
meal. If you were flying that night you were airborne at 7 p.m. and
you could be up for 12 hours. If you were standing by, you lay around
all night. You might scramble at midnight or 2 a.m. if an enemy ship
was spotted. We did aerial reconnaissance one night and the next
night we were in a torpedo-dropping role."

If an Axis vessel was sighted during a reconnaissance mission,
Baynton's crew would summon attack aircraft, then circle the area,
waiting for help to arrive. Once reinforcements showed up, they
would drop flares, lighting the night up as bright as day over the
enemy ship.

Once, Baynton and his crewmates spotted an Axis destroyer and
swooped down for a closer look. "Being rather zealous, we flew right
over it to get an accurate course and speed, and of course it opened
fire on us and we were hit. The wheels and flaps came down and one
of the crew was wounded. We had to land off the runway without the
undercarriage being functional. I remember that rather vividly. I happened to be working the radio and sent out the SOS when we were
hit."

On another occasion he had a harrowingly close encounter with
an enemy night fighter. "We used to see fighters [from time to time].
They flashed an orange light. You'd see it blinking off to the rear quarter. One night we were heading to Palermo. We got up to 2,000 feet
and this guy stuck to us like glue. We slowed the aircraft down and
dropped the wheels and flaps and did a 360 degree orbit in an attempt
to shake him off, and we did. But it was kind of thought-provoking."

Although Baynton and his mates were obviously talented, he is
convinced luck played a major role in their survival. "The casualty
rate was horrendous. It was just luck [if you finished your tour]. Lots of

brave and highly skilled crews didn't make it. If a flak burst was another 20 feet to port or starboard, you might not make it. I remember vividly and will never forget a good crew landing on one engine. They were unable to stop the aircraft, and it went off the runway and landed in a quarry. Only one guy got out. The rest all burned. We went to the funeral and they were all in one box. Those guys were all good friends of mine."

It was not long before Baynton found himself rapidly losing energy. "It was pretty tiring, and it was a pretty slim diet. The food was grim. We were rationed two slices of bread a day. We ate a lot of goat meat, but not in large quantities. Cauliflower was pretty popular. You got pretty sick of eating the same stuff all the time. During the short time I was there I lost so much weight I could get two fingers inside my shirt collar. We were hungry and tired all the time. You got one egg, one chocolate bar and 40 cigarettes a week. And there was no social life at all."

Despite the privations, Baynton recalls there were high spirits among the squadron. "Morale was high. Things were starting to change. We'd stopped being turned back everywhere. We were hitting back."[24]

Indeed they were. One night, wireless operator/air gunner Alex Stittle found an enemy convoy below and summoned Allied destroyers. "When our ships got within 12,000 yards we dropped flares on the enemy," he recalled. "They fired at us, their tracers gave away their position, and our destroyers sank them." Their mission had been accomplished, but the Wellington crew did not get away scot-free. "They hit our tail plane, and our pilot put us into a dive to get out of the flak. He had to put his feet on the dash and pull for all he was worth in order to get out of that dive."

As their successes mounted, the Wellington crews became increasingly bold. Stittle recalls his plane making two torpedo attacks on Axis ships from a scant 20 metres above the waves. At that height, if the pilot dipped a wingtip even slightly they would go straight into the drink. But as far as Stittle was concerned, it was the enemy night fighters that they had to be most worried about. "I had the fright of my life one night because of a fighter. I was operating the radar for about an hour when it was decided that another wireless operator

Wellington bomber wireless operator/air gunner Wilfred Baynton. Courtesy of Wilfred Baynton

would take over, and I was sent to the tail turret. I just got there when I looked down and there was a Junkers-88 right under us, 50 feet down. I could see right into it. I hollered to the pilot to turn, and I didn't use very flowery language. We got away with it. I said later, 'I could have shot him down.' My pilot said, 'No, you don't! We're not up there to dogfight.' He was right. The German night fighters often operated in pairs. Even if you got one, you'd give your position away and the other guy would get you. As soon as you fired they'd see the flash of your guns."

Stittle also came close to dying at the hands of enemy anti-aircraft gunners. "We went to Naples and had engine trouble," he recalls. "On the way home we were down to 1,000 feet, flying down the Straits of Messina between Sicily and Italy. The straits are lined with anti-aircraft guns and searchlights, including guns on barges out in the middle of it. They plastered us with everything they had, but they never hit us at all. We were lucky because our squadron had quite a high casualty rate. During one week we lost half of our men."[25]

Virtually every Wellington crewman who survived his stint on Malta can recall several narrow escapes. Kenneth Boyle, who joined the RCAF as a 19-year-old, remembers his plane being hit both times that it launched torpedo attacks. "Once, our navigator was knocked over. We took his jacket off and wrapped him in bandages. He had bits of shrapnel in him, but he was back in the mess the next day. The doctors took some of it out and told him the rest would eventually come out on its own."

Attacks on enemy ships were always dramatic. "We would have to go right over the ship at low level. After you dropped your torpedo you couldn't bank or you'd leave your belly wide open. So you came right at it. Our front gunner would be machine gunning the ship and then, as we flew over it, the rear gunner would take over. The whole thing would last 15 seconds at the most but it was scary. You were scared poopless and glad to be back, but it was the most exhilarating time of my life."

Boyle's plane was chased on more than one occasion by fighters, but his pilot shook them off by diving within 8 metres of the water. "At that height the fighters couldn't get under you," he says matter-of-factly. Most missions, he added, were flown a scant 150 metres (500 feet) above the water. "We tried to stay under radar and we were so low that we would never take our parachutes. You can't jump at 500 feet because your chute won't have time to open."

Then there was the problem of finding your way home in the dark, often under great stress. Malta may have been easy to spot in daylight, but it was easy to miss at night. "Once we got lost and decided the only thing we could do was head for North Africa. We force-landed on the beach."

Amid all this horror there were comical moments. "Once we bombed Palermo and a town on the southwest coast of Sicily called Marsala. It was a marshalling yard. After our army took over Sicily an air strip was built nearby and we were sent there to pick up any liquor we could get. We found we were not too popular with the army because the only thing we'd hit was the winery!"

Another humorous incident provided the defenders with the best evidence yet that the enemy was losing his will to continue the fight. "Once, a Mosquito crew was forced to land on an Italian aerodrome," Boyle said. "They were invited into the mess by the commanding officer and treated like royalty. Their aircraft was repaired and five days later the Italians let them fly back to Malta! We all thought they had been lost. We were glad to see them."[26]

By the spring of 1943 it was clear not only that the siege of Malta was over, but that the island's fliers and sailors were strangling the Afrika Korps to death. Sensing victory, British Field Marshal Bernard Montgomery launched a massive offensive along a 65-kilometre front. Desperately short of supplies, Rommel fell back, only to be greeted by a new threat coming at him from the rear. British and American troops had stormed ashore at Algeria and Morocco in late 1942, and now they were closing in on the hard-pressed Axis forces from the west. With nowhere to turn, the Germans and Italians made a mad dash for the northern tip of Tunisia, where they waited in vain for the Axis ships that would take them to Sicily. Once it became clear that Malta's forces were making it impossible for any sort of sea rescue to take place, the once-invincible Afrika Korps had only one option left — humiliating surrender.

So it was that on May 12, 1943, some 267,000 German and Italian soldiers were rounded up and herded into prisoner of war camps. The North African campaign, which had cost the Axis powers a staggering 750,000 troops in all, was finally at an end. The Nazi-Fascist threat to Egypt, the Suez Canal and the oil fields of the Middle East was over. More than that, the way was now clear for an Allied invasion of southern Europe. In a very real sense, the tide of the Second World War had turned. After years of having everything their own way, Hitler and Mussolini had suffered a crushing defeat.

Shortly afterwards a Dakota transport plane flew to Malta to bring Lord Gort out. He had been on the island only a few months, but already the hero of Dunkirk was exhausted and ill. Navigator Doug Appleton was on board the rescue plane. "We were told he was a tyrant, that we were not to speak to him or even look at him unless he looked at us," he told the author. "It turned out to be the complete opposite. It was like taking home your long lost uncle. He was very chatty. He even spent some time in the cockpit talking with us. I think he was very relieved to be getting out of there. We flew him to Cairo."

Appleton flew half a dozen relief missions to Malta around this time, bringing in essential goods that were still in short supply. Even at this late date he could see that the defenders were in a bad way physically. "We used to fly in around midnight and leave around 2 a.m. We might have time for a cup of lukewarm tea in the mess, but that was it. We didn't see much of the place but we knew the food was very, very scarce. I met two former crew members once in the middle of the night and they looked like ghosts. I hardly recognized them."

Although the Germans and Italians were no longer much of a threat on these missions, night flights could still be extremely dangerous. "On one trip we ran into a bad storm, the ice tore our antenna off and we were forced down to 200 feet. We missed the island and were flying down the centre of the Mediterranean. We were debating flying to Sicily to land on the beaches there, when Malta told us to turn onto a course that was very dangerous, towards North Africa. They had us zigzagging all over the sky but we made it to Malta."27

Within months of their capture of the Afrika Korps, Allied leaders turned their attention to Sicily. The island was invaded in July 1943 and capitulated in just 38 days. During that time another 163,000 Axis soldiers were killed, wounded or captured. For the people of Malta, the most satisfying part of the Sicilian campaign came right at the end, when the Italian navy sailed into Grand Harbour under the white flag of surrender. In all, 23 warships were captured, including five battleships, seven cruisers and almost a dozen destroyers. As a direct result, several important British and American vessels were no longer needed in the Mediterranean, freeing them up for duty in the Pacific Ocean against the still-powerful Japanese fleet.

After that, British, Canadian and American troops invaded the Italian mainland, tying down tens of thousands of German soldiers who were desperately needed on the Russian Front. When Allied soldiers attacked the ports of Nettuno and Anzio near Rome in the winter of 1944, they were met by no fewer than 98,000 crack German troops. In the end the German effort was not enough. Rome fell, and the Allies continued their relentless march towards victory.

Many months of hard fighting lay ahead but, thanks in no small measure to the brave defenders of Malta, the outcome of the war was no longer in doubt.

EPILOGUE

Malta held out when the Mediterranean was so dangerous that supplies for the British Eighth Army were being carried around the Cape of Good Hope. One would think it might have been taken by paratroopers and glider troopers, as Crete was. The attempt was not made. The island remained unconquered, a light and a symbol. If we want to find the spot where the tide began to turn, Malta is as good a spot as any.

If the British had been capable of surrender, they would have surrendered there. If they had surrendered there Mussolini might still be in Rome and Hitler still be free to wash his red hands in the waters of the English Channel. The United States might be fighting a defensive war. But the flame did not go out. It spread.

So wrote the *New York Times* in an editorial published shortly after Germany surrendered in May 1945. And the *Times* was right. Malta's brave defenders *had* played a key role in saving the free world. Few historians would dispute that even now. The real question that needs to be answered is, *How* did they do it? What was in their character that allowed them to overcome famine, disease, fear and exhaustion to vanquish a swaggeringly confident, well-rested and well-fed enemy who outnumbered them as much as 10 to one? And more to the point, what lessons can we learn by studying their heroism today?

I wrote this, my fourth war book, with some trepidation. I am not anxious to be seen as a "war buff." We all know the type — the fully grown adult who enjoys running around in the woods on weekends with an air pistol, firing red paintballs at fellow enthusiasts. Or the re-enactment zealots who dress up in colourful 19th-century costumes and pine after the days when thousands of young boys routinely slaughtered one another on foreign battlefields. The serious student of warfare knows that true stories of combat can be painful to read or write about. The only thing that makes the tales of brutality and inhumanity bearable at all are recollections of courage and self-sacrifice that so often accompany them.

In the end, I decided to write about the siege of Malta because I felt it tells us a great deal about the true nature of heroism and where it comes from. Like it or not, we need heroes. They are important role models for the young and an inspiration to those of all ages. Unfortunately, it seems to me, our modern world produces precious few genuine heroes, military or otherwise. The brave young man who sailed forth in his propeller plane has been overtaken by a faceless figure in a concrete bunker, poised to press a button that will send a computer-guided missile halfway across the globe. On the civilian front, great inventors like Thomas Edison, who toiled for countless hours in cramped, dingy laboratories, have been replaced by teams of anonymous scientists working in posh glass towers for giant corporations. Bereft of true heroes, we have turned to celebrities instead. It's sad, really, because while the celebrity may be famous, there is often little that is particularly heroic about him or her. Perhaps even more serious is the fact that the cult of celebrity has diminished the worth of the so-called ordinary person. Worse than that, it challenges the democratic notion that everyone is created equal. While the 1940s generation admired regular folks who stood up to the Nazis and won, today's society has been reduced to worshipping overpaid professional athletes, musicians and actors.

It is important that we recapture our appreciation for the courage and worth of ordinary people, because they are the backbone of every successful society. One of the main reasons the Allies won the Battle of Malta — and the war, for that matter — was that the democracies placed a high value on the worth of the individual person, however low his or her station in life. You can see this clearly in the propaganda films of the era. Nazi newsreels showcased thousands of firm-jawed, goose-stepping soldiers marching with machine-like precision. Shot from the waist up, they look for all the world like cement-headed automatons. Allied films, on the other hand, tended to praise people like "Rosie the Riveter," the fictional female war factory worker, or G.I. Joe, the unshaven but heroic *individual* soldier.

On the surface, there was nothing very exceptional about the men and women who saved Malta. Few of them were community leaders before the war, and few became so after the fighting ended. So what was it about them that allowed them to triumph against all odds?

Fighter pilot Eric Crist believes fear helped the defenders rise to the occasion. "Anybody who says he wasn't afraid has a bad memory, but being frightened isn't bad if you don't let it overwhelm you," he said. "It gets your adrenalin up, it gets you going. It can be a useful tool. It sharpens your senses, the excitement, call it what you will." Anger, too, motivated people to stick it out, no matter how tense the situation became. "At first you're frightened," civilian George Porter recalled. "Then you get mad." George Scerri, who was just a school-boy at the time, also believes the more enraged people became, the more grimly determined they were to win. "I remember my father had a shotgun and he said, 'I'm going to kill at least one of them if they invade. After that I don't care what happens. We will fight to the end.' We never thought for one minute about surrendering."

Friendship and an intense feeling of loyalty for comrades were other crucial factors. "Morale was always good on our squadron," Crist noted. "Inevitably we had more pilots than planes, so we had one day on and one day off. When it came your turn to go up, you didn't want to be bypassed. There was real *esprit de corps* in the fighter squadrons. We were a band of brothers. That sounds like a cliché, but you really did develop a great feeling among the pilots. You didn't want to let the other guys down." Belief in their cause was also important. "It was a combination of youth and the fact that we felt our case was just. Everybody always thinks they're on the right side of the angels."

Perhaps most crucial of all was the fact that the defenders of Malta were allowed to be rugged individuals. There was a refreshing lack of regimentation in both the fighter and bomber squadrons. "With the RAF, basically all they wanted you to do was fly every other night," bomber crewman Kenneth Boyle recalled. "The rest of the time you did exactly what you wanted to do." That meant wearing casual cloth-ing, growing your hair a little longer than regulations permitted, and generally feeling more relaxed during off hours than was the case in other theatres of war. In other words, Malta's defenders won because they were less "military" in their outlook than their enemy. Or as Bob Middlemiss noted, the leadership was good because there was not too much of it. Men like George Beurling and Adrian Warburton thrived in such an atmosphere, running up tremendous records in a short time. Once they left Malta, they ran headlong into old-school regimentation, and their effectiveness suffered noticeably. Beurling had such difficulty coping with life on a fighter squadron in England that he was sent back to Canada by unimaginative airforce officials who could not wait to get rid of him. Warburton, too, was never the same pilot after he left the Mediterranean.

Strangely enough, the defenders were also helped by the fact that, prior to ariving in Italy, the attackers had had it too easy. Many of the German and Italian fliers faced very little adversity before they arrived on Sicily. This was especially true for Luftwaffe units that had been making mincemeat out of the Soviet Union's airforce. The Germans were so accustomed to beating up on poorly trained Russian pilots flying obsolete aircraft that they were not prepared for death struggles with determined British Commonwealth aviators equipped with Spitfires. As a result, an ace like Heinz Golinski could shoot down 46 Red Air Force planes, but bag only one Malta Spitfire before being killed himself. The famous Heinz Baer scored only four victories over Malta, after arriving on Sicily with an incredible 113 kills to his credit. In all, 10 Axis aces were shot down over Malta during the height of the siege in 1942.

All of this is not to say the German and Italian airmen were not good. "By and large the Germans were excellent," Canadian fighter pilot Johnny Sherlock says. "They had many more flying hours than we did. There were some good Italian pilots, too. They had done a lot of flying before the war." Eric Crist agrees, although he does not think the Italians had their hearts in the campaign. The Italians also suffered from a lack of good equipment. It is almost impossible for aviators to maintain high morale if they do not have faith in their aircraft. And both the Italians and the Germans were hampered by poor leadership. By the end of April 1942, they had all but won the air battle, which should have paved the way for an invasion. But misled by the overly optimistic reports of General Kesselring, Hitler decided that an amphibious assault was not necessary. By the time he realized his mistake, it was too late.

Looking back across the years, survivors of the siege are almost all of the opinion that the sacrifices were worthwhile. "I lost a lot of friends there," Johnny Sherlock says. "We arrived as eager young kids and we left pretty hard-nosed and calloused. But if we had lost Malta it would have been all over in the Western Desert. Rommel would have gone to Egypt."

Eric Crist agrees, with reservations. "It was worthwhile, but in retrospect war doesn't seem to answer too many questions. We should make sure we never have to come to that. Still, it was an exciting time. I wouldn't have missed it for the world, and I wouldn't do it again for the world."

In the final analysis, the defenders of Malta triumphed because they possessed simple but important virtues such as courage, honour, loyalty and selflessness in abundance. Their less materialistic society was far more successful at nurturing such noble traits than ours is today. The younger generation would be wise to try to recapture some of those virtues because, like it or not, the time will surely come when they will be needed again.

Aircraft Glossary
and Ace Lists

Allied Aircraft

BEAUFORT — This was a twin-engine torpedo bomber capable of carrying a 1,600-pound torpedo. It was defended by four machine guns but was a slow, cumbersome machine that stood little chance against any Axis fighter of the day.

BRISTOL BEAUFIGHTER — This twin-engine two-seater was a versatile plane that was used to attack Axis shipping by day and enemy bombers by night. It had a top speed of more than 510 kilometres per hour. Armed with four cannons and six machine guns, it packed a powerful punch. Malta's leading night fighter pilot, Moose Fumerton, shot down nine enemy planes with a Beaufighter. It had a ceiling of more than 8,500 metres and a range in excess of 2,400 kilometres which gave it the ability to fly all over the Mediterranean.

GLOSTER GLADIATOR — This biplane fighter was obsolete the day it was introduced by the Royal Air Force in the winter of 1937. A full 30 squadrons were equipped with Gladiators before the British realized their mistake and began rushing faster, more modern Hurricane and Spitfire monoplanes into production. When war came in 1939, the few Gladiators still on active service were shunted off to places such as Norway and Malta, where little fighting was expected. In fact, when Italy declared war on England in June, 1940, Malta's only fighter defence consisted of nine Gladiators. They were painfully slow machines with fixed undercarriages, but on the plus side they were highly manoeuvrable. Armed with four machine guns, they proved to be a serious threat to the unescorted Italian bombers that first appeared over the island. After a few weeks of fighting, only three of the Gladiators were left. The deeply religious Maltese civilians dubbed them Faith, Hope and Charity, and the names stuck. In all, Gladiators accounted for nine enemy planes over Malta before they were replaced by the more modern Hurricane fighters.

HAWKER HURRICANE — This rugged, eight-gun fighter could reach speeds of about 545 kilometres per hour and could turn tightly. In the hands of a good pilot it could be a dangerous opponent. Hurricanes downed about 250 Axis planes over Malta for the loss of only about 130 of their own number in aerial combat. The Hurricane was more than a match for the lumbering Italian Cants or the bomb-laden German Stukas and Junkers-88s that it so often encountered. Former Hurricane pilot Dennis Parker remembers it as being "very heavy, but very solid." Although it was a vast improvement over the old Gladiator, it must be admitted that, overall, the Hurricane was inferior to both the German Messerschmitt-109 and the Italian Macchi-202.

MARYLAND — Designed as a light bomber, the twin-engine Maryland proved to be an excellent reconnaissance machine. It had a long range that allowed pilots to search far and wide for their targets. Adrian Warburton proved it could be a surprisingly good dogfighter as well, consistently coming out on top during engagements with enemy fighters.

SPITFIRE — This was the plane that won the Battle of Malta. An elegant, easy-to-fly fighter equipped with two cannons and four machine guns, it gave the Axis fighter pilots all they could handle. The Spit could reach speeds of 600 kilometres per hour and could climb to 11,300 metres. All of the top Allied aces on Malta flew it, including George Beurling, who used its excellent turning ability to gain the upper hand on dozens of opponents.

SWORDFISH — Nicknamed the "Stringbag" by those who flew it, this was the most unlikely looking aircraft of the war. It was a wood-and-fabric open-cockpit biplane that could reach a top speed of just 225 kilometres per hour. Its cruising speed was a pathetic 160 kilometres per hour, which made it a sitting duck for any enemy plane it encountered. It was so obsolete, in fact, that it would not have looked out of place in the skies of the First World War. Nevertheless, it proved to be a highly effective torpedo bomber. It was an agile plane that could weave in and out of flak barrages as it closed in on Axis ships. Swordfish crews sunk many enemy vessels in the Mediterranean, most notably the three Italian battleships sent to the bottom of Taranto harbour in November 1941.

WELLINGTON BOMBER — Nicknamed the "Wimpy" after cartoon character of the era, the Wellington proved to be effective in attacks on U-boats and surface vessels. It was an underrated aircraft that served all through the war. On Malta it was used to both locate and attack convoys, and to bomb targets in Sicily and on mainland Italy.

Axis Aircraft

CANT Z.1007 — Made entirely of wood, the Cant was a tri-motor bomber that could fly 450 kilometres per hour. It was protected by four machine guns and carried a bomb load of 1,270 kilograms. Its engines were not very powerful, however, and its lack of armour plating placed the crew in grave danger any time they were over enemy territory. Many have been critical of the Italian bomber crews for not pressing home their attacks with the same vigour as their Luftwaffe counterparts, but the criticism is unfair. The Cant was not nearly as reliable as the principal German bomber, the Ju-88. It was not designed for low-level bombing, and the Italians did not use it that way.

FIAT BR2OM — A biplane fighter, it saw action over Malta with the Regia Aeronautica in 1940 and early 1941 before being replaced by the Macchi and Reggiane. Like the Gloster Gladiator, the Fiat was agile but slow. Its top speed was only 425 kilometres per hour, which was woefully inadequate for a Second World War fighter.

JUNKERS-88 — A twin-engine aircraft with a crew of four, the Ju-88 proved to be an excellent medium bomber. Defended by five machine guns, it carried a bomb load of 1,800 kilograms. It had a top speed of 450 kilometres per hour when fully loaded, but could retreat at 500 kilometres per hour after jettisoning its bombs.

MACCHI-202 — A highly manoeuvrable Italian fighter that could take a lot of punishment, the Macchi had a top speed of 500 kilometres per hour and a ceiling of 8,800 metres. It was a rugged, agile ship that suffered from a lack of firepower, coming equipped with only four machine guns. Had it been armed with a couple of cannons as well, it might have been a major menace to the Maltese defenders. As it was, Italian ace Furio Doglio Niclot claimed 10 Spitfires with a Macchi, including nine that were officially confirmed. The American ace Claude Weaver was among the pilots on Malta to be shot down by this ship.

MESSERSCHMITT-109 — This was the most formidable opponent faced by the Malta defenders. Armed with one cannon and two machine guns, the ME-109 could fly 625 kilometres per hour and had a ceiling of 11,300 metres. It was clearly superior to the Hurricane, but there was little to choose between it and the Spitfire. It could out-climb and outdive the Spit but could not turn as tightly as the fabled British fighter.

MESSERSCHMITT-110 — This twin-engine, two-seater fighter had four machine guns and two cannons in the nose, and another machine gun in the back seat for use by the rear-gunner. Despite its formidable fire-power, however, it was no match for either the Spitfire or the Hurricane. It had a top speed of 545 kilometres per hour, but was a slow-turning machine that pilots found difficult to fly. It was with-drawn from daylight service over Malta soon after it arrived on Sicily.

REGGIANE — Like the Macchi, the Reggiane was an Italian fighter equipped with only four low-calibre machine guns. It had a ceiling of 11,950 metres and could reach a top speed of 540 kilometres per hour. Although by no means a bad airplane, it was not a match for the Spitfire.

STUKA JU-87 — The Stuka could drop its bombs with almost pin-point accuracy, but it was so slow and clumsy to fly that it proved to be an easy target for both anti-aircraft gunners and Allied fighter pilots. It suffered so heavily at the hands of British Spitfires that it had to be withdrawn from daylight raids over Malta after May 1942. It continued to be used as a night bomber by the Italian airforce for some time after that.

Ace Lists

Although Allied soldiers, sailors, anti-aircraft gunners, bomber crews, aircraft mechanics and even ordinary civilians played crucial roles in winning the siege of Malta, the most important individuals were undoubtedly the fighter pilots. Only a few hundred of them saw action over the island during the long struggle, but they turned the tide of history by shooting down more than 1,000 Axis planes. Every fighter pilot on the island did his part, but the most successful were the aces — the aviators who shot down five or more enemy aircraft each.

Lists of the highest scoring pilots of both sides follow. They differ in some respects from those published elsewhere in that they count "shared" kills as whole victories. However, in cases where more than one pilot is credited with the same number of victories, the man who had no shared kills is listed first. For example, Canadian Wally McLeod appears in the number two position here because none of his 13 conquests were shared with other pilots. P.A. Schade and Tony Goldsmith, on the other hand, both counted one "shared" victory in their totals. It should be noted also that the lists only include planes claimed by pilots during the siege. Victories scored before an airman got to Malta or those obtained after he left the island have been omitted. For instance, while George Beurling finished the war with 32 victories, including four German fighters bagged over Western Europe, the list published here recognizes only the 28 aircraft he destroyed over Malta.

Leading Allied Aces

Name	Nationality	Victories
George Beurling	Canadian	28 (one shared)
Wally McLeod	Canadian	13
P.A. Schade	British	13 (one shared)

Tony Goldsmith	Australian	13 (one shared)
R.B. Hesselyn	New Zealander	12
Slim Yarra	Australian	12
J.A. Plagis	Rhodesian	11
Claude Weaver	American	11 (one shared)
Nigel Park	New Zealander	11 (one shared)
John McElroy	Canadian	10
John Williams	Canadian	10
Adrian Warburton	British	10
F.N. Robertson	British	10
P.A. Nash	British	10 (one shared)
Carl Fumerton	Canadian	9
A.C. Rabagliati	British	9 (one shared)
Ron West	British	9

Leading Axis Aces

Name	Nationality	Victories
Gerhard Michalski	German	26
Siegfried Freytag	German	25
Herbert Rollwage	German	20
Rudolf Ehrenberger	German	16
Walter Brandt	German	14
Gunther von Maltzahn	German	14
Heinz Berres	German	11
Franz Schiess	German	10
Fritz Geisshardt	German	9
Furio Doglio Niclot	Italian	9 (three shared)
Teresio Martinoli	Italian	8
Helmut Belser	German	8
Ennio Tarantola	Italian	8 (three shared)
Aldo Buvoli	Italian	6
Fritz Dinger	German	6

George Beurling's Victory Log

Canadian ace George Beurling was the only Allied pilot of the Second World War who outscored his top Luftwaffe rival in his theatre of battle. In every major conflict of the war, with the exception of Malta, the leading ace was a German. Beurling took top honours in the epic siege by destroying 28 enemy aircraft and damaging at least five others. By way of contrast, the leading Luftwaffe ace on Sicily, Gerhard Michalski, had 26 confirmed kills. Following is a complete list of Beurling's victory claims over the island. In all cases, the date given is for the year 1942. The names of his victims are from Shores, Cull, and Malizia, *Malta: The Spitfire Year 1942.*

Abbreviations used:

KIA — Killed in action.
WIA — Wounded in action.
POW — Prisoner of war.
Flamer — Shot down in flames.

No.	Date	Type	Result	Remarks
1	June 12	ME-109	Damaged	Tail blown off
2	July 6	Cant Z.1007	Damaged	One crewman KIA
3	July 6	Macchi-202	Destroyed	Flamer
4	July 6	Reggiane	Destroyed	Romano Pagliani, KIA
5	July 6	ME-109	Destroyed	Toni Engels, KIA
6	July 8	ME-109	Destroyed	
7	July 8	Ju-88	Damaged	One engine ablaze
8	July 8	ME-109	Destroyed	
9	July 10	Macchi-202	Destroyed	Sgt. Visentini, WIA

10	July 10	ME-109	Destroyed	Hans-Jurgen Frodien, KIA
11	July 12	Reggiane	Destroyed	Aldo Quarantotti, KIA
12	July 12	Reggiane	Destroyed	Carlo Seganti, KIA
13	July 23	Ju-88	Damaged	
14	July 23	Reggiane	Destroyed	
15	July 27	Macchi-202	Destroyed	Falerio Gelli, POW
16	July 27	Macchi-202	Destroyed	Furio Doglio Niclot, KIA
17	July 27	ME-109	Destroyed	
18	July 27	ME-109	Damaged	
19	July 27	ME-109	Destroyed	Karl-Heinz Preu, KIA
20	July 29	ME-109	Destroyed	Karl-Heinz Witschke, KIA
21	Aug. 8	ME-109	Destroyed	
22	Aug. 13	Ju-88	Destroyed	(shared kill, Hans Schmiedgen and crew KIA)
23	Sept. 25	ME-109	Destroyed	
24	Sept. 25	ME-109	Destroyed	
25	Oct. 10	ME-109	Destroyed	
26	Oct. 10	ME-109	Destroyed	
27	Oct. 13	Ju-88	Damaged	
28	Oct. 13	ME-109	Destroyed	
29	Oct. 13	ME-109	Destroyed	Pilot bailed out
30	Oct. 13	Ju-88	Destroyed	Anton Wilfer and crew, KIA
31	Oct. 14	Ju-88	Destroyed	
32	Oct. 14	ME-109	Destroyed	
33	Oct. 14	ME-109	Destroyed	Josef Ederer, WIA

CHRONOLOGY OF EVENTS

The Siege of Malta

JUNE 10, 1940 — Italy declares war on England. Twenty-four hours later, 35 Regia Aeronautica bombers launch the first air raids on Malta with attacks on Valletta, Kalafrana and Hal Far. One bomber is shot down by a British pilot flying one of Malta's three Gladiator biplanes. The deeply religious Maltese quickly dub the Gladiators Faith, Hope and Charity.

AUGUST 1940 — A dozen Hurricanes fly into Malta, providing much-needed help for the antique Gladiators. Nevertheless, the old biplanes stay in operation until early 1941, shooting down a total of nine enemy aircraft.

SEPTEMBER 1940 — A convoy of supply ships sails unmolested into Grand Harbour. The Italian airforce is providing the only opposition to Malta at this stage of the war and it has relatively few planes on Sicily.

NOVEMBER 1940 — Reconnaissance planes from Malta take photographs of the Italian fleet that lead to a devastating raid on Taranto harbour by British Swordfish torpedo-bombers. Enemy losses are so severe that the Italian surface fleet is never again a major force in the Mediterranean.

JANUARY 1941 — British aircraft carrier HMS *Illustrious* limps into Grand Harbour after being heavily bombed, giving the first indication that Allied ships will no longer be able to sail in and out of Malta with impunity. More than 200 men on *Illustrious* are killed or wounded, but the ship is repaired and sent back to Alexandria.

NOVEMBER 1941 — Luftwaffe units arrive on Sicily. German air-craft begin bombing Malta heavily in December.

FEBRUARY 13, 1942 — Adolf Hitler approves Operation Hercules, the proposed invasion of Malta. Hundreds of German planes are ordered to Sicily to prepare for a major blitz of the island.

FEBRUARY 16, 1942 — The RAF sends Canadian ace Stan "Bull" Turner to Malta to help organize the defenders.

MARCH 1942 — German and Italian aircraft launch the March Blitz, pounding Malta hard throughout the month. A major attempt to run a convoy through to the island ends in failure.

MARCH 7, 1942 — Fifteen Spitfires fly into Malta from the aircraft carrier HMS *Eagle*. Sixteen more arrive before the month is out.

APRIL 1942 — Enemy pilots fly more than 10,000 sorties against Malta. Much of Valletta is destroyed or seriously damaged. The month ends with Malta down to three fighters.

APRIL 15, 1942 — King George VI awards the George Cross to the people of Malta in recognition of their great courage under fire.

MAY 9, 1942 — Sixty-four Spitfires fly to Malta from British carrier *Eagle* and American carrier *Wasp*. Malta has a powerful fighter force for the first time. Next day, the Spitfires and Maltese anti-aircraft gunners shoot down or damage a combined total of more than 60 German and Italian aircraft.

JUNE 1942 — Two merchant ships make it to Grand Harbour after a savage convoy battle that saw the Allies lose 15 vessels. Nevertheless, the two survivors bring in enough food to ward off starvation. Canadian pilot George Beurling flies into Malta this month to begin a tour of operations that will become legendary.

JULY 1942 — The heaviest air fighting of the siege takes place, with the Allies losing more than 50 planes while claiming 137 victories.

JULY 27, 1942 — George Beurling shoots down three planes, one of them flown by leading Italian ace Doglio Niclot. In all, the Canadian ace destroys 16 enemy planes in July.

AUGUST 1942 — Another major convoy battle is fought. Allied shipping losses are again heavy, but five merchant ships reach Grand Harbour, once again saving Malta from starvation.

OCTOBER 1942 — The Germans and Italians launch their final blitz on Malta. It rages for 10 days. There are heavy losses on both sides, but the battle ends in defeat for the Axis.

NOVEMBER 1942 — Five merchant ships make it to Malta, encountering little opposition. Next month, four more supply ships sail in completely unopposed. The 31-month siege is finally over.

MAY 12, 1943 — With ships and planes from Malta constantly sinking Axis ships headed for North Africa, the vaunted Afrika Korps is forced to surrender to the Allies. Some 267,000 Axis soldiers are taken prisoner.

ENDNOTES

Chapter One

1   John Dedomenico, interview.

2.   Cajus Bekker, *Hitler's Naval War* (London: MacDonald, 1971), 255.

3.   Anthony Martienssen, *Hitler and His Admirals* (London: Secker and Warburg, 1948), 124.

4.   B.H. Liddell Hart, *The Rommel Papers* (London: Collins, 1953), 288.

5.   David Irving, *Hitler's War* (New York: Viking, 1977), 399.

6.   Charles Jellison, *Besieged: The World War II Ordeal of Malta, 1940-42* (Boston: University Press of New England 1984), 153.

7.   Winston Churchill, *The Second World War: The Hinge of Fate* (Boston: Houghton Mifflin, 1950), 308.

8.   Philip Vella, *Malta: Blitzed but Not Beaten* (Valletta, Malta: Progress Press, 1985), 56.

9.   Hajo Herrmann, *Eagle's Wings: The Autobiography of a Luftwaffe Pilot* (Osceola, WI: Motorbooks International, 1991), 73.

10.   Werner Baumbach, *The Life and Death of the Luftwaffe* (New York: Ballantine Books, 1949), 149.

11.   Helmut Zlitz, interview.

12.   Herrmann, 123.

13.   Johannes Steinhoff, *Straits of Messina: Diary of a Fighter Commander* (London: Andre Deutsch, 1971), 22.

14.   *Ibid.*, 106.

15.   *Ibid.*, 27.

16.   Ronaldo Scaroni, interview.

17.   *Ibid.*

Chapter Two

1.   Bill Olmsted, *Blue Skies* (Toronto: Stoddart, 1987), 99.

2.   Max Arthur, *There Shall Be Wings: The RAF from 1918 to the Present* (London: Hodder and Stoughton, 1993), 123.

3.   George Brown and Michel Lavigne, *Canadian Wing Commanders of Fighter Command in World War Two* (Toronto: Ballantine Books, 1984), 307.

4.   Christorpher Shores, Brian Cull, and Nicola Malizia, *Malta: The Spitfire Year, 1942* (London: Grub Street, 1991), 87.

5.   Hugh Halliday, *The Tumbling Sky* (Stittsville: Canada's Wings, 1978), 259.

6.   Robert Jackson, *Douglas Bader: A Biography* (London: Arthur Barker, 1983), 89.

7.   Halliday, 262.

8.   Laddie Lucas, *Flying Colours: The Epic Story of Douglas Bader* (London: Hutchinson, 1981), 182.

9.   Brown and Lavigne, 303.

10.   *Ibid.*

11.   Shores, Cull, and Malizia, 96.

Chapter Three

1.   Shores, Cull, and Malizia, 98.

2.   Arthur, 89.

3.   Eric Crist, interview.

4.   Noel Ogilvie, interview.

5.   Harry Kennedy, interview.

6.   Eric Crist, interview.

7.   Johnnie Johnson, *Full Circle* (London: Pan Books, 1968), 141.

8.   Laddie Lucas, *Flying Colours*, 174.

9.   John Frayn Turner, *Famous Air Battles* (London: Arthur Barker, 1963), 150.

10.   *Ibid.*, 156.

11.   Laddie Lucas, *Malta: The Thorn in Rommel's Side* (London: Penguin Books, 1992), 90.

12.   Arthur Inch, correspondence with author.

13. Myriam Mifsud, interview.

14. George Porter, interview.

15. Vincenza Desira, interview.

16. George Porter, interview.

17. Myriam Mifsud, interview.

18. George Scerri, interview.

19. Milo Vassallo, interview.

20. Myriam Mifsud, interview.

21. Ed Cauchi, interview.

22. Myriam Mifsud, interview.

23. George Scerri, interview.

24. Harry Kennedy, interview.

25. Lex McAulay, *Against All Odds: RAAF Pilots in the Battle for Malta, 1942* (Milsons Point: Century Hutchinson Australia, 1989), 31.

26. Jack Fletcher, interview.

Chapter Four

1. Jack Fletcher, interview.

2. Francis Gerard, *Malta Magnificent* (New York-London: Whittlesey House, 1943), 117.

3.   Noel Ogilvie, interview.

4.   George Scerri, interview.

5.   John Dedomenico, interview

6.   Paul Stellini, interview.

7.   George Porter, interview.

8.   Ed Schranz, interview.

9.   George Scerri, interview.

10.   Eric Crist, interview.

11.   McAulay, 47.

12.   John Dedomenico, interview.

13.   *Times of Malta*, April 15, 1942.

14.   George Scerri, interview.

15.   Eric Crist, interview.

16.   John Dedomenico, interview.

17.   Johnson, 206.

18.   John Dedomenico, interview.

19.   George Scerri, interview.

20.   Johnny Sherlock, interview.

21.   Eric Crist, interview.

22.   Johnson, 209.

23.   B.H. Liddell Hart (ed.), *History of the Second World War* (Somerset: Purnell and Sons, 1966), 1012.

24.   Thomas Foley, letter to his mother, Feb. 17, 1942.

Chapter Five

1.   Paddy Schade, interview.

2.   Johnny Sherlock, interview.

3.   George Scerri, interview.

4.   Vincenza Desira, interview.

5.   Carmel Portelli, interview.

6.   Arthur Inch, correspondence with author.

7.   John Dedomenico, interview.

8.   *Ibid.*

9.   Liddell Hart, *History of the Second World War*, 1012.

10.   Shores, Cull, and Malizia, 239.

11.   Steinhoff, 217.

12.   John Dedomenico, interview.

13.   Tony Ferri, interview.

14.   Johnny Sherlock, interview.

15.   Noel Ogilvie, interview.

16.   Eric Crist, interview.

Chapter Six

1.   George Hogan, *Malta: The Triumphant Years, 1940-43* (London: Robert Hale, 1978), 128.

2.   Churchill, 304.

3.   Cajus Bekker, *The Luftwaffe War Diaries* (New York: Ballantine Books, 1969), 353.

4.   Johnny Sherlock, interview.

5.   *Ibid.*

6.   George Beurling and Leslie Roberts, *Malta Spitfire: The Story of a Fighter Pilot* (Toronto: Oxford University Press, 1943), 3.

7.   *Ibid.*, 116.

8.   Laddie Lucas, *Wings of War* (London: Hutchinson, 1983), 182.

9.   Lucas, *Out of the Blue.*

10.   Frank Kerley, correspondence with author.

11.   *Ibid.*

12.   J.R. Colville, *Man of Valour: The Life of Field Marshal Lord Gort, V.C.* (London: Collins, 1972), 251.

13. Beurling and Roberts, 122.

14. Kenneth Boyle, interview.

15. Johnny Sherlock, interview.

16. Carl Fumerton, interview.

17. David Bashow, *All the Fine Young Eagles: In the Cockpit with Canada's Second World War Fighter Pilots* (Toronto: Stoddart, 1996), 231.

18. Churchill, 383.

19. Johnny Sherlock, interview.

20. Arthur Thurston, *Bluenose Spitfires* (Hantsport: Lancelot Press, 1979), 46.

21. Bob Middlemiss, interview.

Chapter Seven

1. Ronaldo Scaroni, interview.

2. Noel Ogilvie, interview.

3. Ronaldo Scaroni, interview.

4. Bob Middlemiss, interview.

5. Beurling and Roberts, 139.

6. Bob Middlemiss, interview.

7. Beurling and Roberts, 150.

8.   Brian Nolan, *Hero: The Buzz Beurling Story* (Toronto: Lester and Orpen Dennys, 1981), 85.

9.   *Ibid.*

10.   *Airforce: Magazine of the Air Force Association of Canada,* 20 (no. 1): 14.

11.   *Ibid.*

12   D.J. Dewan, correspondence with author.

13.   Bob Middlemiss, interview.

14.   *Airforce,* 20 (no. 1): 14.

15.   Johnny Sherlock, interview.

16.   McAulay, 133.

17.   Ronaldo Scaroni, interview.

18.   Bob Middlemiss, interview.

Chapter Eight

1.   Thurston, 21.

2.   Vella, 167.

3.   Noel Ogilvie, interview.

4.   Johnny Sherlock, interview.

5.   Myriam Mifsud, interview.

6.   George Porter, interview.

7.   Milo Vassallo, interview.

8.   Larry Milberry and Hugh Halliday, *The RCAF at War* (Toronto: Canav Books, 1990), 376.

9.   *Ibid.*, 378.

10.   *Ibid.*, 378.

11.   Bashow, 82.

12.   Carl Fumerton, interview.

13.   *Ibid.*

14.   *Ibid.*

15.   Bashow, 148.

16.   Halliday, 99.

17.   Carl Fumerton, interview.

18.   *Ibid.*

19.   Helmut Zlitz, interview.

20.   Tony Ferri, interview.

21.   *Ibid.*

Chapter Nine

1.   William Keen, interview.

2.   Myriam Mifsud, interview.

3.   W.G.G. Duncan Smith, *Spitfire into Battle* (London: John Murray, 1981), 137.

4.   *Ibid.*

5.   *Ibid.*

6.   Wilfred Baynton, interview.

7.   Alex Stittle, interview.

8.   Wilfred Baynton, interview.

9.   Eric Crist, interview.

10.   *London Free Press*, August 7, 1997.

11.   Alistair Mars, *British Submarines at War, 1939-1945.*(London: William Kimber, 1971), 130.

12.   William Keen, interview.

13.   John McIntyre, correspondence with author.

14   Harry Kennedy, interview.

15.   *Ibid.*

16.   *Ibid.*

17.   John McIntyre, interview

18   Harry Kennedy, interview.

19.   Harry Kennedy, interview.

20.   John McIntyre, interview.

21.   Harry Kennedy, interview.

22.   John McIntyre, interview.

23.   Harry Kennedy, interview.

24.   *Ibid.*

25.   William Keen, interview.

26.   Harry Kennedy, interview.

27.   *Ibid.*

Chapter Ten

1.   John Dedomenico, interview

2.   George Scerri, interview.

3.   Bashow, 124.

4.   *Globe and Mail* [Toronto], October 14, 1942.

5.   Beurling and Roberts, 215.

6.   Lucas, *Wings of War*, 183.

7.   *Globe and Mail* [Toronto], October, 1942.

8.   Lucas, *Out of the Blue*, 164.

9.   Baumbach, 155.

10.   Ronaldo Scaroni, interview.

11. Adolf Galland, *The First and the Last: The Rise and Fall of the German Fighter Forces, 1938-45* (New York: Ballantine Books, 1967), 114.

12. *Ibid.*

13. Baumbach, 159.

14. Vella, 132.

15. *Time*, October 1942.

16. George Porter, interview.

17. Bob Taggart, interview.

18. *Ibid.*

19 *Ibid.*

20. Reg Thackeray, correspondence with author.

21. Peter Hoad, interview.

22. Reg Thackeray, correspondence with author.

23 *Ibid.*

24. Wilfred Baynton, interview.

25. Alex Stittle, interview.

26. Kenneth Boyle, interview.

27. Doug Appleton, interview.

BIBLIOGRAPHY

Arthur, Max. *There Shall Be Wings: The RAF from 1918 to the Present.* London: Hodder and Stoughton, 1993.

Bashow, David. *All the Fine Young Eagles: In the Cockpit with Canada's Second World War Figher Pilots.* Toronto: Stoddart, 1996.

Baumbach, Werner. *The Life and Death of the Luftwaffe.* New York.: Ballantine Books, 1949.

Bekker, Cajus. *The Luftwaffe War Diaries.* New York: Ballantine Books, 1969.

Bekker, Cajus. *Hitler's Naval War.* Translated by Frank Ziegler. London: MacDonald, 1971.

Beurling, George and Roberts, Leslie. *Malta Spitfire: The Story of a Fighter Pilot.* Toronto: Oxford University Press, 1943.

Bishop, Arthur. *Courage in the Air.* Whitby: McGraw-Hill Ryerson, 1992.

Bowyer, Chaz. *The Men of the Desert Air Force, 1940-43.* London: William Kimber and Co. Ltd., 1984.

Bradford, Ernle. *Siege: Malta 1940-1943.* London: Hamish Hamilton, 1985.

Brown, George and Lavigne, Michel *Canadian Wing Commanders of Fighter Command in World War Two.* Toronto: Ballantine Books, 1984.

Churchill, Winston. *The Second World War: The Hinge of Fate*. Boston: Houghton Mifflin Co., 1950.

Coffin, H. M. *Malta Story*. New York: Dutton.

Colville, J.R. *Man of Valour: The Life of Field Marshal Lord Gort, VC*. London: Collins, 1972.

Constable, Trevor, and Toliver, Raymond. *Horrido! Fighter Aces of the Luftwaffe*. New York: Ballantine Books, 1968.

DeDomenico. F.S. *An Island Beleaguered*. Malta: Givo Muscat, 1946.

Dunmore, Spencer. *Above and Beyond: The Canadians' War in the Air, 1939-45*. Toronto: McClelland and Stewart, 1996.

Galland, Adolf. *The First and the Last: The Rise and Fall of the German Fighter Forces, 1938-45*. New York: Ballantine Books, 1967.

Gerard, Francis. *Malta Magnificent*. New York-London: Whittlesey House, 1943.

Halliday, Hugh. *The Tumbling Sky*. Stittsville: Canada's Wings Inc., 1978.

Halliday, Hugh, and Milberry, Larry. *The RCAF at War*. Toronto: Canav Books, 1990.

Herrmann, Hajo. *Eagle's Wings: The Autobiography of a Luftwaffe Pilot*. Osceola, WI.: Motorbooks International, 1991.

Hogan, George. *Malta: The Triumphant Years, 1940-43*. London: Robert Hale , 1978.

Irving, David. *Hitler's War*. New York: The Viking Press, 1977.

Jackson, Robert. *Douglas Bader: A Biography*. London: Arthur Barker 1983.

Jellison, Charles. *Besieged: The World War II Ordeal of Malta, 1940-42*. Boston: University Press of New England, 1984.

Johnson, Johnnie. *Full Circle*. London: Pan Books, 1968.

Kesselring, Albert. *A Soldier's Record*. New York: Morrow, 1954.

Liddell Hart, B.H., editor-in-chief. *History of the Second World War*. Somerset: Purnell and Sons, 1966.

Liddell Hart, B.H., *The Rommel Papers*. London: Collins, 1953.

Lucas, Laddie. *Flying Colours: The Epic Story of Douglas Bader*. London: Hutchinson, 1981.

Lucas, Laddie. *Malta: The Thorn in Rommel's Side*. London: Penguin Books, 1992.

Lucas, Laddie. *Out of the Blue*. London: Grafton Books, 1987.

Lucas, Laddie. *Wings of War*. London: Hutchinson, 1983.

Martienssen, Anthony. *Hitler and his Admirals*. London: Secker and Warburg, 1948.

Macksey, Kenneth. *Kesselring: The Making of the Luftwaffe*. London: B.T. Batsford, 1978.

Mars, Alistair. *British Submarines at War, 1939-1945*. London: William Kimber, 1971.

McAulay, Lex. *Against All Odds: RAAF Pilots in the Battle for Malta, 1942*. Milsons Point, New South Wales: Century Hutchinson Australia, 1989.

McCaffery, Dan. *Air Aces: The Lives and Times of Twelve Canadian Fighter Pilots*. Toronto: James Lorimer & Co., 1990.

Nolan, Brian. *Hero: The Buzz Beurling Story*. Toronto: Lester and Orpen Dennys, 1981.

Olmsted, Bill. *Blue Skies*. Toronto: Stoddart, 1987.

Shores, Christopher; Cull, Brian; and Malizia, Nicola. *Malta: The Hurricane Years, 1940-41*. London: Grub Street, 1987.

Shores, Christopher; Cull, Brian; and Malizia, Nicola. *Malta: The Spitfire Year, 1942*. London: Grub Street, 1991.

Smith Duncan, W.G.G. *Spitfire Into Battle*. London: John Murray, 1981.

Spooner, Tony. *Warburton's War: The Life of Wing Commander Adrian Warburton*. London: William Kimber, 1987.

Steinhoff, Johannes. *Straits of Messina: Diary of a Fighter Commander*. Translated by Peter and Betty Ross. London: Andre Deutsch, 1971.

Tantum, W. H., and Hoffschmidt, E.J. *The Rise and Fall of the German Air Force, 1933 to 1945*. Old Greenwich, CT: W. E. Inc., 1969.

Thurston, Arthur. *Bluenose Spitfire*. Hansport, Nova Scotia: Lancelot Press, 1979.

Turner, John Frayn. *Famous Air Battles*. London: Arthur Barker, 1963.

Vella, Philip. *Malta: Blitzed But Not Beaten*. Valletta, Malta: Progress Press, 1985.

Wismayer, J.M. *The History of the King's Own Malta Regiment and the Armed Forces of the Order of St. John*. Valletta, Malta: Said International, 1989.

Newspapers/Magazines

Airforce Magazine

London *Free Press*

MacLean's Magazine

New York Times

Time Magazine

Times of Malta

Toronto *Globe and Mail*

INDEX

Photographs are indicated in italics.